A VILLAGE TO V

HIKING THE JESUS TRAIL

AND OTHER BIBLICAL WALKS IN THE GALILEE

ANNA DINTAMAN
DAVID LANDIS

Jesus Trail Route Network

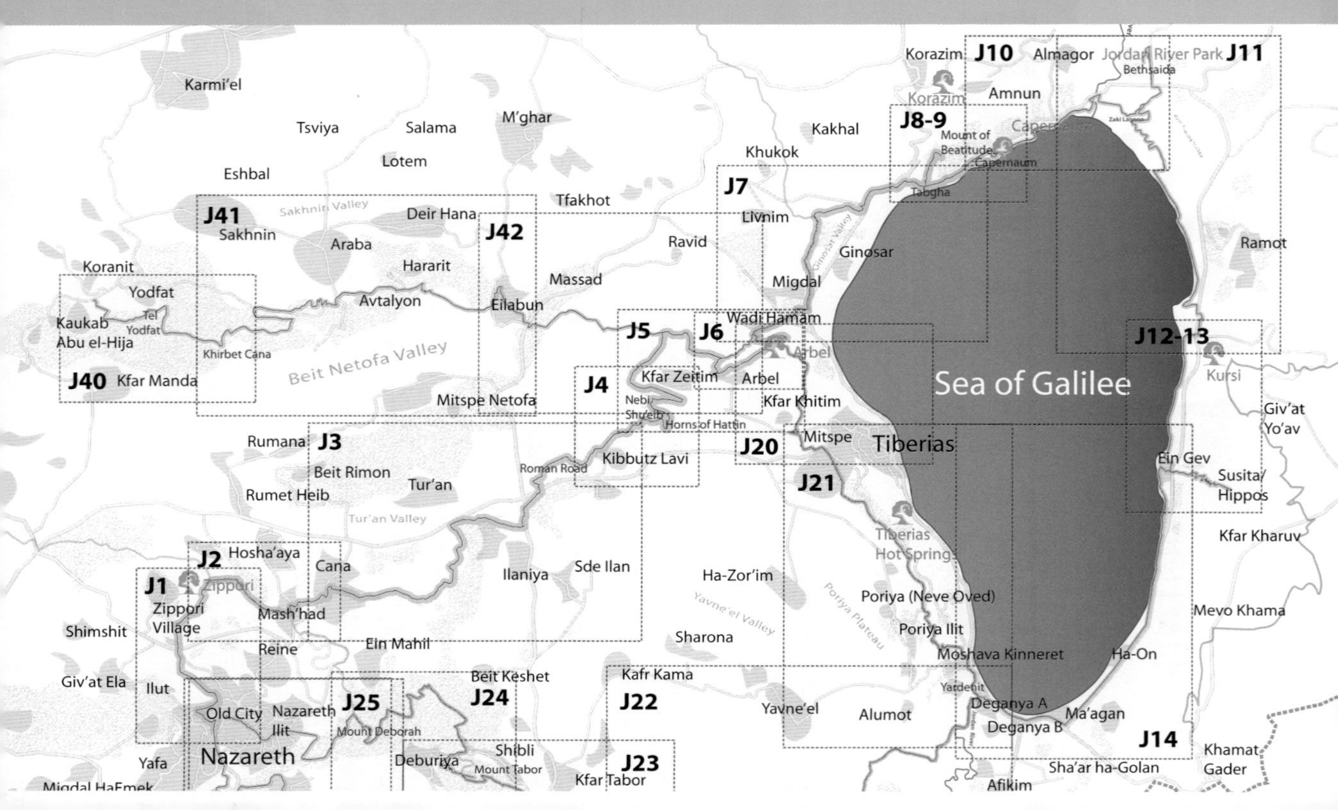

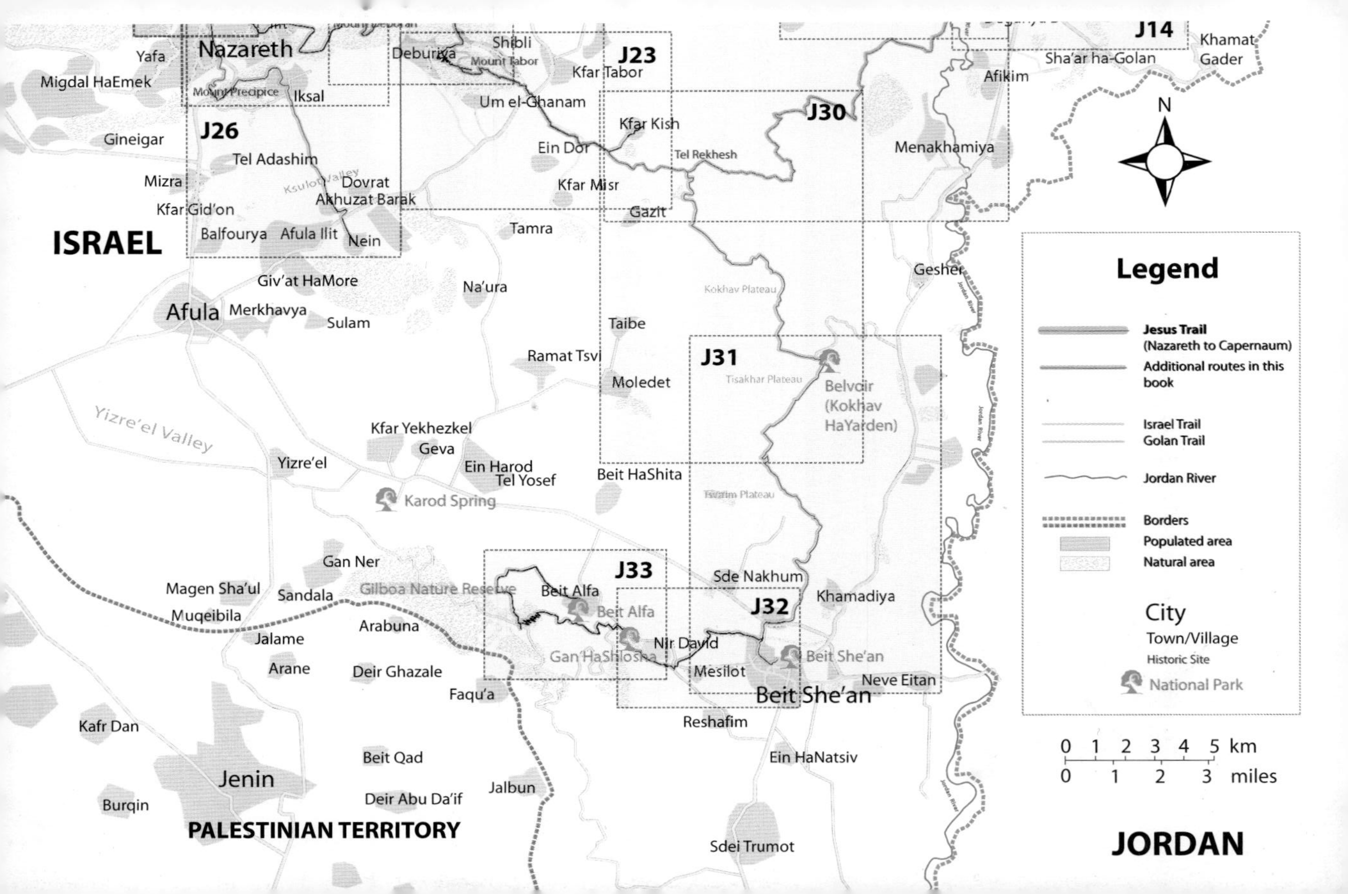
Legend
Jesus Trail
(Nazareth to Capernaum)
Additional routes in this book
Israel Trail
Golan Trail
Jordan River
Borders
Populated area
Natural area
City
Town/Village
Historic Site
National Park
0 1 2 3 4 5 km
0 1 2 3 miles
N
ISRAEL
JORDAN
PALESTINIAN TERRITORY
J14
J23
J26
J30
J31
J32
J33
Nazareth
Yafa
Migdal HaEmek
Mount Precipice
Iksal
Deburiya
Mount Tabor
Shibli
Kfar Tabor
Um el-Ghanam
Kfar Kish
Ein Dor
Tel Rekhesh
Kfar Misr
Gazit
Gineigar
Tel Adashim
Mizra
Ksulot Valley
Dovrat
Akhuzat Barak
Kfar Gid'on
Balfourya
Afula Ilit
Nein
Tamra
Giv'at HaMore
Na'ura
Afula
Merkhavya
Sulam
Taibe
Ramat Tsvi
Moledet
Kokhav Plateau
Tisakhar Plateau
Belvoir
(Kokhav
HaYarden)
Yizre'el Valley
Kfar Yekhezkel
Geva
Yizre'el
Ein Harod
Tel Yosef
Beit HaShita
Karod Spring
Tsvaim Plateau
Gan Ner
Magen Sha'ul
Sandala
Muqeibila
Gilboa Nature Reserve
Beit Alfa
Arabuna
Jalame
Arane
Deir Ghazale
Faqu'a
Gan HaShlosha
Nir David
Mesilot
Sde Nakhum
Khamadiya
Beit She'an
Neve Eitan
Reshafim
Ein HaNatsiv
Kafr Dan
Beit Qad
Jenin
Jalbun
Deir Abu Da'if
Burqin
Sdei Trumot
Sha'ar ha-Golan
Khamat
Gader
Afikim
Menakhamiya
Gesher
Jordan River

Hiking the Jesus Trail and Other Biblical Walks in the Galilee
1st edition, April 2010

Village to Village Press, Harleysville, PA 19438
www.villagetovillagepress.com

Photographs/Diagrams
All photographs and diagrams © David Landis and Anna Dintaman except:
p. 33 © Craig Lorge, p. 56 © Alexander Fröhlich, p. 174, 183 © Kevin Butrick,
p. 87, 99, 186, 187 Wikimedia Creative Commons/Public Domain

Cover Photographs
Front: Overlooking the Sea of Galilee from Mount Arbel © Anna Dintaman
Back (left to right): Wildlife on Mt. Gilboa, Abu Ashraf's restaurant in Nazareth,
Franciscan church on Mt. Tabor © David Landis

Many of the images in this guide are available for licensing.
Visit www.biblephotos.org for more information.

ISBN 978-0-9843533-0-9
Library of Congress Control Number: 2010923692

A Note on Name Variations

Many of the place names mentioned in this book can be spelled in a variety of ways in English. This is partly due to the transliteration of the name from its original alphabet (usually Hebrew or Arabic) and also due to changes in the pronunciation of the place name throughout history, and pronunciation of place names in different languages.

For example, modern-day Zippori (the Hebrew pronunciation) is known as Saffuriya in Arabic, and was known as Sepphoris (a Greek name) during the time of Jesus. Beit She'an, a Galilean Decapolis city, was known in biblical times as Beth Shan and is referred to in Arabic as Beisan. We have attempted to use the most standardized spelling of these place names by spelling them as they appear on road signs and/or entrance signs. These standardized names tend to favor the Hebrew pronunciation. When relevant we have tried to list both the Arabic name and ancient name as legitimate variations.

A Note on Terminology

To indicate dates, we use the commonly accepted academic terms of BCE (Before the Common Era) and CE (Common Era). For dates when the era is not specified, assume Common Era.

We use the term "Palestine" to refer to the historic region of the Middle East stretching between the Mediterranean Sea and the Jordan River. Palestine has been a regional name since the Roman era. Within the region of Palestine, smaller relevant regions are Judea (Jerusalem area), Galilee (area of Jesus' ministry), Samaria (between Judea and Galilee), and the Decapolis area (south and east of Galilee). We do not use this term with political motive, or to disregard the modern country of Israel, but as a commonly-accepted academic term for the historic region.

Contents

Leaving Nazareth,
he went and lived in Capernaum,
which was by the lake
in the area of Zebulun and Naphtali—
to fulfill what was said
through the prophet Isaiah:

"Land of Zebulun and land of Naphtali,
the way to the sea,
along the Jordan,
Galilee of the Gentiles—
the people living in darkness
have seen a great light;
on those living in the land of the shadow of death
a light has dawned."

Matthew 4:13-16

Meet the Faces of the Jesus Trail

Ever since the idea of the Jesus Trail started to circulate, it received an encouraging amount of support from many diverse communities, though a few folks have been dubious over the use of the name of Jesus, and suspected the name of being a cheap marketing move, or exploitation of religion for financial gain.

We were even once asked, "Who is the face of the Jesus Trail?" We were uneasy, unsure how to respond. The question seemed to imply a slick and charismatic salesman charming people into purchasing a package deal.

The obvious (if perhaps sanctimonious) answer would be, of course, Jesus. But we believe there are many faces to the Jesus Trail—the faces of the people we meet upon it. The faces of Arabs and Jews, of native-born Israelis and recent immigrants, of the young, the old, people from all walks of life. People who suffer and people who prosper. Palestinians, kibbutzniks, Thai migrant workers. Christians, Muslims, Druze, Bahá'í. Fellow travelers and pilgrims from all walks of life. The list could go on.

As Jesus walked this land in his ministry, we imagine that he met a similarly eclectic mix of people—peasants, soldiers, religious elite, Samaritans, merchants, travelers from the ends of the empire. Jesus received hospitality from people, perhaps surviving economically almost solely on the grace and generosity of others. We wonder what kind of people Jesus spoke with along the road, who offered him cold water or to share a portion of their food. What kind of philosophy and musing did he hear in idle talk along the road?

Abdullah Nasser and Liad Inon at the Fauzi Azar Inn in Nazareth

Jesus did not travel with fear of those different from himself, but accepted hospitality from a tax collector (Luke 19:1-8), a sinful Samaritan woman (John 4:1-22), a Roman official (John 4:43-54) and other Gentiles and outsiders to his people group.

Experience hospitality and conversation with the many faces of the Jesus Trail.

We hope that you also experience hospitality and conversation with the many faces of the Jesus Trail. Articles and books about this region invariably begin with adjectives like "war-torn" and "conflict-ridden," but we are constantly humbled and blessed by the goodness of the people we meet. Once, separated by no more than five minutes, we sat down for coffee and cookies with Arab Bedouin and then were greeted warmly with offers of help by a group of Jewish young adults. A few days later we were invited to a meal by two Arabs from Nazareth—a Christian and a Muslim, childhood friends.

We are convinced that walking is a humble, non-threatening way to encounter new people, bring to life historical and spiritual texts and, through the physical challenge and removal from ordinary life, also grow to know ourselves better. We hope that stereotypes and preconceptions will melt away in the smelting of sweat, tired limbs, conversation and extraordinary encounters with others.

We invite you to fearlessly step into this challenge, following the example of Jesus. Trust in God and the image of God reflected in the people you meet. Be blessed and be a blessing.

Anna Dintaman
David Landis

#1: Classic Jesus Trail

Nazareth to Capernaum: J1-J9, 62 km, 4 days

Difficulty: Best-developed multi-day trail with accommodations, water and food readily available. Trail well-marked with orange blazes.

Highlights: Old World ambiance in Nazareth, fascinating Byzantine mosaics at Zippori, charming Cana churches, forest scenery, ancient roads, 360° views from the Horns of Hattin, Nebi Shu'eib shrine, view of Sea of Galilee from Mt. Arbel, churches on the Sea of Galilee

Begin in bustling Nazareth, boyhood home of Jesus. Take one day to explore Nazareth and prepare supplies for your walk. Plan your walking days as follows:
DAY 1: Nazareth to Cana via Zippori, 13.4 km, +3 km if entering park (J1-2)
DAY 2: Cana to Kibbutz Lavi, 14.4 km (J3)
DAY 3: Kibbutz Lavi to Moshav Arbel, 15.7 km (J4-5)
DAY 4: Moshav Arbel to Capernaum via Mount of Beatitudes, 18.8 km (J6-J9)
Extend this itinerary with #2 (+4-5 days), #3 (+5 days) or #5 (+7 days).

Tours, Guides and Groups

If you're not keen on setting up your own logistics, you can purchase a self-guided tour package from Jesus Trail Tours which includes lodging, luggage transfer, entry fees, shuttle and other support, with an option to add meals. There are also packages for guided tours and mountain bike tours. See www.jesustrailtours.com for details. The self-guided option in dorm lodging starts at $299 for 6 days/5 nights.

If you're looking for a partner or group to hike with, check out the forum on the Jesus Trail website. You can post your dates and details and see if others are interested in joining you.

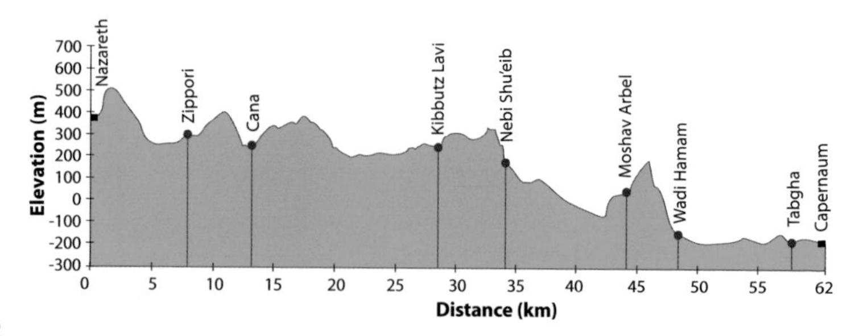

A hiker crests the Horns of Hattin and takes in the view of the Arbel Cliffs.

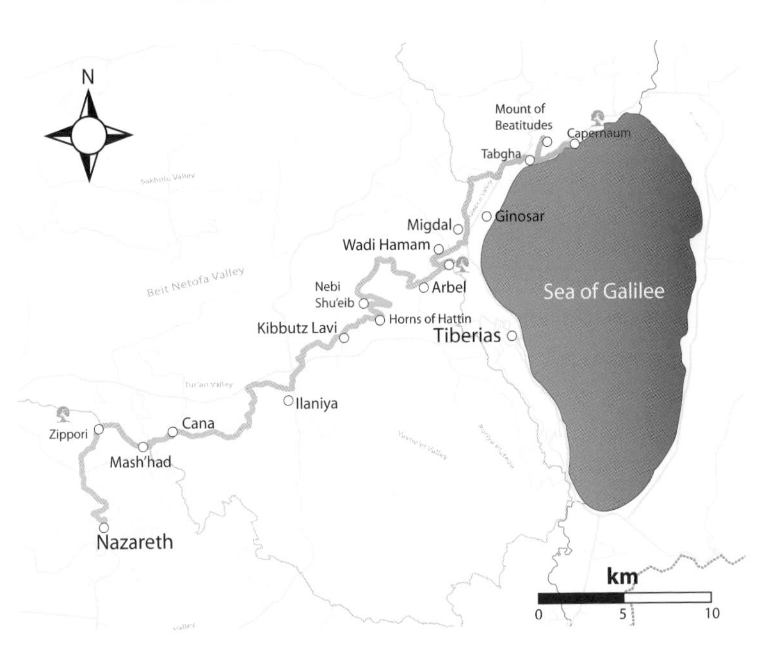

#2: There and Back Again

Nazareth to Capernaum with Return Loop: J1-9 and J21-25, 129 km, 8-9 day loop

Difficulty: Accommodations on return loop are limited, camping or taxi to accommodations required. Prolonged stretch without drinking water refill. Significant elevation change.

Highlights: Stunning Sea of Galilee views, Jordan River baptismal site, ancient excavations, Rift Valley scenery, Mt. Tabor views and churches, forest walking over Mt. Deborah, view from Mt. Precipice

DAYS 1-4: Classic Jesus Trail (J1-9), 62 km from Nazareth to Capernaum.
Optional: Backtrack to Tiberias from Capernaum (+1 day) or take the bus to save time.
DAY 5: Tiberias to Yardenit (J21), 13.1 km
DAY 6: Yardenit to Kfar Kish (J22), 19.4 km
DAY 7: Kfar Kish to Deburiya via Mt. Tabor (J23, part of J24), 15 km
DAY 8: Deburiya to Nazareth via Mt. Deborah (J24-25), 19.0 km

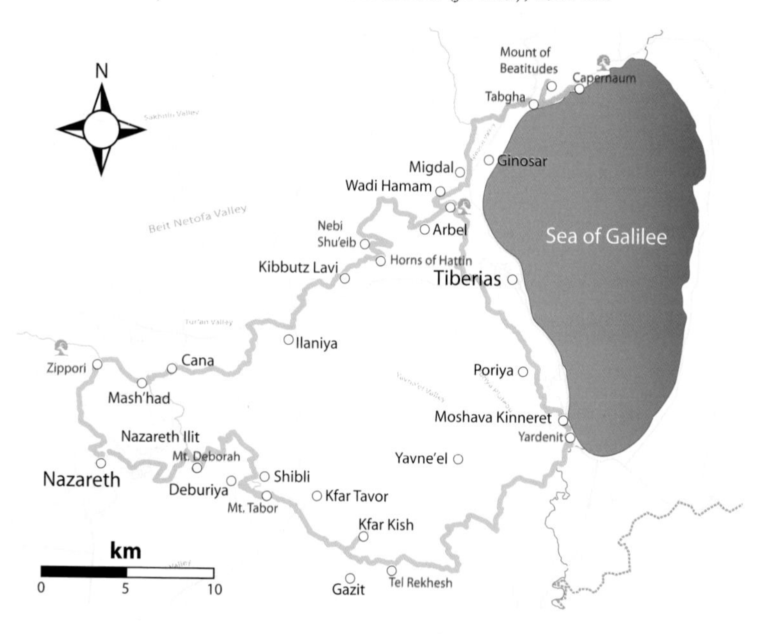

#3: "Sea"-nery

Loop around the Sea of Galilee:

J20 in reverse and J6-J14, J21 in reverse, 91 km, 7 day loop

Difficulty: ▬□□ Accommodations, food and water available. Flat terrain, with optional steep ascent of Susita.

Highlights: View from Mt. Arbel, churches at Tabgha, Mount of Beatitudes and Capernaum, ancient ruins at Bethsaida, Jordan River, Byzantine monastery at Kursi, Roman city of Susita, Sea of Galilee beaches, hot springs and nightlife in Tiberias

The church on the Mount of Beatitudes, situated on the north side of the Sea of Galilee

DAY 1: Tiberias to Arbel (J20 in reverse), 6.1 km
DAY 2: Arbel to Capernaum via Tabgha and the Mount of Beatitudes (J5-9), 15.2 km
DAY 3: Capernaum to Bethsaida (J10), 12.4 km
DAY 4: Bethsaida to Kursi (J11), 15.8 km
DAY 5: Kursi to Ein Gev, Ein Gev to Susita and back (J12-J13), 13.8 km
DAY 6: Ein Gev to Yardenit (J14), 14.5 km
DAY 7: Yardenit to Tiberias (J21 in reverse), 13.1 km

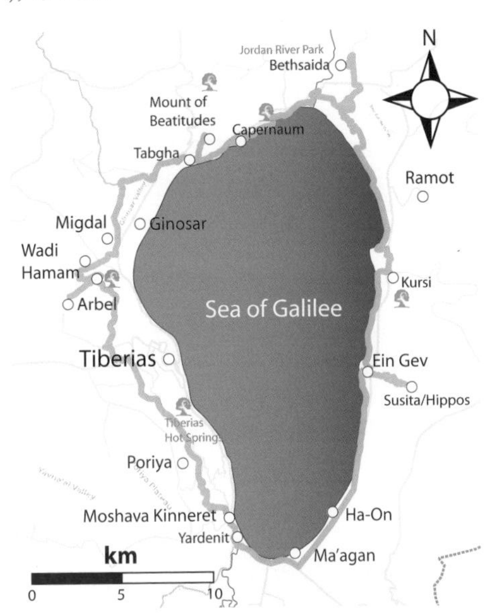

#4: Off the Beaten Track

Nazareth to Gilboa via Belvoir and Beit She'an: J25-23 in reverse and J30-33, 6 days, 87 km

Difficulty: Significant elevation change. Some long stretches between water refills. Camping or taxi to accommodations required.

Highlights: Sweeping views from Mt. Precipice and Mt. Tabor, vast savannas full of gazelle, Crusader castle with a view, massive Roman city, natural hot springs, wildflowers galore on Mt. Gilboa

DAY 1: Nazareth to Deburiya (J25 & part of J24 in reverse), 19.0 km
DAY 2: Deburiya via Mt. Tabor to Tel Rekhesh (J24-J23 in reverse), 16.9 km
DAY 3: Tel Rekhesh to Belvoir (J30), 12.7 km
DAY 4: Belvoir to Beit She'an (J31), 16.5 km
DAY 5: Beit She'an to Gan HaShlosha (J32), 8.0 km
DAY 6: Gan HaShlosha to Mt. Gilboa to Beit Alpha (J33), 13.6 km

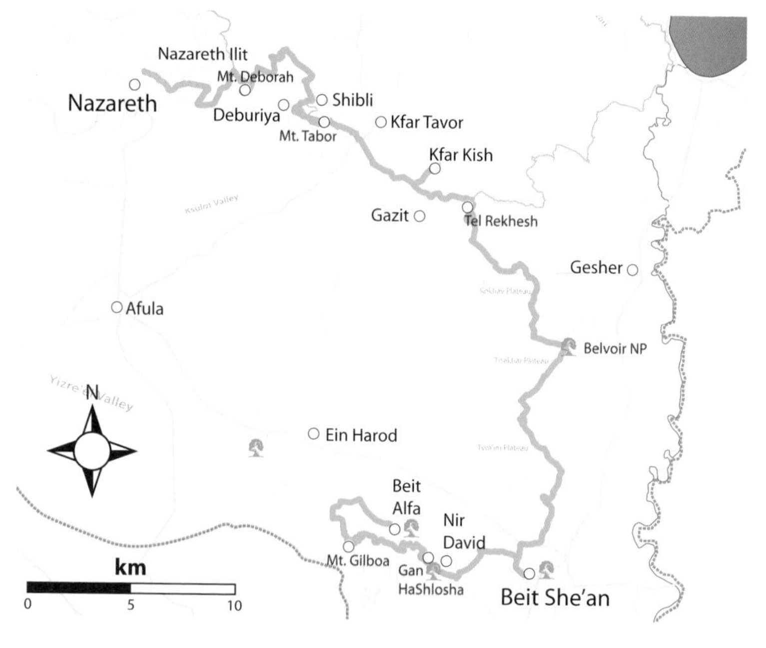

#5: Ruins Walk

Explore ruins at Khirbet Cana

Kaukab to Wadi Hamam:

J40-42, 2 days, 36 km

Difficulty: ▬■□ Significant ups and downs.

Highlights: Sculpture garden, shrine of Saladin's lieutenant, ancient ruins at Yodfat, ruins at alternate location for biblical Cana, peaceful space at Lavra Netofa Monastery, friendly Eilabun village, "Jesus scenery" in Wadi Arbel

DAY 1: Kaukab to Eilabun via Yodfat and Khirbet Cana (J40-41), 23.0 km
DAY 2: Eilabun to Wadi Hamam (J42), 12.9 km

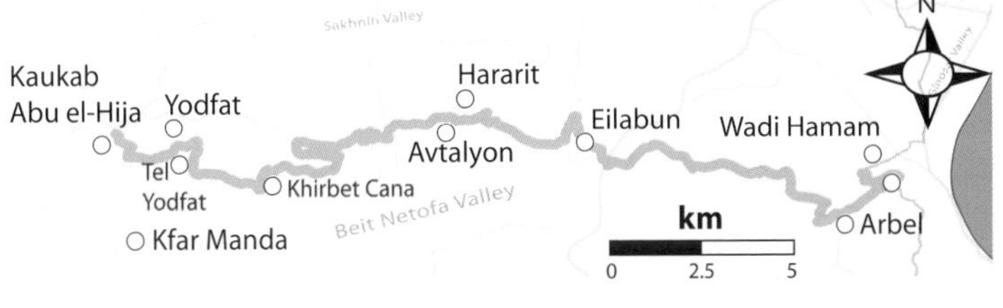

Mt. Gilboa bursts with spring wildflowers.

#6: The Jesus Marathon

A 2-Week Sojourn between Biblical sites in the Galilee: J1-14, J22 and J30-33, 194 km

Difficulty: Significant elevation change. Some long stretches between water refills. Camping or taxi to accommodations required.

DAYS 1-4: Follow the Classic Jesus Trail, Nazareth to Capernaum (J1-9), 62 km
DAY 5: Capernaum to Bethsaida (J10), 12.4 km
DAY 6: Bethsaida to Kursi (J11), 15.8 km
DAY 7: Kursi to Ein Gev, Ein Gev to Hippos and back (J12-13), 13.8 km
DAY 8: Ein Gev to Yardenit (J14), 14.5 km
DAY 9: Yardenit to Kfar Kish/Tel Rekhesh (J22), 19.4 km
DAY 10: Kfar Kish/Tel Rekhesh to Belvoir (J30), 17.7 km
DAY 11: Belvoir to Beit She'an, 16.5 (J31)
DAY 12: Beit She'an to Gan HaShlosha (J32), 8.0 km
DAY 13: Gan HaShlosha to Mt. Gilboa to Beit Alpha (J33), 13.6 km
DAY 14: Bus back to Nazareth for some well-deserved rest!

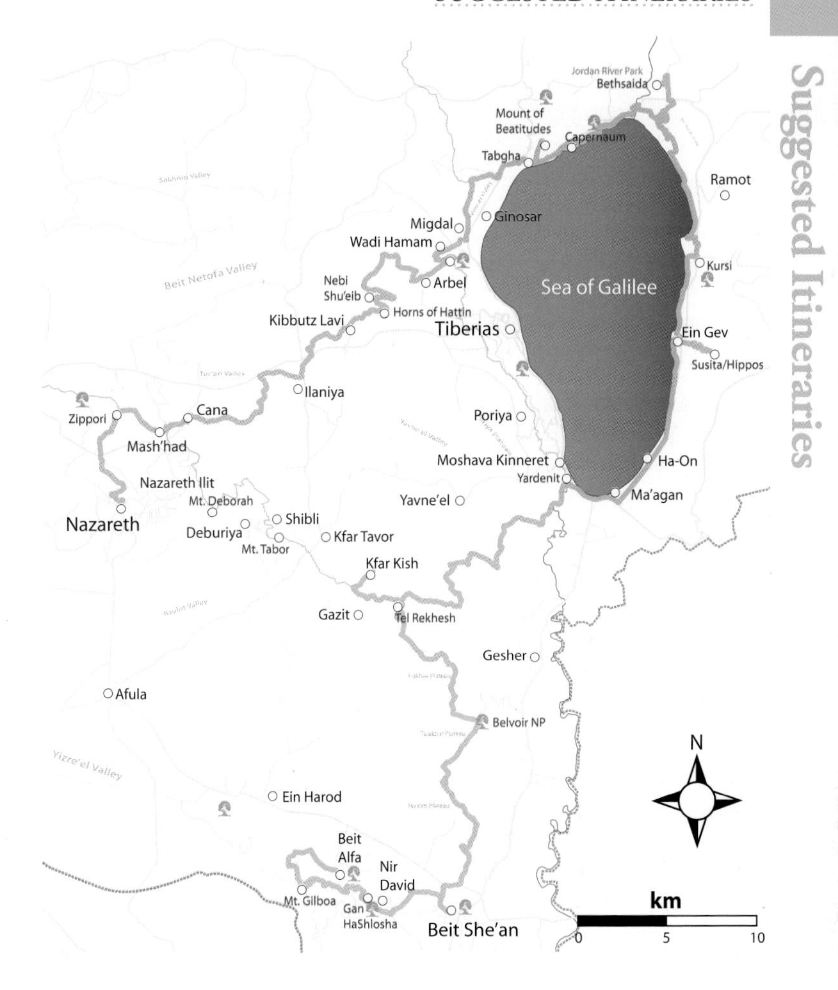

Still haven't had enough?

You can continue hiking for months on any of Israel's other 10,000+ km (6,000+ miles) of marked hiking trails. See pp. 45-47 for a description of a few of the long distance routes in the region.

A hiker pauses to enjoy the view descending Arbel Cliff (opposite).

Day Hikes

Only have one day? Don't like to carry your gear? This book is designed so that each segment could be hiked as a day or half-day hike. Here are a few of our favorite sections for day hikes:

1. Village Walk: Nazareth to Cana (J1-J2, +3 km for park)
4-6 hours, 13.6 km
Start in Nazareth and take J1 to Zippori. After exploring the ruins and mosaics, eat a picnic lunch before continuing on J2 to Cana. See the churches, renew your wedding vows, eat a plate of falafel, then catch a local bus back to Nazareth.

2. Battlefield Walk: Lavi to Nebi Shu'eib (end of J3, J4)
3.5-4.5 hours, 9.6 km
Begin at Golani Junction and walk along ancient Roman road, then pass by a religious kibbutz and ascend the Horns of Hattin, site of a decisive Crusader battle, for a dazzling 360° view. Finish by descending to the Druze shrine of Nebi Shu'eib and take a taxi to town or a bus stop on the Nazareth-Tiberias road.

3. Sea View Walk: Tiberias to Yardenit (J21)
3-5 hours, 13.1 km
This gentle scenic walk follows the Israel Trail, with elevated views of the Sea of Galilee. End in Yardenit for an encounter with the Jordan River, then catch a bus back to Tiberias.

4. Cave and Cliff Walk: Tiberias to Wadi Hamam (J20 in reverse, J6)
4-6 hours, 9.7 km
Begin in Tiberias and follow the northbound Israel Trail from Sapir Boulevard. Dip through a valley before ascending the gentle slope up to Mt. Arbel. Enjoy the stunning view, then descend the cliffs and explore the caves carved into the rock face. End at Wadi Hamam spring and take a taxi or walk to the road to catch a bus back to Tiberias.

5. Mountain Walk: Mount Tabor Ascent (J23)
2-3 hours, 4.0 km
Begin in Nazareth and take a bus to Gazit Junction near Kfar Tavor. Ascend Mt. Tabor by the Israel Trail marked footpath. Explore the churches, watch a sunset and taxi back down the mount to take a bus back to Nazareth.

The Sea View Walk affords marvelous panoramas of the Sea of Galilee, where much of the ministry of Jesus took place 2000 years ago.

Jesus of Galilee

The Galilee region of Israel has been a crossroads of cultures, an agricultural breadbasket and a gateway for trade for as long as humans have lived there. Some of the earliest remains in the broader region were found in the valleys and lakeshores of Galilee, and evidence suggests it may have been the first area in the world where plants and animals were domesticated. Some of its earliest sedentary inhabitants were the Canaanites, and since then a multitude of people groups have called Galilee home or passed through its boundaries. The Bible calls the region "Galilee of the Gentiles," as it was a region that bordered exclusively Gentile territories, where Jews were rarely the majority.

Ever since the time of Abraham, an important trade route known as the *Via Maris,* or Way of the Sea, stretched through the Galilee, connecting Europe to Africa and Asia. Cultures met and mingled as merchants and militants traveled through the area for economic or political gain. The region was settled by Canaanites, Philistines, Israelites, Persians, Egyptians, Greeks, Romans, Muslims, Crusaders, Mamluks, Ottomans, the British and most recently, the state of Israel.

As is common in rugged landscapes, the Galilee developed a two-fold reputation: first, that of being somewhat of a backwater or hinterland (not a highly developed urban or administrative area), and second, that of fierce independence, determination to be autonomous, and resistance to foreign occupation or obligation.

First-Century Travel

"Jesus wept" (John 11:35) is generally referred to as the shortest verse in the Bible, but "Jesus walked" could just as easily be part of the canon. The gospels are a story of movement, following Jesus as he travels from village to village preaching, teaching and healing. The range of Jesus' travels as an adult extends at least 80 km (50 mi) east to west and 240 km (150 mi) north to south through present-day Israel, the West Bank, Jordan, Lebanon and Syria. In the course of his ministry he probably walked thousands of kilometers.

Jesus called his disciples to action: *"Come, follow me"* (Mark 1:17), *"Go and make disciples of all nations"* (Matthew 28:19). He also gave them specific instructions about how to travel: *"Take nothing for the journey except a staff—no bread, no bag, no money in your belts. Wear sandals but not an extra tunic"* (Mark 6:8-9).

Jesus was not the only one traveling in the Galilee in the 1st century. The *Via Maris* may have passed through the Jezre'el Valley near Nazareth, connecting the

Mediterranean to Damascus, and ultimately connecting as far as Egypt to present-day China. The *Pax Romana* extending across the empire encouraged trade and the movement of people and ideas.

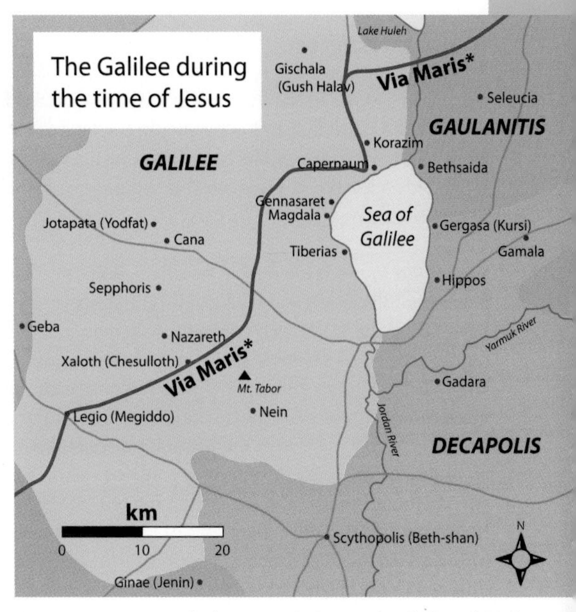

**Approximate route, also known as the International Coastal Highway*

We might imagine that as a boy, Jesus may have walked up to Mt. Precipice and peered down into the expansive Jezre'el Valley at the diverse travelers below—camel caravans, Roman legions, merchants and tradesman. As he walked the paths between villages and cities, whether via Roman roads or unregulated back routes, we can visualize the multiplicity of people he may have met and walked with for a time. The hours of walking may have been full of self-reflection, conversation and pondering the natural world around him. The multiple-day walk from Nazareth to Capernaum leaves plenty of time to consider the birds of the air and the lilies of the field (Matthew 6:25-34).

In recent years there has been a resurgence of interest in the historical Jesus, as scholars have examined everything from the politics, economy and sociology of 1st-century Palestine, to what Jesus may have eaten (see p. 166). In recreating Jesus' lifestyle in one small way, we hope that the act of traveling as Jesus did will bring new insights into this search, both devotionally for the pilgrim and intellectually for the academic.

Did Jesus Really Walk the Jesus Trail?

For thousands of years merchants have pocketed money selling pieces of the "true cross" or leading gullible pilgrims to supposedly holy places. There are clear economic gains for a town to be identified as a place of pilgrimage. For the purposes of this book, we have included sites traditionally identified as the places Jesus visited in the New Testament that do not necessarily stand up to rigorous academic and archeological criticism. Two thousand years after the life of Jesus we often have no way of knowing where specific events took place. Sometimes more than one traditional site exists for the same event, one claimed by the Catholic Church and one by the Orthodox, and occasionally even a third Protestant site! Jesus did not leave us a road map or GPS coordinates of his walking habits, so we must rely on tradition and a bit of guesswork as we piece together historical routes with the biblical narrative.

But we do know Jesus walked in this region. A lot. We know that he traversed fields and hills, rivers and villages. It is interesting to speculate whether Jesus would have taken the safer, well-established Roman roads or smaller back paths. It is highly probable that Jesus spent time along certain portions of the path, particularly where the trail follows ancient roads and at the sites from the 1st century. In modern Israel, many of these historic routes overlap roads and highways. Our preference is to stay as close to the historic routes as possible, but not at the expense of an unsafe or unpleasant walking experience. Some sections of the Jesus Trail trace paved Roman roads and ancient paths, but where this is not possible we sought trails that emulate the experiences of ancient travelers. While we have considered historical accuracy as much as possible, ultimately we believe it is more important to travel in the spirit and ethos of Jesus than in his literal footsteps.

One difference between Christianity and other monotheistic religions is the lack of emphasis on physical places. In Judaism, Israel is the most important place on earth, the dwelling place of God and God's people. In Islam, places are equally important, with Mecca as the spiritual hub of the religion, the direction to which all prayer is oriented. While many Christians hold places from the New Testament as important and special, there is no formal theology of land. As Jesus told the Samaritan woman,

> *"Believe me, woman, a time is coming when you will worship the Father neither on this mountain nor in Jerusalem... Yet a time is coming and has now come when the true worshipers will worship the Father in spirit and truth, for they are the kind of worshipers the Father seeks."* John 4:21, 23

These sites are clearly valuable for their fascinating history, but more valuable still are the "living stones," the people of the region that Jesus cared so deeply for in his life, and the many people around the world who have been inspired by the message of Jesus.

As Archbishop of the Galilee, Elias Chacour, says, "Living stones are more important than holy shrines."

Pilgrimage

Blessed are those whose strength is in you, who have set their hearts on pilgrimage.
Psalm 84:5

The ancient practice of pilgrimage has made a surprising comeback in recent years. Thousands of people have chosen to forego the tour bus for an experience of walking between historical, religious and spiritual sites all over the world. The *Camino de Santiago*, an 800-km trail across northern France and Spain, has become the hallmark of the resurgence and now hosts well over 100,000 walkers a year.

Most of the world's major religions have a tradition of pilgrimage. The *Hajj*, a pilgrimage to Mecca with specific symbolic actions, is one of the five pillars of Islam. In Judaism, pilgrimage centers around Jerusalem and the site of the former Jewish temple. Buddhist pilgrims flock to important places from the life of the Buddha. Bahá'í pilgrims walk the steps of the Bahá'í temple in Haifa, Israel.

Pilgrimage also has a rich history in Christianity. The Bible, even from its beginning in Hebrew scripture, speaks of a people on the move, wandering through the desert being led by and provided for by God. Abraham, the father of monotheism, set out from his native land allowing God to lead him. Some say the Magi who traveled from the east to visit baby Jesus were the first Christian pilgrims. Others in the New Testament made journeys to see Jesus for healing or to hear him teach.

Early Christians traveled to the Sea of Galilee and other sites from the life of Jesus. In the 4th century, the Roman emperor Constantine promoted tolerance for Christianity and eventually was baptized. His mother, Helena, traveled the Middle East searching for the exact locations of events from the life of Jesus so that they could be remembered. Today many of the traditional Christian sites in the Middle East are built on the places found by Helena. During Byzantine times, pilgrimage became popular and many pilgrims left records of their journeys. During the Crusader era, many places of pilgrimage became battlefields as European warriors fought violently to keep them under Christian control. During times when pilgrimage became too dangerous for European Christians, other "surrogate" pilgrimage locations were identified in Europe so that the practice of pilgrimage could continue.

What is Pilgrimage?

Different faiths, time periods and philosophies give varying nuance to the concept of pilgrimage. We attempt here to lay down a general framework while also recognizing that pilgrimages can be unique and diverse.

First of all, **pilgrimage moves.** Pilgrims are not static, but active and dynamic. The pilgrim journey by definition involves movement from one place to another, be it across the street or across a continent. This movement may be physically challenging, such as walking great distances. This movement may be personally challenging, bringing interactions with people or customs beyond our comfort zones. This movement may be disorienting and humbling, as we enter a place we have not been and must rely on others to guide and assist us.

Pilgrimage remembers. Pilgrimages lead us to places of sacred and historical value where we remember events and ideas that have impacted our lives, beliefs and philosophy. The Hajj to the Ka'ba remembers the triumph of monotheism over polytheism. The Hill of Crosses in Lithuania remembers that Christianity survived and outlived the Soviet Union despite Soviet attempts to eradicate religion. Jewish pilgrims to Jerusalem are reminded of their covenant with God. Christian pilgrimage to sites from the life of Jesus remembers the importance and challenge of the life and teachings of Jesus.

Pilgrimage inspires and transforms. Pilgrims do not move just for movement's sake or remember for remembering's sake, but with the goal of being inspired and transformed in their daily life. Some pilgrims come with a specific goal—to find peace about a recent troubling event, to seek guidance for a big decision, to refresh a sense of spiritual connection to God.

The association of places, particularly mountaintops, with experiences of divinity or proximity to the divine is a pervasive theme across cultures and religions. George MacLeod, founder of the Iona community in Scotland, refers to these locations as "thin places," where the separation between humans and God dissipates and communication between them comes more easily. The Old Testament speaks frequently of pagan "high places" of worship in the surrounding area. Many significant biblical events take place on mountains. Moses received the Ten Commandments on Mt. Sinai. Abraham offers to sacrifice Isaac on Mt. Moriah. The transfiguration takes place on an unspecified mountain (traditionally thought to be Mt. Tabor). The Sermon on the Mount has even taken on the name of its elevated place of preaching. Jerusalem was built on a hill.

Pilgrimage seeks out these thin places, physically pursuing locations that facilitate spiritual experience, healing, direction and other types of brushes with the divine. In the journey, pilgrims are removed from the distractions of everyday life, possessions and relationships and go to a new spiritual and physical place of encounter. The sacrifice and pain of the journey embody the pilgrim's longing for spiritual renewal.

Sacred Travel: Make your Trip a Pilgrimage

Prepare for an Inward Journey

Before you leave for the trail, it may be helpful to block out some time to mentally prepare for your journey. This might include spending a few hours in nature in silence. You might also write in your journal, reflecting on what has drawn you to embark on a pilgrimage and what you hope to find, experience or achieve through your pilgrimage. Other ways to prepare yourself could include reading from the Bible or other inspirational books, spending time in prayer and meditation and speaking about your pilgrimage with a trusted mentor or friend who has also completed a pilgrimage.

> "The geographical pilgrimage is the symbolic acting out of the inner journey. The inner journey is the interpretation of the meaning and signs of the outer pilgrimage. One can have one without the other. It is best to have both."
>
> —Thomas Merton

Focus on a Theme

Pay attention to themes that emerge as you prepare for pilgrimage. Think back over the past six months or year and identify which moments were the most life-giving for you and which the most challenging. Choose a theme to focus on that fits your experience and also your hopes for completing the pilgrimage. Ancient pilgrims were often seeking healing, penance or an answer to prayer. You might also feel drawn to complete a pilgrimage to seek physical or spiritual healing for yourself or a loved one. If you have had a difficult or traumatic year, perhaps your pilgrimage will center around seeking forgiveness, direction, peace or equilibrium. If you have had a blessed year, perhaps the focus of your pilgrimage can be thankfulness. It can be helpful to choose a symbol that represents your theme and carry it with you on your journey. This can also be a conversation starter to share the reason for your pilgrimage with others you meet along the way.

Be Open to New Experiences

Even as you meditate and focus on a theme, keep your eyes open and senses alert for surprises. Things will never all turn out as planned, but the challenges and inconveniences can also be a vehicle for growth. Be mindful with each person you encounter, remembering that you have an opportunity to show kindness to them, and they may have something to share with you. At its best, pilgrimage entails a community of people willing to care for one another.

The Jesus Trail Story

The Jesus Trail began as a collaborative project between two friends with a converging mission. Maoz Inon traveled the world trekking in some of its most exotic corners, observing how trekking served to stimulate local economies and preserve local culture. He returned to his native Israel with the dream of developing a religious and historical trekking route aimed at international visitors. Maoz founded a guesthouse in the heart of the Old City of Nazareth, attracting foreign tourists as well as other Israelis to discover the historic center of the largest Arab city in Israel.

David Landis, an American outdoor adventure enthusiast, met Inon as Landis traveled around the world after university and sought help in completing the 940-km Israel Trail (see p. 45) in 2005. The two remained friends, and when Landis returned to Israel in 2007 with a vision of using communications and tourism to connect people, the idea of the Jesus Trail began to hatch.

Both felt that with the high level of tourism in Israel, there should be a means for tourists to experience the Galilee and the sites from the life of Jesus in a more authentic and relational way than in a large impersonal tour bus. They also felt that more of the tourism money coming into the country should reach the hands of small local businesses in the economically struggling villages of the Galilee. Their own appreciation for the beauty of the region inspired their desire to protect the environment and educate others to maintain it.

From its beginning, the Jesus Trail has been a small-scale operation. Landis spent thousands of hours studying maps and walking trails, searching for the most beautiful, logical and feasible way to walk between important biblical sites in the Galilee. The results were logged by GPS and offered free to download from a simple website, designed by Landis and packed with practical and historical information available for free to anyone who wanted to walk the trail. Inon stocked his Nazareth guesthouse with information about the route and purchased a GPS to have available for walkers.

The first big break for this humble trail was a burst of media attention in the summer of 2008, less than a year after the idea of the trail was conceived. The Associated Press ran a story that was picked up by hundreds of newspapers around the world. Interest in the trail grew and many hikers contacted Landis and Inon for information. Later in 2008, Inon recruited volunteers to accompany hikers on a walk of the first day of the Jesus Trail, from Nazareth to Zippori and Cana.

Landis and Inon began a conversation with the Society for the Protection of Nature in Israel (SPNI) in late 2008, and requested that SPNI mark the trail with paint blazes in the same system that other trails are blazed and marked on official 1:50,000 scale hiking maps of the region. SPNI was supportive of the project and, in spite of difficulties and delays in receiving permission to paint blazes across a mosaic of private, public and municipal land, succeeded in blazing the trail in the summer of 2009. Finally, hikers could come and walk without dealing with a GPS and with little chance of getting lost.

David Landis and Maoz Inon at Mt. Precipice

This completion coincided with an important event for the people of Nazareth—the visit of Pope Benedict XVI to perform an outdoor Mass. The Jesus Trail story was picked up once again and featured in *Agence France-Presse* and *The Washington Post*, and on ABC News and NBC's *The Today Show*. The trail continues to draw interest from around the world, and new resources (available at www.jesustrail.com) are constantly being developed to meet the needs of Jesus Trail walkers.

Responsible Tourism

Tourism is a $5-trillion-a-year industry, making up almost 10% of the global economy, according to the World Travel and Tourism Council. Unfortunately, the huge amounts of money involved in the tourism industry rarely reach those who need it most, and too often set up exploitative and unbalanced relationships between citizens of a host country and visitors to that country. Some tours are set up so that tourists see only one aspect of the country they visit—luxurious hotels, air-conditioned buses, impressive historical sites—without any interaction with local people or understanding of how they live. In this model, the tourist is the customer and "the customer is always right," so tours aim for customer satisfaction without considering the well-being of the host community.

A new movement in the tourism industry focuses on socially responsible tourism, which aims to educate travelers about local issues and conditions, and also to foster positive interaction between residents and visitors. Rather than viewing the relationship between locals and tourists as purely financial between provider and customer, ethical tourism frames that relationship as one of mutual respect between host and guest.

Socially responsible tourism also involves respect and care for the local environment, striving to minimize the environmental impact of tourism while promoting conservation in local communities by providing an economic incentive to maintain and preserve the natural world.

The Jesus Trail was designed with responsible tourism in mind. Walking is a non-threatening, low-environmental-impact means of travel that stimulates interaction with local people. The trail encourages locals to take an active role in caring for the environment as stakeholders in a project that provides business for the community. Several small family-run guesthouses that directly benefit local families have opened their doors in Cana, Ilaniya and Deburiya to provide an alternative to impersonal chain hotels. When local business owners and international visitors interact face to face, more tourism money can stay in and benefit communities along the trail.

Some guidelines for responsible tourism:

- Focus on taking the posture of a student of local culture, seeking to learn rather than reinforce preconceptions.
- Think local: hire local guides, eat local foods, try to live in a way similar to local people rather than seeking out what is familiar or comfortable.
- Show respect for the local culture by learning a few key phrases in the local language (see phrasebook on pp. 236-243).
- Pay fair prices and appreciate expertise with adequate tips (10-15%). When possible, buy handicrafts through a fair trade co-op to ensure that artists are paid a living wage for their work.
- Select a balanced itinerary that allows interaction with different ideologies, religions or ethnic groups, rather than favoring one group or narrative.
- Learn about and respect local customs. Wear appropriate clothing, especially at religious sites. Ask permission before taking photos of local people.
- Select tour providers based on their philosophy of travel rather than only considering the cheapest price.
- Respect shortages in water, electricity and other limited resources by restricting your own use.
- Follow Leave No Trace environmental principles (see opposite page).

Leave No Trace:

"Take only photos, leave only footprints."

We highly encourage all hikers to closely follow the principles of Leave No Trace, a set of guidelines designed to minimize the environmental impact of outdoor activities. This not only protects the environment from pollution and disruption, but preserves natural areas for the enjoyment of other hikers and people living nearby.

Plan Ahead and Prepare:

- Minimize packaging waste and bring adequate trash bags.
- Plan a route that is realistic for the skill level of your group, allowing plenty of time to find a suitable camping space.
- Try to keep the size small, or split a larger group into two groups.
- The more you plan for your trip, the less likely you are to break environmental guidelines out of fatigue or desperation.

Travel and Camp on Durable Surfaces:

- Avoid causing erosion by walking only on established paths.
- Camp in designated areas, without disturbing flora and fauna.

Dispose of Waste Properly:

- Pack out everything that you pack in.
- Carry a trash bag and deposit all trash in proper receptacles, including organic waste (orange peels, egg shells, etc).
- Go at least 60 m (200 ft) away from water, camp site and trails to use the bathroom.
- Dig a hole 15-20 cm (6-8 in) deep to dispose of solid human waste.
- Throw used toilet paper in a trash bag to pack out, not on the ground.

Minimize Campfire Impact:

- We do not advise using campfires at all on the Jesus Trail.
- Use a camping stove for food preparation.

Respect Wildlife:

- Don't feed or approach wild animals.
- Store food and garbage securely, so animals don't come across it and eat anything that could damage their health.

Leave Anything You Find:

- Respect history—do not damage or remove pieces of historical structures.
- Do not take or move rocks, plants or other natural objects.
- Do not build, dig, stack or otherwise mutilate the natural surroundings.

Be Considerate of Other Visitors:

- Respect other people using trails and facilities.
- Try to be quiet and let the sounds of nature prevail for others.
- Be kind and polite to locals as you walk through their towns and near their properties. Remember that you are a guest, and treat locals as your generous hosts!

Travel in Israel

Israel is an ideal location for independent travel, with extensive public transportation, many English-speaking locals and a network of budget accommodations throughout the country. In addition to a strong outdoor adventure culture, many Israelis have spent time abroad and are familiar with backpacking and independent travel. Accessibility combined with rich cultural and historical sites of interest offer months of options for exploration and learning. The following section briefly outlines what to expect as you plan your hiking trip to Israel.

Traveling to and from Israel

Visas

Citizens of the United States, Canada, Australia, New Zealand and most of Europe do not need a visa prior to arrival in Israel and are usually given three months entry upon arrival at Ben Gurion International Airport in Tel Aviv or land borders. This tourist visa can be extended for an additional three months at the Ministry of the Interior, which has offices in Tel Aviv, Jerusalem, Haifa and Nazareth. Travel to and from the Palestinian Territories requires transit through Israel and the same entry and exit policies apply. No special immunizations are required.

Entry Stamps

Those planning future travel to Arab countries, except Jordan and Egypt, should ask for their passports not to be stamped upon arrival and departure in Israel and on both sides of land border crossings. Many Arab countries, including Syria and Lebanon, will deny entry to anyone with an Israeli stamp in their passport or an adjacent country's stamp from a land border with Israel (Jordan/Egypt). For example, a person may enter Israel from Jordan through a land border, but even if that person does not receive an Israeli passport stamp, the exit stamp from the Jordanian land border will be an obvious tip-off that the person has been to Israel. Some countries, including the United States, allow a second passport for dealing with this issue.

Border Crossings

Travelers crossing from Israel to Jordan at the Allenby/King Hussein Bridge need a Jordanian visa prior to arrival at the border. Both northern (Sheikh Hussein) and southern (Yitzhak Rabin/Arava) crossings sell Jordanian visas at the border. It is possible to enter Egypt by land at the Taba crossing near Eilat, but you must get an Egyptian visa either in Eilat or Tel Aviv in advance. There are currently no land crossings between Israel and Syria or Lebanon.

Accommodations

A variety of accommodations to fit your style and price range are available throughout the country, from campgrounds to five-star hotels. Expect to pay about 50-120NIS for a single dorm bed and 300-500NIS for a double private room. Costs tend to be more on weekends and holidays. For a list of accommodations relating to the hiking routes in this book (1-32), refer to pp. 232-233.

For general options throughout Israel, we recommend starting your search with ILH—Israel Hostels, a network of privately owned accommodations with exceptional character aimed at independent travelers. The Israeli Youth Hostel Association (IYHA) runs a set of hostels with rooms that are clean and affordable, but somewhat sterile. A system of family stays (see below) is being developed in the Galilee. The hospitality and social networking website CouchSurfing provides an means for meeting other travelers and staying in their homes.

BOOKING ONLINE

ILH
www.hostels-israel.com

IYHA
www.iyha.org.il/eng

HOSTEL WORLD
www.hostelworld.com

HOSTELS.COM
www.hostels.com

COUCHSURFING
www.couchsurfing.com

Camping

Israelis generally have a relaxed attitude regarding wild camping (sleeping in areas not officially designated for camping such as picnic areas, fields or forests), which is permitted almost anywhere except for unauthorized areas in National Parks and Nature Reserves. If you're unsure about the camping regulations for a specific

What is a Family Stay?

Many of the small towns along trails in the Galilee do not have a formal hotel, hostel or B&B. In these cases, trail organizers have worked with local families to provide homestay accommodations in spare apartments or rooms. This win-win situation provides accommodations for the weary hiker as well as a side income for local families. Visitors also have the opportunity to meet local people for a more authentic glimpse into life in the Galilee. All of the homestay families on the trails speak English. Many of the accommodations have a separate entrance, private bathroom and guest kitchen.

A Jesus Trail hiker gets to know her hostess at the Cana Wedding B&B.

location, don't hesitate to ask locals nearby. They may even invite you into their home for the night! Official campsites, both paid and free, are marked on route maps. Free campsites generally have water and picnic tables and sometimes bathrooms. Pay campgrounds have bathrooms, hot water showers and sometimes other amenities like a snack bar.

Transportation

Public transportation runs to most locations across Israel with a combination of buses, trains and shared taxis, also called *sheruts* or *services* (pronounced sair-**vees**). The largest bus company is Egged, which runs routes to all regions of Israel. Many routes in the Galilee are run by Nazareth Transport and Tourism (NTT) which also runs a route to Amman, Jordan several times per week.

Buses

Public buses run regularly except holidays and Shabbat, which begins each Friday at sundown and ends on Saturday evening. Most buses will run routes until late Friday afternoon and resume service Saturday evening. NTT and other Arab-owned bus companies run routes on Saturdays and most Jewish holidays, but are less frequent on Muslim holidays. **See pp. 234-235 for detailed information on bus routes relevant to the hikes outlined in this book.**

Train

Israel has a clean, convenient train system that runs primarily along the coast. The main line between Ben Gurion Airport and Nahariya runs about every half hour except on Shabbat. Prices are similar to bus journeys, but trains are usually faster and more comfortable. Be aware that train cars can be very crowded during rush hour, especially in the hours before Shabbat begins. Accurate time tables and prices can be found at Israel Railways website: www.rail.co.il/en.

Taxis

Taxis can be arranged from any point on the trail. Most hotels and guesthouses are happy to arrange taxis for you, or you can use the phone numbers to the left. Van-sized taxis are available for larger groups.

Israeli Public Buses

- **Egged** (All areas), ☎03-694-8888, ☎*2800, www.egged.com
- **Nazareth Transport & Tourism**, ☎04-657-0577 (Galilee), ☎04-601-0458 (Amman reservations)
- **GB Tours**, ☎04-657-0745
- **Dan** (Tel Aviv), ☎03-639-4444, www.dan.co.il/english

Israel Trains

- Direct and easy connection to Ben Gurion Airport
- Schedules at www.rail.co.il/EN
- Tel: ☎*5770 or ☎03-611-7000

Taxis in the Galilee

- Josef: ☎050-753-5661
- Rami David: ☎050-543-5324
- David Meir: ☎050-523-7086
- Nazareth Taxi: ☎04-655-5536

Sample fares:

- Nazareth to Capernaum 150NIS
- Nazareth to Zippori: 60NIS
- Capernaum to Tiberias: 60NIS

Car Rental

Rental cars are available from all major cities including Tel Aviv, Jerusalem, Haifa, Tiberias and Nazareth. Daily rental fees are reasonable (as low as $30/€20 a day in low season, starting at twice that in high season), but bear in mind that fuel costs in Israel are high—around 6NIS a liter ($6.15/gallon; €1.10/liter).

On the bright side, Israel is a small country, so no in-country distance is all that far. Some credit cards offer Collision Damage Waiver (CDW) Insurance on rental cars, but this coverage is usually void in Israel. Budget (www.budget.co.il), Avis (www.avis.co.il) and Hertz (www.hertz.co.il) all have offices in larger cities. In Nazareth try GoodLuck rentals (www.goodluckcars.com), located on Paulus the 6th St.

Hitching/Tramping

Hitchhiking is fairly common in Israel, especially in more remote regions in the north and south. It is best done from existing bus stops by reaching your arm out and casually pointing in the direction you wish to go—no thumbs-up needed. If you choose to hitchhike, use common sense. It's safer to hitchhike in pairs, especially for women. Do not hesitate to turn down a ride from anyone that makes you uncomfortable. If you are at a popular site, such as a national park, you might ask around in the parking lot if anyone is going toward your next stop. Any hitchhiking you undertake is at your own risk!

Communication ☎

There are more cell phones than people in Israel, and we strongly recommend that you bring one along on your hike. Service is available on all of the hikes outlined in this guide, and it can be crucial to have a phone in case of an emergency as well as very helpful when making reservations. Israel's country code is +972. When dialing local numbers from abroad, be sure to drop the leading 0 before the area code.

If you have an unlocked tri- or quad-band GSM cell phone, you can purchase an Israeli SIM card with a local number for 20-80NIS, with Cellcom and Orange as the two most popular carriers. Purchase prepaid phone credit at kiosks and convenience stores. Having a local SIM card lets you make calls and send texts within Israel and send texts internationally, with all incoming calls and texts for free. You can buy a SIM card ahead of time from www.israelsims.com. You can also rent a cell phone at the airport or from Israel Phones (www.israelphones.com) or Amigo (www.amigo-us.com). Many cell phones from your home country offer international roaming, but costs for these services are usually very high.

The Internet is accessible at most hotels and hostels, many offering wifi if you choose to bring your own laptop. Larger towns usually have an Internet cafe, but their number has decreased as wifi has become more popular. Post offices are available in every town and offer international shipping.

Money and Budgeting

The unit of currency in Israel is the New Israeli Shekel (NIS or ₪), which is made up of 100 *agorot*. Some tourist areas also accept US dollars and Euros. Ben Gurion Airport and all major towns in Israel have ATMs (cash machines), which are the best way to obtain shekels upon arrival. For up-to-date conversion rates, check www.xe.com. Credit cards are accepted in most accommodations and provide a good backup to your ATM card. Many credit cards charge a currency conversion fee of up to 3%, so consider a card with free conversion, such as Capital One.

The budget for your hiking trip to Israel depends mostly on your personal style. For travelers camping out and making their own food, it is possible to hike and hitch for as little as $15/€10 per day. For hostelers with a meal or two out and public transportation, costs are more like $40-60/€25-40 per day. For private hotel rooms, nicer restaurants and transport by rental car, $100/€75+ per day is likely.

Business Hours

Since the Jewish Sabbath (Shabbat) is observed on Saturday, the "weekend" for most Israelis is Friday/Saturday and the dreaded first day back at work is Sunday, not Monday. Business hours are generally 8am-7pm Sunday through Thursday. Stores close early on Friday, and almost nothing is open on Saturday.

In Arab towns, the weekend looks a little different, as shops tend to be closed on Friday (the Muslim holy day) and Sunday (the Christian holy day), with Saturday as the most lively market day.

Traveling with Children

Israel is a very child-friendly destination with good infrastructure, smooth roads and generally high standards of living. Diapers, baby food and other supplies can be bought in any city. If you plan to hike the trail with children, think through how much walking your child can realistically handle in a day, or for younger children, how far you can carry them. Choose an itinerary with a realistic distance and difficulty rating. The terrain is mostly suitable for all-terrain strollers with a few minor adjustments in route.

Garbage and Recycling

As soon as you set out on the trail out of Nazareth you will notice one of Israel's worst environmental problems: garbage. Outside of towns along the trail you may see improvised garbage dumps, construction debris and miscellaneous junk interfering with the serene natural views. Many garbage disposal sites are reaching maximum capacity and have not been maintained properly.

While there are recycling facilities in a few cities, less than 5% of Israeli waste is recycled and over 90% is buried in landfills, placed in official or unofficial dumps or burnt. Disposing of construction waste correctly is expensive, so many companies cut costs with illegal dumping. A goal of the Jesus Trail is to encourage environmental awareness and draw attention to environmental issues such as this, with the hope that outdoor tourism will give locals a stake in maintaining the natural beauty of the Galilee.

Safety in Israel and on the Jesus Trail

While the media often portrays Israel and Palestine as perpetual hot spots of violence, the tourist areas of the region are generally very safe with a high level of security. In fact, the statistically most dangerous part of a trip to Israel is probably your drive to the airport in your home country. Tourists have not ordinarily been targets of violence in Israel, and politically motivated violence in Israel has been low for the past five years. Crime rates in Israel are very low, on par with western European countries like Germany. Israel is a popular tourist destination, with almost three million foreign visitors each year, and the overwhelming majority complete their trip without incident.

The Galilee region is very stable and local people are by and large remarkably hospitable and helpful. Israelis generally enjoy the outdoors, so hiking and backpacking are common and acceptable activities. There is always some risk associated with hiking and camping alone in any part of the world, but the risk in the Galilee region is very minimal.

Female hikers have occasionally reported unwanted attention from some young men in towns. This attention can be annoying, but is usually not dangerous and is best ignored. If the problem persists, walk into a shop or other area with people and enlist their help. Older locals are often frustrated and embarrassed by any mistreatment of visitors and can take care of the problem. If serious harassment occurs, call the police at ☎100.

Environment of the Galilee

הגליל الجليل

Geography and Ecology

The 1st-century historian Josephus Flavius (see p. 205) wrote that the Galilee was "wonderful in its characteristics and in its beauty. Thanks to the rich soil there is not a plant that does not flourish there, and the inhabitants grow everything: the air is so temperate that it suits the most diverse species."

The name Galilee comes from the Hebrew word *Galil*, which means "cylinder" or "district," and was sometimes referred to as *ha-Galil ha-goyim*, or the "district of the nations" or "district of the Gentiles." In biblical times the Galilee region was roughly circle shaped, while today the term usually refers to a slightly different territory which includes the northern coast of Israel and extends only to the northern Israeli border (not into Lebanon as it would have in biblical times). The Galilee measures approximately 100 km from north to south, and 70 km west to east.

Present-day Galilee consists of three subregions—*Upper Galilee, Lower Galilee* and *Western Galilee.*

Lower Galilee stretches from the Jezre'el Valley in the south up to the Beit HaKerem valley, and from the Mediterranean Sea in the west to the Sea of Galilee in the east. The landscape of Lower Galilee consists of low rugged hills and valleys, mostly made up of soft limestone and dolomite. *Upper Galilee* is delineated by the Beit HaKerem Valley up to the Lebanese border (and in biblical times continued up to the Litani River in Lebanon, including the cities of Tyre and Sidon), and includes more dramatic mountains and more isolated areas. Around the Sea of Galilee and further north, dark volcanic basalt rock and rich volcanic soil make up much of the landscape. *Western Galilee* refers to the section along the coast from Haifa up to Rosh Hanikra on the Lebanese border.

Most of the Galilee falls into the Mediterranean zone of vegetation, characterized by high rainfall, low temperature and green areas. Vegetation varies in hills, plains and valleys. Evergreen trees, such as Palestinian oak, characterize the hill country as their hearty roots can penetrate the limestone and dolomite. Tabor oaks once thrived in lower Galilee until they were largely deforested by the Ottomans to use as fuel for railway engines.

On the eastern slope of the Galilee, as the landscape plunges below sea level, the climate begins to transition into the Irano-Turanian zone. Farther north the climate shifts to a moist-temperate zone, where laurel, arbutus, Judas trees and walnut trees flourish. Jerusalem pines still dot the landscape in areas with soft bedrock. The coastal plain provides ideal conditions for carob trees. In the early 20th century, eucalyptus trees were introduced from Australia to aid in the draining of the Hula swamp region. After World War II, conifers were introduced to the region to combat erosion.

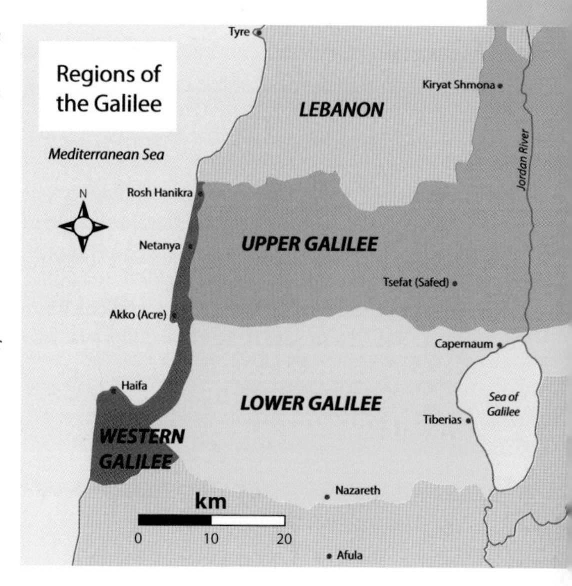

Birds

Consider the ravens: They do not sow or reap, they have no storeroom or barn; yet God feeds them. And how much more valuable you are than birds!
Luke 12:24

Israel lies directly on the migratory path of many rare and interesting birds that travel between Europe and Asia, making it an ideal place for bird watching. Over 500 different species have been recorded as living in or migrating through Israel, with annual traffic of over 500 million birds. This phenomenon was observed even in biblical times, with over 100 references to birds in the Bible. Several birding stations are set up in different regions of Israel, but anyone with binoculars and a bird book can get started in amateur bird watching in any natural area of Israel.

On the Jesus Trail, spring and autumn are a good time to observe storks. The small distinctive hoopoe bird was crowned the national bird of Israel in 2008, and can be observed during any season. The lesser kestrel, a small endangered bird of prey, visits the Galilee in spring and has been part of a regional education project to set up nesting boxes and protect the habitat of its dwindling population.

There are many bird watching tours available through nature societies, or you can purchase a guide to birds in Israel and do your own exploring.

Flowers

Consider how the lilies grow. They do not labor or spin. Yet I tell you, not even Solomon in all his splendor was dressed like one of these. Luke 12:27

In the spring, a stunning array of wildflowers carpets the Galilee in lush green and jewel tones. Israel's national flower, the cyclamen (see p. 82), peeks its pink and white head above ground, followed by the red poppy-like anemones. Many varieties of irises flourish in the Galilee, including the Nazareth iris, unique to a small area outside of Nazareth, and the Gilboa iris, found in a small reserve on Mt. Gilboa. The best time to enjoy the wildflowers is early spring after the flowers have been nourished by the winter rains.

Animals

Jesus replied, "Foxes have holes and birds of the air have nests, but the Son of Man has no place to lay his head." Matthew 8:20

The Galilee is home to many species of animals, in spite of industrialization that has radically reduced viable habitat. On the Jesus Trail you're most likely to see gazelles, turtles, foxes, rabbits and possibly a harmless (or harmful...) snake or two. Outside of Nazareth, a camel herder occasionally tends his flocks, though most camels live further south in the Negev. Further north, herds of wild boar can occasionally be seen as well as jackals, whose piercing barks punctuate the night silence. Hyenas supposedly still live in the region, though sightings are rare.

Galilean Food

The Mediterranean climate and fertile ground of the Galilee make it the main food production area of Israel. Olives, wheat and grapes, known as the Mediterranean Triad, are grown in abundance. The Galilee has a reputation for high-quality natural foods, from local wines and honeys to homemade cheeses and breads. *Freekeh*, a green cracked wheat, is a popular local ingredient. Among Palestinian communities, *maklube* (which means "upside-down" in Arabic) is a common dish, in which layers of spiced rice, meat and vegetables are cooked in a pot which is then inverted over the serving dish. Delicious sweets like *baklava* and *kanafeh*, a warm syrupy dessert featuring goat or sheep's cheese, are definitely worth sampling. You can even take a "culinary tour" of the Galilee to sample some of the lesser-known delights (www.galileecuisine.co.il).

People of the Galilee

Though known for being a Jewish state, Israel is home to a colorful mosaic of people from diverse religious and ethnic backgrounds. About 76% of the population of Israel are Jewish, of which the majority are secular. **Ashkenazi** is a term for the descendents of European Jews who follow the European-style practice of Judaism. Jews who follow the religious tradition developed on the Iberian peninsula before the 15th-century expulsion of Jews from Spain are known as **Sephardi**. Those Sephardi Jews who settled in the Middle East, North Africa, Central Asia and the Caucasus became known as **Mizrahi,** though many of these also follow the Sephardic religious practices. Religious observance among Jewish Israelis ranges from Orthodox to Reformed to atheist and every possible variation between.

After the partition of the region into a Jewish and Arab state and subsequent war in 1948 (see historical timeline p. 221), Arabs living in what became the state of Israel were granted Israeli citizenship. These Arab citizens of Israel are often referred to as **Arab Israelis** or Arabs of '48, though some would still identify themselves as Palestinians. Most Arab-Israelis are Sunni Muslim, though about 10% are Christian (mostly traditional churches such as Catholic and Orthodox) and 9% Druze.

Arab citizens of Israel make up about 20% of Israel's population, and live mainly in Arab towns as well as mixed cities, such as Haifa. Arab Israelis make up 52% of the population of the Galilee. As citizens, they officially have the same rights and privileges (such as voting) as Jewish Israelis, but discrimination is still common and Arab cities frequently receive less government spending than nearby Jewish cities. While Jewish-Israelis perform a mandatory 2-3 years of military service, Muslim and Christian Arab-Israelis are exempt from military service. **Druze** (pp. 94-95) are required to serve in the military and many **Bedouin** (p. 216) do so voluntarily.

The **Circassians** are another minority population in the Galilee, with about 3000 centralized in two Galilean towns: Kfar Kama and Rehaniya. Circassians migrated to Israel in the 19th century after being exiled from the Caucasus region by the Russians. While Circassians are mainly Sunni Muslim and speak Arabic, they have a distinct culture and also have their own Circassian language.

Palestinian is a term for Arabs with family origins in Palestine, such as those in the West Bank and Gaza as well as Arab refugees from the wars in 1948 and 1967 who do not have Israeli citizenship. Palestinians in the West Bank and Gaza are not allowed to enter Israel without special permits that are difficult to obtain. Also, Israeli citizens are legally banned from entering Palestinian territory. To add even more confusion to the mix, Arabs in East Jerusalem were granted residency in Israel but not citizenship.

Hiking in the Galilee

Israel Nature and National Parks Protection Authority

Israel has a well-developed and maintained national park system with over 65 sites spread across the country run by the Israel Nature and National Parks Protection Authority (www.parks.org.il). These range from archeological sites to nature reserves to recreational areas such as hot springs.

Entrance fees range from 10-60NIS depending on the size and importance of the site. You can also purchase park passes that can be used for multiple sites. For 90NIS, an orange card gets you into any six parks within a two-week period. The green card, at 130NIS, gets you unlimited entrance into national parks for two weeks. If you plan on sticking around longer, year-long park passes cost 250NIS per individual, 275NIS per couple and 330-360NIS per family.

National parks generally open at 8am and close at 5pm, or 4pm in winter and on Fridays and the eve of national holidays. Facilities usually include bathrooms, places to refill water and a gift shop with snacks, drinks and souvenirs. English brochures are usually provided, and other languages are also often available.

The only national parks directly on the Jesus Trail are Zippori and Arbel; others mentioned in this book are Capernaum (entrance free), Kursi, Korazin, Beit She'an, Belvoir (Kokhav HaYarden), Gan HaShlosha (1/2 price with a park pass) and Beit Alpha. Vatican-owned Capernaum and the Mount of Beatitudes requires separate nominal entrance fees. Entering Jordan River Park and Bethsaida by car requires an entrance fee, but not if arriving on foot or bicycle.

Trail-blazing supplies

Society for the Protection of Nature in Israel (SPNI)

The Society for the Protection of Nature in Israel (SPNI) is an environmental organization established in 1953 to oppose the draining of the Hula Valley swamp in northern Israel. Though the swamp was drained to make way for more farmland, SPNI succeeded in re-flooding portions of the valley. SPNI has been at the forefront of environmental education and legislation in the region, with membership of over 100,000. They have several field schools throughout the country and lead environmental education seminars, outdoor trips and a variety of other projects related to environmental protection and education.

Mountain biking the Jesus Trail down from the Horns of Hattin

Another role of SPNI is marking and maintaining official hiking trails in Israel. They produce excellent regional topographic maps with all hiking trails marked (including the Jesus Trail on the next map scheduled for release summer of 2010).

Israeli Hiking, Biking and 4x4 Trail System

Trails in Israel are marked with paint blazes made up of three stripes. Ordinary short trails are marked with a solid black, blue, red or green stripe between two white stripes, and commonly referred to by the color of the center stripe (blue trail, green trail, etc). The Israel Trail (blue/orange/white) is a unique long-distance trail that stretches from Eilat on the southern border to Dan on the northern Lebanese border. Recently, longer regional trails have been added such as a trail circumnavigating the Sea of Galilee (white/purple/white).

The Jesus Trail is Israel's first long-distance historical route and bears the distinction of its own unique blaze color—white/orange/white or an orange dot (see diagram on next page). These paint colors will guide you through the towns and villages and sites of the trail. Itineraries beyond the Classic Jesus Trail are not marked in orange blazes, but follow various other marked trails. Pay close attention to section maps and directions to make sure you are following the correct blaze colors.

Figure 1: Jesus Trail goes straight

Figure 2: Jesus Trail turns right

Figure 3: Jesus Trail (orange dot) and blue trail turn right

Figure 4: Jesus Trail (orange dot), red trail and Israel Trail veer right together. Green trail joins from left

Jesus Trail Markings

Hiking trails in Israel are marked with paint blazes of three stripes of color indicating the direction of the path. The Jesus Trail (J1-9) blaze colors are white/orange/white (fig. 1). The stripes bend at a right angle to the left or right to indicate turns (fig. 2). Sometimes the trail follows along other marked trails—the Jesus Trail blazes will either alternate with the blaze of the other trail, or an orange dot will be added above the other trail blaze (fig. 3). Sometimes the Jesus Trail intersects other trails, as indicated above (fig. 4).

Only J1-9 (Classic Jesus Trail) are blazed in orange. Additional trails in this book are blazed in a variety of colors indicated on maps and route descriptions.

From each blaze, the next one should be visible. Train your eyes to look for these symbols on rocks, trees, walls, curbs and fences. Be aware that occasionally paint blazes are altered or destroyed by weather, animals or local graffiti artists. We do our best to make sure the trail and its blazes are well-maintained, so please inform us if you find a section with missing or damaged blazes.

Other Hiking Trails in the Region

Israel Trail
(Hebrew: Shvil Yisra'el)

שביל ישראל
مسيرة درب البلاد

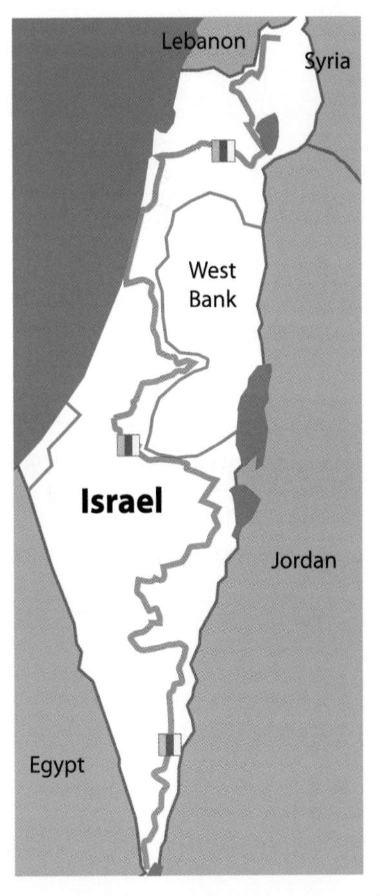

Israel's most prominent long-distance hiking trail, the Israel Trail, is a marked 940-km route stretching from Eilat in the south on the Red Sea to northernmost Dan near the Lebanese border. The trail was marked in 1991 and has become a popular activity for Israeli youth to complete after military service.

The colors of the blaze represent sections of the trail; orange for the Negev desert, blue for the Mediterranean Sea, and white for the snow of Mt. Hermon.

The trail can be hiked independently, though tent camping is necessary as well as water drops at some points in the Negev. Most hikers complete the trail in five to eight weeks.

There is one guidebook to the Israel Trail in English (p. 228) that can be purchased in Nazareth. For more information see www.israeltrail.org.

Snow-capped Mt. Hermon

Golan Trail (Hebrew: Shvil HaGolan) שביל הגולן مسار الجولان

The mountains of Bashan are majestic mountains; rugged are the mountains of Bashan. Psalm 68:15

In 2008, another long-distance trail was added to Israel's repertoire: the Golan Trail. Though the Israel Trail was purposefully routed around the contested Golan Heights (biblical Bashan) which Israel captured from Syria in the Six-Day War of 1967, some felt that the beauty of the region warranted its own trail.

Stretching 125 km from Mt. Hermon on the Syrian/Lebanese border to the Sea of the Galilee, the trail traverses some of the most remote and lushly vegetated landscape in Israel. The trail is blazed in blue, green and white, representing the Sea of Galilee, fertile vegetation, and Mt. Hermon. To download the GPS track see www.golantrail.com.

Jerusalem Trail مسار القدس שביל ירושלים

Our feet are standing in your gates, O Jerusalem. Psalm 122:2

The Jerusalem Trail, a new and lesser-known path, winds through the city of Jerusalem and the surrounding landscape, connecting ancient history with a surprising amount of natural beauty. The 42-km loop trail is marked with a combination of colored blazes (mostly blue) and metal signs with the emblem of a lion with a walking stick, but the blazes are difficult to follow. Connecting to the Israel Trail on both sides, the trail is a useful add-on for through hikers. To download the GPS track see www.jerusalemtrail.com.

Nativity Trail مسار الميلا

So Joseph also went up from the town of Nazareth in Galilee to Judea, to Bethlehem the town of David, because he belonged to the house and line of David. Luke 2:4

The Jesus Trail isn't the first biblical walking trail in the region. In 1999, the Alternative Tourism Group, a Palestinian tour agency, developed a trail from Nazareth through the northern West Bank (biblical Samaria) to Bethlehem. Dubbed the

Nativity Trail, the path was designed to recreate the journey of Mary and Joseph leaving their hometown of Nazareth to be counted in a census in Bethlehem, where Jesus was born. It was developed in conjunction with a variety of celebratory activities to usher in the year 2000. Unfortunately, the Second Intifada broke out just prior to the festivities, and many tourists canceled their plans to come to the region. The Nativity Trail lay dormant for the next eight years as the political situation made it impossible for tourists to walk between Israel and the West Bank.

In 2008, the trail was revived after being rerouted to skirt new Jewish settlements. The northern border between Nazareth and the Palestinian town of Faqu'a is seldom open, so hikers usually begin in Faqu'a after traveling up from a Jerusalem border. The 160-km trail is unmarked and only accessible by hiring a guide. It passes through Nablus, Jericho, Bethlehem and various ruins, tombs and archeological sites, many of which have not been excavated. An excellent (though now outdated) guide for the trail is *The Nativity Trail and other Walks in Palestine* by Tony Howard and Di Taylor. To hire a guide, see www.atg.ps.

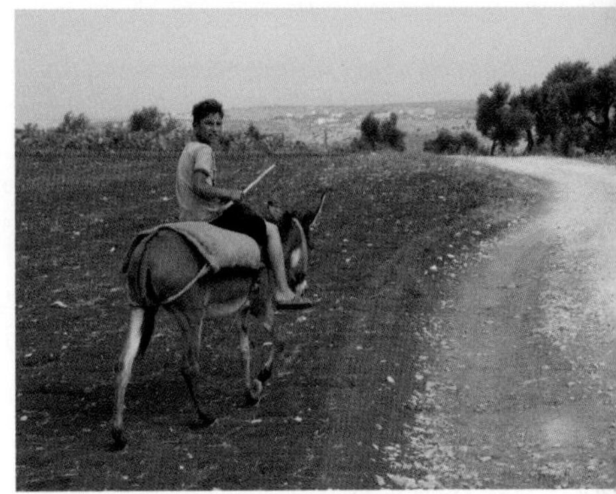

A local boy rides his donkey through fields along the Nativity Trail.

Abraham's Path מסار إبراهيم الخليل נתיב אברהם

The Lord had said to Abram, "Leave your country, your people and your father's household and go to the land I will show you." Genesis 12:1

Another long-distance cultural path in the region, Abraham's Path, was initiated by Harvard University's Global Negotiation Project in 2007. The path recreates the journey of Abraham, father of Judaism, Christianity and Islam, leaving his homeland of Ur/Urfa, traveling to Canaan and to his final resting place in Hebron. Goals of the Path include providing economic benefit to towns and villages along the trail and encouraging increased understanding between diverse people.

So far, segments of Abraham's Path are open in Turkey, Jordan, Israel and Palestine, which can be walked with a guide. For more information see www.abrahampath.org.

Preparing to Hike the Jesus Trail

Choosing your Itinerary

The routes described in this book are designed to be walked by average people. You don't need to be a mountain climber, super athlete or hard-core camper to enjoy the trail! The trail has something for everyone, whether your goal is Christian pilgrimage, historical learning, physical fitness, enjoyment of nature, encountering other cultures and religions or any combination of these.

Your own pace, fitness, interests and time constraints will factor into which itinerary you choose. If you're short on time, select a day hike or half-day hike. If you want to sleep in a bed and eat a restaurant meal each night, select a route that has these amenities. If you'd rather walk shorter amounts and have more time to spend at points of interest, split up a one-day section into two days. If there are certain sites that you don't want to miss, be sure to select a route that includes them. Any itinerary can also be walked in reverse, though note the changes in elevation when reversing a route (refreshing downhills turn into rugged uphills).

When to Go

Israel has a Mediterranean climate characterized by hot, dry summers and cool, wet winters. The rainy winter season begins around November and the intensity increases through December and January. Spring rains usually end in March, transforming the brown countryside into lush, green hills bursting with a variety of colorful flowers. During the spring, streams and rivers are also at their peak, making this the ideal time to hike the Jesus Trail.

Israel's climate offers two great hiking seasons—March to May and mid-September to mid-November. Hiking during the remainder of the year is not ideal due to the greater extremes in weather and temperature. June to August is very hot in the

The difference between hiking in spring versus summer at Susita (Hippos).

Galilee and the sun's intensity combined with high temperatures require that hikers walk shorter distances, rest during the middle of the day and carry more water. Although cooler in December and January, frequent and prolonged periods of rain can bring gloom to any hiking experience and turn otherwise pleasant paths into sticky mud pits. You can count on rain-free walking from May to September.

Another factor to consider in the timing of your trip are the various holidays that may impact your travel. During Jewish holidays, public transportation shuts down and during Ramadan, the Muslim month of fasting, some stores and restaurants might be closed during the day. Christians may wish to combine their visit with the Holy Week festivities surrounding Easter, which bring many tourists and travelers from around the world. However, note that Easter often coincides with Passover, during which accommodations will be scarcer and more expensive. For a list of religious holidays in Israel, refer to the chart on p. 245.

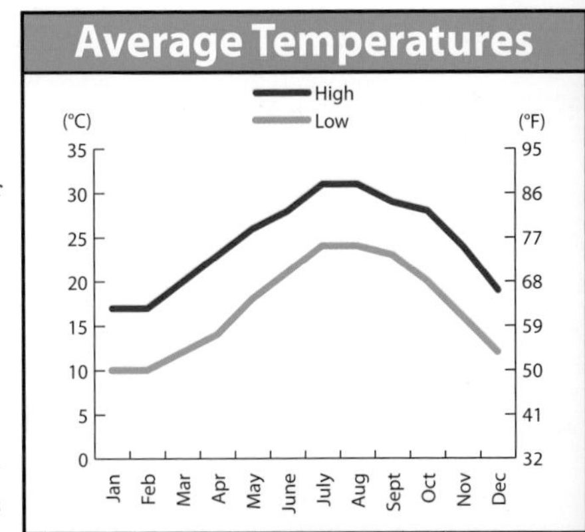

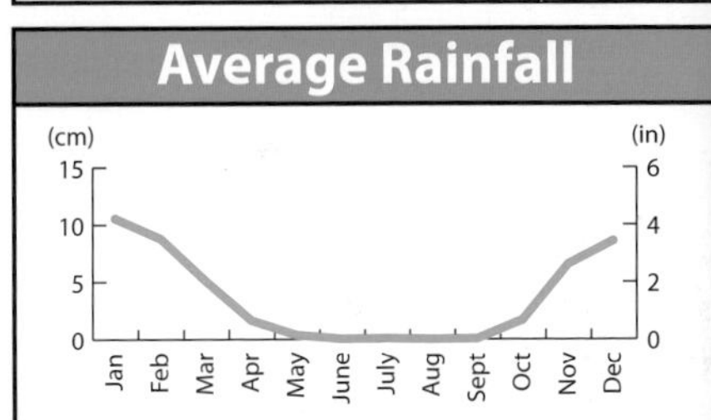

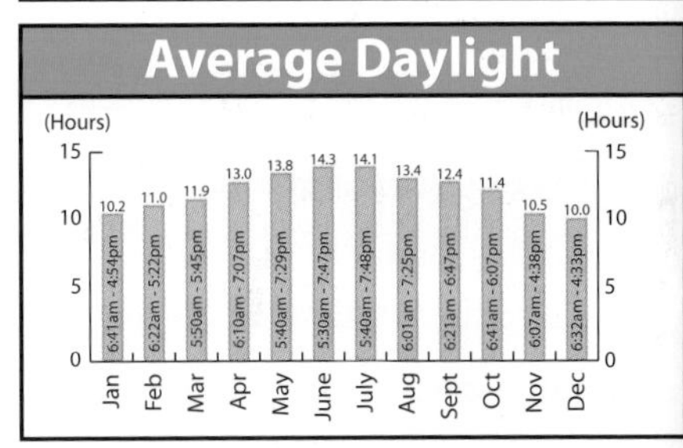

*Nazareth averages, other Galilee statistics are similar.

Packing for the Trail

In the spirit of Jesus' instructions in Mark 6:8, we encourage packing simply and lightly, as you will become painfully aware of each unnecessary possession after a few hours on the trail.

REI (Recreation Equipment Inc.) is a large American consumer cooperative that sells outdoor gear. A large section of their website is a database devoted to knowledge on outdoor equipment and skills. We recommend consulting this resource for choosing a specific backpack, hiking shoe or learning more about how to use a GPS. Available online at www.rei.com/expertadvice.

Day Hiking Gear

- ☐ Backpack (15-25L)
- ☐ Navigation: guidebook (optional: GPS, maps, compass)
- ☐ Knife
- ☐ Fire starter
- ☐ Light: headlamp or flashlight
- ☐ Sun protection: hat, sunglasses, sunscreen and lip balm
- ☐ First aid kit with foot care and toilet paper
- ☐ Fleece or jacket (not necessary in summer)
- ☐ Waterproof jacket during rainy season
- ☐ Personal/optional: journal & pen, pocket Bible, camera, cell phone, wallet

Clothing (Multi-Day)

- ☐ Footwear (boots or trail sneakers)
- ☐ Lightweight sandals
- ☐ Hiking socks, wicking sock liners
- ☐ Quick-drying pants/shorts
- ☐ Short-sleeved wicking shirts
- ☐ Underwear
- ☐ Swimsuit
- ☐ Warm hat*
- ☐ Long-sleeved shirt or fleece layer*
- ☐ Long underwear top/bottom*
- ☐ Waterproof shell*

**only necessary in rainy/cold season*

Camping Gear

- ☐ Large backpack (40-60L)
- ☐ Tent, sleeping pad, sleeping bag
- ☐ Stove, cookware, utensils, soap and cleaning supplies
- ☐ 10 m accessory cord
- ☐ Personal items (toothbrush, toothpaste, soap, etc.)
- ☐ Insect repellent

Footwear

The most important part of any trek is comfortable, broken-in footwear. Make sure you break in your footwear significantly by doing several day hikes with a loaded pack before you begin a multi-day trek. Your feet will thank you! Since the Jesus Trail routes are mostly day hikes and overnight trips with light loads, trail shoes or light hiking boots are your best choice. Although many of the trails in this book are on 4x4 tracks devoid of thorny plants and loose dirt, we do not recommend exclusively wearing sandals unless you are accustomed to doing so and have a sturdy and reliable pair.

Blisters, caused by friction, are a frequent consequence of poor-fitting footwear, a problem exacerbated by having wet feet. Wool and synthetic socks keep your feet dry by wicking moisture away from your skin, which prevents blisters. Cotton socks should be avoided. Liner socks also provide a helpful extra layer to reduce friction. Make sure to wear your intended footwear (shoes, socks and liners) thoroughly on a variety of terrain for the months before your trip in order to work out the kinks and avoid the misery of blisters on your trip.

Clothing

Think about your hiking clothes as layers, with the inner layer for moisture management, the middle layer for insulation and the outer layer for weather protection. The general rule for outdoor clothing is to avoid cotton fabrics (jeans and most T-shirts) as they do not retain insulating properties when wet. Synthetic materials (polyester, nylon, spandex) and wool will dry faster than their cotton counterparts and are the best choice in wet weather.

We recommend bringing a rain jacket with a waterproof breathable membrane such as Gore-Tex®. Plastic ponchos are a good backup option if rain is possible but unlikely. Hypothermia is possible if you run into wet weather during the winter season, so be prepared with the right clothing. Always have a dry set of clothes (socks included) to change into after a rainy day. If your body is wet it will be difficult to stay warm.

In warm weather seasons, choose lightweight breathable clothes that provide sun protection. Remember that you can save weight by hand-washing clothes on the trail and drying them on your pack as you hike.

In every season, be prepared for the sun with a wide-brimmed hat and sunglasses. Be sure to use sunscreen regularly, and never underestimate the sun's strength. Severe sunburn will make the rest of your trip uncomfortable and increase chances of dehydration.

As you pass through Arab villages and religious Jewish areas, respect conservative local norms by wearing pants at least below the knee and shirts that cover shoulders. Covered knees and shoulders are also required to enter the religious sites along the route, including Nebi Shu'eib and the churches around the Sea of Galilee. A pair of pants that can zip off into shorts provides flexibility.

Sample First Aid Kit:

- ☐ Variety of adhesive bandages
- ☐ Antibiotic ointment
- ☐ Sterile gauze pads
- ☐ Pain reliever/fever reducer (such as acetaminophen or ibuprofen)
- ☐ Antihistamine (such as Benadryl)
- ☐ Moleskin or other blister treatment
- ☐ Safety pins
- ☐ Baby powder (helps with chafing)
- ☐ Instant cold compress
- ☐ Anti-diarrheal medicine
- ☐ Small scissors
- ☐ Optional: insect bite treatment

Gear

For day hikes, see the day hiking gear list on the opposite page. For overnight trips, use a larger pack instead of a day pack and add camping gear. The Jesus Trail is not particularly technically challenging and does not require special gear beyond normal backpacking supplies.

Backpacks

Packs designed for day use range in volume from 500-2500 in^3 (10-40 L) and multi-day packs range from 2500-6000 in^3 (40-100 L), depending on the length of your trip. Since supplies are available every day on the Jesus Trail and frequently on other routes in this book, a 40-60 L pack should be sufficient for multi-day treks. For a day trip, a standard school-sized backpack should be fine (900-1500 in^3, 15-25 L). It's important to have a pack that fits you well, so get fitted in a gear store or measure your own torso length before purchasing a pack.

Sleeping Pad, Sleeping Bag and Tents/Tarps

If you plan to camp, it is essential that you carry at least a sleeping pad and sleeping bag. In addition to comfort, a sleeping pad insulates you from the ground during the night and sleeping bag temperature ratings assume you are using a pad under the bag. Simple foam pads can be purchased at any Israeli gear store for 20-60NIS.

For any season, a three-season (15-35°F/-10-0°C) sleeping bag will be plenty to keep you warm at night. From May-September, a summer bag should be sufficient (+35°F/0°C). Down sleeping bags insulate better for their weight but not at all when wet. Synthetic sleeping bags retain insulating properties when wet, which is advisable for camping during the winter months.

We recommend that you carry a tarp or tent, especially from October through April. A simple three-season backpacking tent will do the job. Lightweight options include tarp tents, bivy sacks or fly tarps with a simple ground sheet. Although mosquitoes and flies do not pose a great problem in the Galilee, it may also be worth the tent's weight to keep away pesky buzzing in your ears that might keep you up all night.

Food Ideas

- Dehydrated pasta or rice meals
- Granola
- Instant oatmeal
- Canned beans or vegetables
- Tuna or other canned meat
- Nuts and seeds
- Dried fruit
- Olives
- Salami
- Peanut butter and jelly
- Pita bread
- Coffee
- Powdered milk
- Drink mix with electrolytes
- Fruits and vegetables that don't bruise easily (apples, oranges, cucumbers)

Stoves and Cookware

A backpacking stove is essential for cooking hot meals on the trail. Individuals and small groups may prefer screw-on canister stoves for their simplicity and lighter weight. Larger groups may prefer a sturdier liquid fuel model such as the classic MSR® WhisperLite™. It is prohibited to fly with fuel canisters or flammable liquids, but all of these fuel types are available at any gear store in Israel.

Don't forget to pack appropriate cookware and utensils. The more a group can consolidate these items, the better. The lightest options are made of titanium, but aluminum and stainless steel options will get the job done. Lexan soup spoons or spork combinations can serve as a universal utensil. A pocket knife aids in a variety of cooking and repair tasks, and most include can and bottle openers.

Outdoor Gear Stores

Israel has a variety of quality outdoor gear stores with many international brands of both clothing and equipment.

If you don't want to carry gear over on the flight, you can completely outfit yourself to hike the trail once you arrive in Israel. Be aware that imported brands are typically marked up 20-50%. Gear stores are available in Nazareth at the Dodge Center shopping area (p. 177), the Camping Store in Tiberias (p. 153) and other major cities.

Food

The ideal foods for backpacking have light packaging, are calorie-dense and provide carbohydrates and protein.

In lower Nazareth, there are many small grocery stores that are open daily with reduced hours on Sundays. All types of fresh fruit and vegetables are available in the Old City's market. In one trip to Nazareth Ilit's Dodge Center commercial area, you can find just about everything you need for the hike: a large Mega supermarket, an outdoor gear store and a large chain bookstore with a reasonable English language section. In Tiberias, there are many large supermarkets near the downtown commercial region. See the map on p. 153. Other towns along the trail also have food stores for restock.

Jesus Trail Mix

To figuratively walk in Jesus' culinary footsteps, the following trail mix recipe is made up of ingredients that would have been common in a 1st-century Galilean diet.

Grain, especially wheat, was the base of the 1st-century diet, and toasted whole grain traveled well. Adding almonds to the grain results in a complete protein combination. Raisins are included for a bit of a sugar kick and because raisins would have been plentiful in 1st-century Galilee.

Trail mix base:

- 2 parts toasted wheat berries*
- 1 part raisins
- 1 part almonds

*To toast the grain, first heat 2.5 mL (1/2 tsp) of oil for each 120 mL (1/2 cup) of grain. When the oil is hot, add grain and stir constantly over medium-low heat for about five minutes. Add salt to taste, and cool grain by spreading flat on a plate.

Optional add-ins/substitutions: chopped, dried figs, apricots, or dates; walnuts; toasted sesame seed; toasted pearl barley.

Water on the Trail

Water is the most important resource on earth, and you may never realize this more than when you are hiking. Make sure to always have plenty of water with you. Most international hikers underestimate the strength of the heat and sun in the Galilee and easily become dehydrated, leading to fatigue, headaches and possible heat stroke and hospitalization. Drink mixes that add flavor and replenish electrolytes, such as Gatorade, help to encourage drinking.

If camping, be sure to bring a carrying capacity of at least three to five liters of water for overnight and cooking use. This can easily be done without wasting pack space by bringing collapsible water bottles to fill up before hiking to your campsite.

A simple option is to buy a 1.5 L bottle of water and refill along the trail. Many hikers prefer hydration systems with a tube and bite valve which can easily be sipped without stopping to take a bottle out of the pack.

For most hikes, you will not need to carry more than three liters of water per day if you are not camping overnight. If you need to carry water for camping or cleaning, plan accordingly. In the summer, you should try to drink a minimum of five liters per day. If you feel thirsty, you are already dehydrated. Pay attention to water refill locations on each section map.

With a few exceptions, it is not an option to obtain water from natural sources. We recommend filling up from the tap, as tap water in Israel is generally safe to drink. It's not possible to buy bottled water consistently for all of the hikes in this guide, and we encourage the environmentally-friendly practice of reusing bottles.

When walking through agricultural land you may see what look like water faucets out in the agricultural fields. Do not drink from these faucets, as they may contain pesticide or fertilizer-treated water. Water filters or purification tablets are only helpful if you are thinking of hiking J22 or J30-32 in the rainy season. The water from the spring at Wadi Hamam is drinkable.

Using Our System of Hiking Routes

Stage Numbering and Route Network

In organizing the network of hikes in this book, we have chosen to break down longer hikes into numbered "J" sections grouped by color. Each J represents a partial or full-day hike that can be coupled with other J routes into multiple-day itineraries. Each J has a chapter in this book with an accompanying map, elevation profile, transportation and accommodations information and points of interest.

By referencing the appendices in the back of the book, you can easily see which accommodations (pp. 230-233), buses (pp. 234-235), and scripture references (p. 244) are relevant to each J route.

All J routes are accessible on either end by bus or taxi except two. Route J30 at Tel Rekshesh requires a 4x4 vehicle for access or can be reached on foot from the J23/24 intersection at Kfar Kish. Khirbet Cana at the J40/41 intersection, is only accessible by foot or 4x4 vehicle from Kafr Manda.

Distances and Pace

Distance are measured in metric units (kilometers and meters). For rough conversion, remember that 10 km equals 6.2 miles and 100 meters (or 0.1 km) and 100 yards are approximately the same distance, the length of a football field. Pay close attention to changes in blaze colors to anticipate your next turn or landmark.

Estimated duration of walking time for each route is listed assuming a pace of 3-5 km/hr (1.8-3 mph) with difficulty in terrain and elevation change taken into consideration. As you plan, remember to factor in extra time for breaks and to explore points of interest. We encourage you to plan your itinerary according to the pace that meets your personal goals and fitness level.

Difficulty Ratings

Each J route is assigned a level of difficulty from 1-3 and a brief description. All difficulty ratings are relative, as all of the hikes in this book would be "easy" for a professional mountaineer and, conversely, "difficult" for a 90-year-old grandfather. If you are in doubt as to whether you can handle a certain route, be sure to examine the elevation change and water access points. Also, consider the location of the nearest road if you would need to leave the route early due to fatigue. These ratings consider an "average" walker, who is reasonably fit but not necessarily athletic.

- ■□□ **Easy.** Slight elevation change. Sturdy footing. Water easily accessible.
- ■■□ **Moderate.** Some elevation change. Moderately challenging terrain.
- ■■■ **Challenging.** Significant elevation change. Possibly rocky or narrow path with less stable footing. Water sources may be scarce.

Mountain Biking the Jesus Trail

Most of the routes in this guide are possible on a mountain bike, but some require slight modification. Check each chapter to see if there are detours necessary for mountain bikes. Sections that cannot be biked are marked on the maps with 🚳, while detours are marked 🚲. We recommend that you bring your own mountain bike with front suspension. Biking the route greatly increases the amount of kilometers possible each day and enables day trips with less gear to carry. If you wish to carry overnight camping gear on your bike, add a rack and set of rear panniers or take bare necessities in a daypack.

Bikes are available for rent in Tiberias at Aviv Hostel and Tiberias Hostel (p. 150), but their quality and maintenance record is questionable. Higher quality mountain bikes are available from the Hooha Cyclist's House in Kfar Tavor (p. 162).

A tool Jesus didn't have: Download the Jesus Trail route to your GPS for foolproof navigation.

Maps, Google Earth and GPS

A variety of navigational tools are available through this guide and the Jesus Trail website at www.jesustrail.com. This book contains the following maps:

- Full trail network, which shows all routes with boxes around each J (pp. 2-3)
- 26 J route maps
- Detailed maps of relevant cities, parks and ancient sites
- Map Index: alphabetical listing of all maps and diagrams in book (p. 251)

Topographical Hiking Maps

SPNI makes accurate topographical maps (scale 1:50,000), which are more detailed than maps in this book. While only available in Hebrew, these maps are still very helpful in showing land contour, including all paved roads, 4x4 paths and hiking trails in the region. Each SPNI map section (80-100NIS) can be bought in any outdoor gear store or many Steimatsky's bookstores. All of the J routes outlined in this book can be found on map #3 with the exception of routes J10-14 which require map #1. Proceeds from SPNI map sales are directed into trail marking efforts. Another helpful secondary option is the Mapa Israel road atlas in English, which is available at most bookstores in Israel and updated annually, though hiking trails are not directly marked on these maps (scale 1:150,000 to 1:225,000).

Google Earth

We recommend that part of your trail preparation includes viewing the Jesus Trail route on Google Earth, a free software program that uses your Internet connection to access an image database for street-level detail of global sites. This allows you to see the exact path overlaid on satellite images with 3D topographical detail. By exploring the hills and valleys through this virtual tour, you will have a better idea of what to expect when you arrive in the Galilee.

Free GPS and Google Earth downloads available at: www.jesustrail.com/maps

The most current Jesus Trail route network with all hiking tracks and points of interest in this book can be download in Google Earth (KMZ), Garmin (GDB) and GPS exchange (GPX) file formats.

GPS Navigation

GPS stands for Global Positioning System, a technology developed for surveying and navigation purposes. The system works like traditional celestial navigation as GPS units receive signals from high-orbiting satellites to calculate specific coordinates at any given location. Accuracy is +/- 3 m, depending on each specific receiving unit's capability. GPS units are now relatively inexpensive ($75-400), and provide the best way to know exactly where you are in relation to a pre-programmed map or track.

In addition to the Google Earth files that are available on our website, we also have all of our routes and points of interest available in GPX format for free download to a personal GPS unit. We recommend using a mapping handheld, and have used Garmin devices for much of our research (eTrex Vista HCx). Most GPS units do not come pre-programmed with detailed base maps, especially of Israel, but with our downloadable file you will still be able to navigate the route easily and precisely.

Each GPS unit has three categories of data that are easily manipulated by users: waypoints, routes, and tracks. A **waypoint** marks the coordinates of an individual notable location, like where you parked your car or pitched your tent. A **route** is a collection of waypoints that are linked by straight lines in a specific order for navigation. A **track** is a detailed record of a walk that demonstrates the curve of a path, sometimes referred to as a "bread crumb trail." Tracks can be saved after each journey or pre-loaded and retraced on the GPS. The Jesus Trail files on the website use the track system as opposed to the route system for more accurate navigation.

We recommend bringing a GPS on your trek in order to guarantee navigational success. Be sure to bring enough batteries to last the duration of your hike. GPS units are available for rent in Nazareth at the Fauzi Azar Inn (p. 62).

JO

NAZARETH OLD CITY נצרת الناصرة

1-2 km
2-3 hours

DIFFICULTY:

NAZARETH TRANSPORT:

To/from Tel Aviv: Egged bus 823 or shared taxis (shorter, better option, from near main bus stop in Nazareth and Tel Aviv's Central Bus Station).

To/from Jerusalem: Direct Egged bus 955 runs twice daily. Connect in Afula for more options.

To/from Haifa: Bus 331 runs every 15-30 minutes from Paulus the 6th St. in Nazareth to outside Haifa's HaShmona train station (easy connection to airport).

To/from Tiberias: Bus 431 runs several times daily from Mary's Well to the Tiberias bus station.

Soak in Old World atmosphere in the Ottoman-style marketplace, satisfy your sweet tooth with local delicacies

This walking tour takes you to the major points of interest in the town. Feel free to deviate down interesting alleys and stop for coffee, tea and sweets in cafes along the way. No one is in a hurry in Nazareth. Begin at the Basilica of the Annunciation and allow 2-3 hours to visit all the sites listed.

Accommodations:

1. **Fauzi Azar Inn:** ☎054-432-2328; www.fauziazarinn.com; dorm 70NIS, double with breakfast 300-400NIS wifi
2. **Al-Mutran Guesthouse:** ☎04-645-7947; www.al-mutran.com; double 470NIS wifi
3. **Sisters of Nazareth:** ☎04-655-4304; dorm 60NIS, double 150-250NIS
4. **St. Margaret's Pilgrim Hostel:** ☎04-657-3507; dorm 140NIS, double 400NIS P

Nazareth

"Nazareth! Can anything good come from there?," Nathanael asked. "Come and see," said Philip. John 1:46

Nazareth, a bustling Arab city, is best-known as the childhood home of Jesus and the place of annunciation where Mary received the message that she would give birth to Jesus (Luke 1:26). The Bible also cites Nazareth as the place where Jesus began his ministry in the synagogue, after which an angry mob attempted to throw him off of a cliff (Luke 4:16-30). Today, Nazareth is the largest Arab city in Israel with over 70,000 people, of which about 2/3 are Muslim and 1/3 Christian. Just up the hill is Nazareth Ilit, a predominantly Jewish city of 43,000.

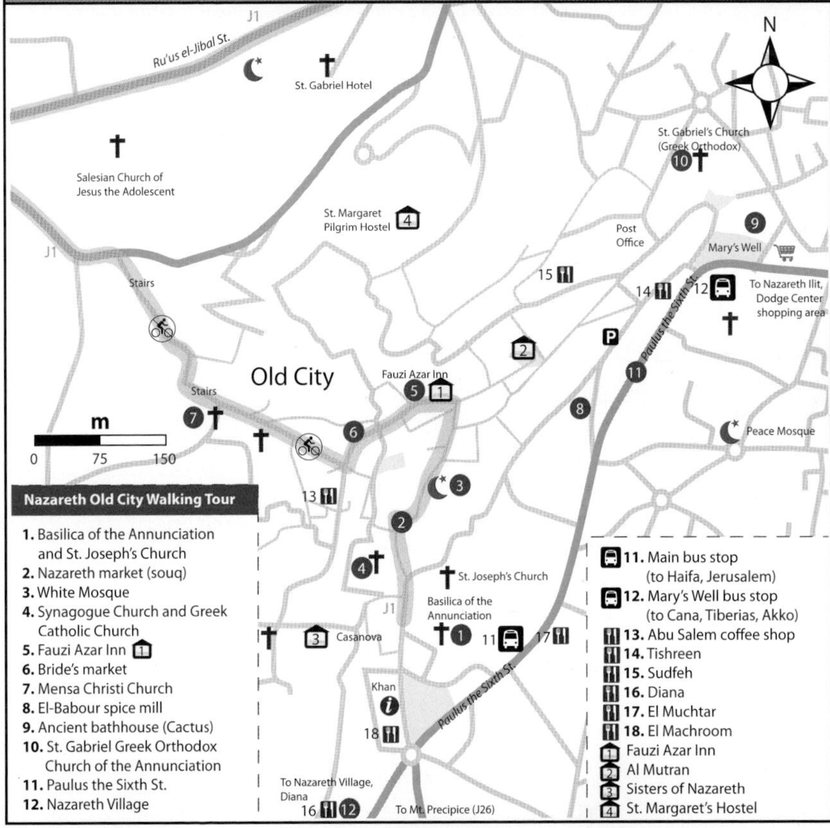

Nazareth Old City Walking Tour

1. Basilica of the Annunciation and St. Joseph's Church
2. Nazareth market (souq)
3. White Mosque
4. Synagogue Church and Greek Catholic Church
5. Fauzi Azar Inn 1
6. Bride's market
7. Mensa Christi Church
8. El-Babour spice mill
9. Ancient bathhouse (Cactus)
10. St. Gabriel Greek Orthodox Church of the Annunciation
11. Paulus the Sixth St.
12. Nazareth Village

11. Main bus stop (to Haifa, Jerusalem)
12. Mary's Well bus stop (to Cana, Tiberias, Akko)
13. Abu Salem coffee shop
14. Tishreen
15. Sudfeh
16. Diana
17. El Muchtar
18. El Machroom
1 Fauzi Azar Inn
2 Al Mutran
3 Sisters of Nazareth
4 St. Margaret's Hostel

The Old City is the most interesting spot for tourists, full of layers of history, winding alleys and exotic Old World atmosphere. It's easy to get lost in the narrow twisting streets which were, until recently, dirt trails trodden by Nazareth's first city planners—donkeys. The Old City streets were paved in the year 2000 in preparation for a visit from Pope John Paul II.

The name Nazareth likely comes from the Hebrew word *netzer*, which means branch or plant shoot.

1. Basilica of the Annunciation

(☎04-657-2501; 8am–5:30pm; free) Nazareth's most prominent landmark, the **Basilica of the Annunciation**, marks the traditional location of Mary's house where she was visited by the angel Gabriel to receive the news of her divine pregnancy.

The current building dates from 1969, incorporating the earlier Byzantine grotto into the lower level. The dome is shaped to resemble a white lily, a symbol associated with Mary. The courtyard features mosaics from around the world portraying Mary and the Christ child in different cultural styles. Sixty meters at its highest, the Basilica is the largest church building in the Middle East.

Religious art in the Basilica of the Annunciation

Myriad shopping opportunities await in the Nazareth market.

2. Nazareth Market

The **Nazareth market**, or *sook*, is alive with hustle and bustle and offers clothes, treasures and trinkets from ancient to modern. Depending on the season, the **fruit and vegetable market** will most likely be heaped with some type of exotic fruit you have never seen before, fresh off the tree or vine. The large house dominating the market is owned by the Fahum family, well-known and historically rooted in Nazareth. The Fahum family also runs a **coffee mill** just down the street—let the rich aroma of coffee and cardamom guide your nose there.

Under the arches of the house are two **bakeries** —one with unique aniseed rolls, and one across the street with tasty olive and za'atar (see p. 187) pizzas for 6NIS. Around the corner is **Abu Ashraf's restaurant**. His *katayef* (fried pancakes filled with cheese or nuts) are highly recommended. Don't worry, you'll burn off the calories on the trail.

Abu Ashraf serves up tasty treats.

The White Mosque is open during daylight hours except during prayers. Modest dress required, remove shoes.

3. The White Mosque

(☎04-656-9061) In the heart of the Old City, the **White Mosque** is Nazareth's first mosque, built in the early 19th century by Abdalla El Nini. Locals recount that he was a respected judge in the Fahum tribe who wrote in his will that the mosque should always preach love and respect. Even today, Ateph El Fahum pre-reads the sermons to make sure they contain nothing offensive to other religions. The mosque houses a small museum featuring historical photos of Nazareth.

4. Synagogue Church and Greek Catholic Church

(Mon/Tues/Thurs/Fri: 9am-12:30, 2:30pm-6pm, Wed/Sat: 9am-12:30, Sunday: closed) The **Synagogue Church** from the Crusader period is the traditional site where Jesus announced his ministry by reading from Isaiah 61 and declaring himself the fulfillment of the prophesy (Luke 4:14-20). In the 19th century, the adjacent **Greek Catholic Church** was added to the structure.

5. Fauzi Azar Inn

(☎04-602-0469, see p. 58) The **Fauzi Azar Inn** is the restored 19th-century Ottomon mansion of the Azar family, now a guesthouse with resources about the Jesus Trail and other travels in the region. Jesus Trail cofounder Maoz Inon manages the inn along with Suraida Shomar Nasser, granddaughter of the wealthy Arab landowner for whom the inn is named. The Azar family was once one of the richest and most influential families in the Galilee.

The three-story mansion features six-meter hand-painted ceilings, a Turkish marble floor, a panoramic view of the Old City from the great hall and a stone-arched courtyard. Even if you don't stay the night, it's right on the trail and worth stopping by to catch a glimpse of Nazareth in its heyday.

Entrance to the Fauzi Azar Inn

6. Bride's Market

Before they were lured away to shopping malls in Upper Nazareth, every Arab bride in Nazareth and the surrounding villages came to the **bride's market** to prepare for her wedding. Though not as active today, you can still see the glittering wares of dresses, jewelry, candles, fabrics and other finery.

For a tea or coffee break, keep straight past the bride's market to **Abu Salem coffee shop** (☎057-533-0103) (unsigned on the right-hand side) and ask for the cinnamon walnut tea from Wisam, the third-generation owner.

7. Mensa Christi Church

To the left as you ascend out of Nazareth on the Jesus Trail, this 1860 Salesian church is built over a slab of stone remembered as the "table of Christ," *mensa christi*, where Jesus enjoyed a meal with his disciples after the resurrection. To see the inside, ask the neighbors opposite the church for the key and leave a small donation. Note the amusing typo on the plaque outside.

8. El-Babour Spice Mill

(☎04-645-5596; Mon-Sat) This delightful 100-year-old flour mill turned spice shop is a mosaic of colors and smells. There is something for everyone with over a thousand types of herbs, spices and grains as well as candies, nuts, teas, *hulva* (sesame candy) and a host of other Middle Eastern specialties. While they now grind with newer equipment, the old steam-powered flour grinder is still on display. The mill was started by a German family who came to Nazareth as part of the Templar movement of the 19th century.

9. Ancient Bathhouse

(☎04-657-8539; www.nazarethbathhouse.org, Mon-Sat)
During renovations to a dilapidated souvenir shop, a local Nazarene stumbled upon the ruins of an ancient bathhouse thought to be Roman-era. Surprisingly, the heating system is much larger than the bathhouse at Beit She'an, one of the Decapolis cities. If the structure is indeed Roman, its discovery may contradict the image of Nazareth as a tiny peasant village and call into question previous perceptions of the boyhood life of Jesus. The bathhouse is entered by way of the Cactus Gallery near Mary's Well. Call ahead for a half-hour tour and snack (120NIS for a group of 1-4).

Photos opposite:
Shooting the breeze in Abu Salem coffee shop (top)
Spice selection at El-Babour (bottom)

10. St. Gabriel Greek Orthodox Church of the Annunciation

(Mary's Well Square; 7am-10am, 12pm-6pm Mon-Sat)
In the Orthodox tradition, Mary received the annunciation not at home but while drawing water from the well. A Greek Orthodox church marks this alternate annunciation spot. Traditional golden icons cover the small church's interior. Water from Mary's well flows through the far room. The present building dates from the 18th century, built on the ruins of an earlier Byzantine church.

St. Gabriel's Orthodox Church, Nazareth

11. Paulus the Sixth Street

The congested main street through Nazareth is full of restaurants and shops, including two famous sweets stores. Locals say that **El Muchtar** is the place for *knaffe* (a cheesy sweet with what looks like shredded wheat on top) and **El Machroom** for *baklava* (flaky phyllo dough filled with nuts and honey).

The world of Jesus comes alive among the olive trees at Nazareth Village.

12. Nazareth Village

If congested present-day Nazareth doesn't evoke for you images of the pastoral youth of Jesus, stop by Nazareth Village for a Parable Walk through their recreation of 1st-century Nazareth, replete with authentic building techniques, costumes, tools, foods and farming practices. Actors in period clothing demonstrate crafts such as olive and wine pressing, weaving, carving and shepherding, all done in the 1st-century technique. Olive and fig trees and other important staples dapple the grounds while donkeys and goats wander the fields. The buildings include a synagogue, oil press, house and workshop, with new sites constantly added.

Pottery shards, the presence of terracing, an ancient wine press, quarries, watch towers and an irrigation system dating from the 1st century all strongly suggest that the land was indeed farmed during the time of Jesus. A team of consultants ensured that the building techniques were as accurate to the time of Jesus as possible, and Nazareth Village staff were consulted for the production of the 2006 movie *The Nativity Story*. The Nazareth Village website includes original research resources about building techniques.

Nazareth Village
☎04-645-6042;
www.nazarethvillage.com;
adult/child/student;
50/22/34NIS

A tour of the village takes about an hour and includes a small oil lamp to take home with you. Call ahead for reservations. Tours are available in a variety of languages.

Where to Eat in Nazareth

Paulus the Sixth Street has plenty of shwarma, falafel and other quick eats. Expect to pay about 12NIS for a falafel and 20NIS for shwarma.

For more sophisticated cuisine, Nazareth offers a surprisingly good array of restaurants that draw diners from surrounding towns and villages.

A few to choose from:

- **Tishreen:** ☎04-608-4666; 56 Bishara St.; mains 35-75NIS; noon-midnight Mon-Sat, 5pm-midnight Sun
- **Sudfeh**: ☎04-656-6611; 908/35 Mary's Well; mains 50-120; noon-1:30am Mon-Sat, 6pm-1:30am Sun
- **Diana:** ☎04-657-2919; 51 Paulus the Sixth St.; mains 75-125NIS; 11am-midnight every day

J1 NAZARETH TO ZIPPORI

7.8 km
2-3 hours

Difficulty:
Steep ascent out of the Old City, gentle grades for the remainder of the walk.

Admission Fees:
Zippori NP.

Biking Detours:
It isn't possible to bike the Old City stairs. Instead ride up HaGalil Street to the promenade on Ru'us el-Jibal street.

Transport for Zippori:
There are no direct buses to Zippori NP. Buses 343 and 28א go to Tsipori branching, which is 3 km from the park. A taxi from Nazareth to Zippori costs 60NIS.

Feel the energy of the Nazareth market, admire Ottoman architecture, breathe deeply through peaceful pastoral fields, gaze at exquisite mosaics in Zippori National Park

Beginning at the Basilica of the Annunciation, the trail enters the Old City market through a stone-arched entryway (see Nazareth Old City and Downtown map p. 59). The trail is informally marked with large orange dots through the market. Walk past the White Mosque and continue through the bride's market. The trail climbs out of Nazareth by way of 406 steps, where the trail is blazed as (white/orange/white) and follows a scenic promenade with a view of the forested hill of Zippori in the valley. At a traffic circle, the trail turns left and leaves Nazareth through a suburb, continuing down a ridge on dirt tracks. The trail meets Route 700 to cross Route 79 and continues to ancient Zippori by way of peaceful agricultural fields. The trail meets a paved road at the entrance to Zippori National Park. Continue straight to Cana, or leave the trail to explore the park.

Accommodations:

- **Zippori Village Country Cottages:** ☎04-646-2647; www.zipori.com; double 450NIS
- **Rish Lakish** (Zippori)**:** ☎052-845-4662; ☎04-645-5021; Ecological farm and olive press house. Camping free on request, dorm coming soon.

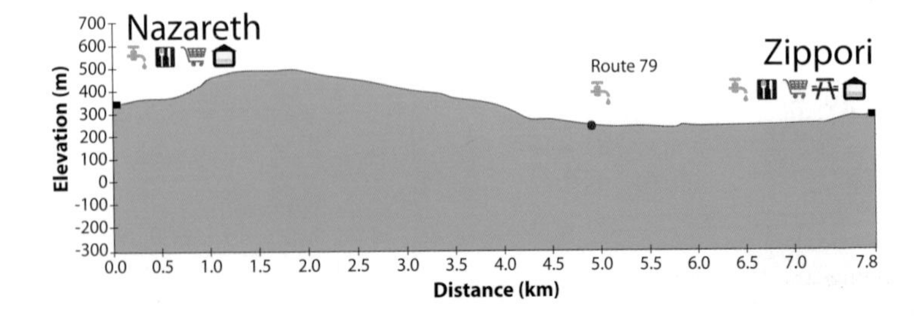

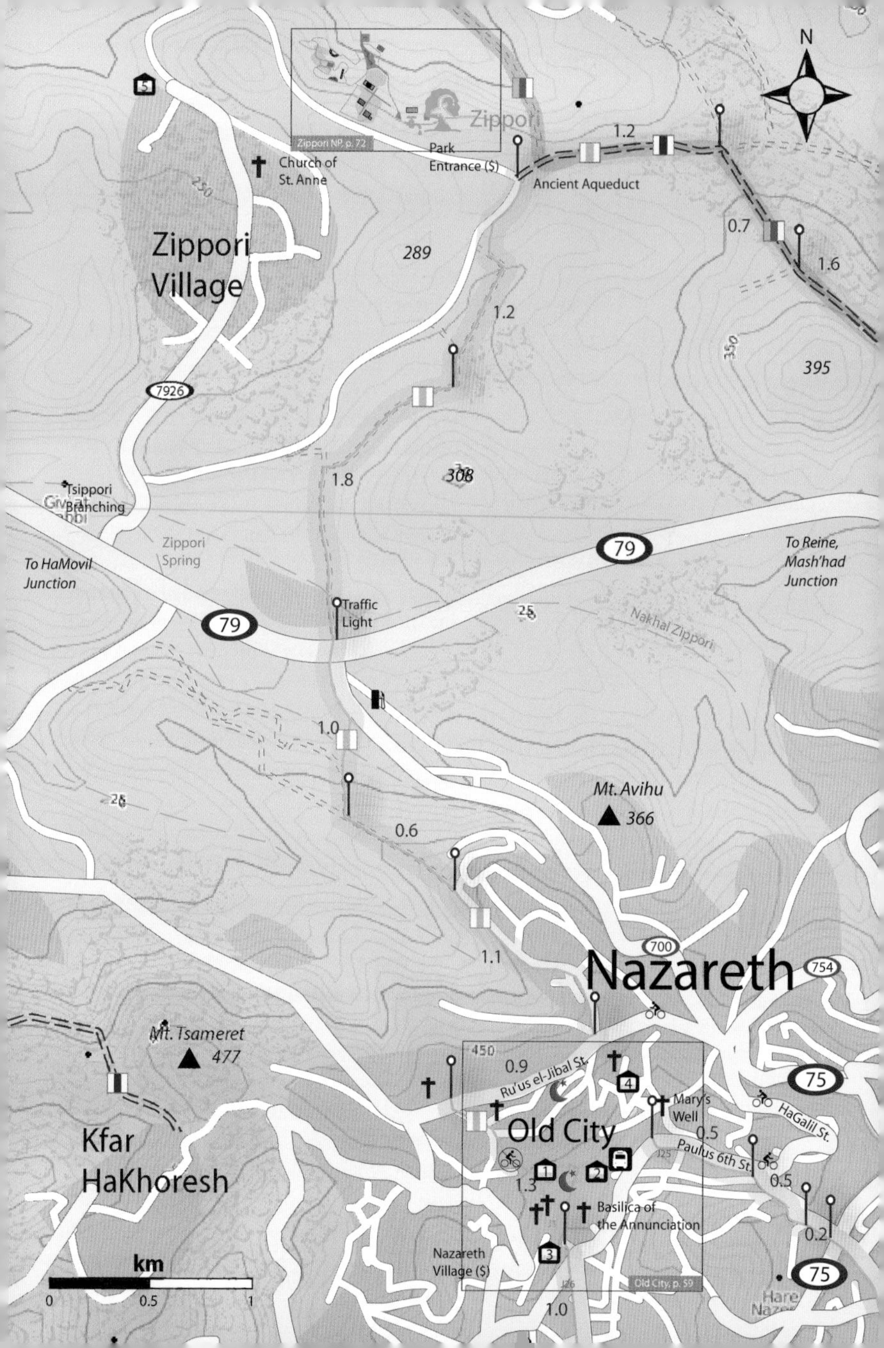

N
Zippori NP, p. 72
Zippori
Park
Entrance ($)
Church of
St. Anne
Ancient Aqueduct
1.2
0.7
1.6
250
Zippori
Village
289
1.2
350
395
7926
308
1.8
Tsippori
Branching
Zippori
Spring
To HaMovil
Junction
79
To Reine,
Mash'had
Junction
Traffic
Light
Nakhal Zippori
1.0
0.6
Mt. Avihu
366
1.1
700
754
Nazareth
Mt. Tsameret
477
450
0.9
Ru'us el-Jibal St.
Mary's
Well
Old City
0.5
HaGalil St.
Paulus 6th St.
0.5
75
Kfar
HaKhoresh
1.3
Basilica of
the Annunciation
0.2
Nazareth
Village ($)
Old City, p. 59
km
0
0.5
1
1.0

Crusader fortress at Sepphoris, including Herodian tombstones

Sepphoris تپوري ציפורי

A city on a hill cannot be hidden.
Matthew 5:14b

The ruins of **Sepphoris** show layers of an ancient city, inhabited as far back as the 7th century BCE. Described by Josephus Flavius as the "ornament of the Galilee," the city was a center of wealth and commerce beginning in the 1st century CE and lasting for centuries. Halfway between the Sea of Galilee and the Mediterranean Sea, Sepphoris was on a major trade route leading to Ptolemais (modern Akko).

According to the Babylonian Talmud, the name comes from the Hebrew word *tsipor*, which means "bird," for the bird's-eye view afforded by the city's position on a hill. The most notable feature of the excavations today are the stunning mosaics dating from the 2nd to 6th century CE.

Sepphoris was conquered by Herod the Great in 37 BCE and was the site of a Jewish revolt upon his death in 4 CE. The revolt was violently crushed, resulting in the city being burned to the ground and the Jewish peasant rebels sold into slavery. Apparently Sepphoris Jews learned their lesson, as they did not participate in the Great Jewish Revolt of 66 CE. In response to this revolt, the Romans destroyed the Jewish Temple in Jerusalem, shifting the cultural and religious center of Judaism to the Galilee.

Again after the Bar Kokhba Revolt (see p. 219), Jewish refugees fled to Sepphoris. By this time the name had been changed to Deocaesarea to pay homage to Zeus and the emperor. The Sanhedrin, the Jewish high court, convened in Sepphoris for some years during the 2nd century. Also, the Mishnah, a codification of Jewish oral religious tradition, was compiled there in the late 2nd century.

What's in a name?
The city of Sepphoris has had many names: Zippori, Le Sephorie, Deocaesarea, Neronias, Eirenopolis and Saffuriya

Sepphoris would have been under construction during the lifetime of Jesus, leading some scholars to speculate that Joseph, and perhaps Jesus as well, were employed as *tectons* in Sepphoris (more accurately translated as "builder" rather than the usual "carpenter").

Water system at Zippori National Park

Tradition cites Sepphoris as the home city of Anna and Joachim, parents of Mary, so some believe Joseph may have met his bride-to-be while laboring in Sepphoris. Not far from the site, the 12th-century Crusader **Church of St. Anne** rests on the traditional site of Anna's house. Sepphoris is also traditionally known as the hometown of Joanna, a follower of Jesus mentioned in Luke 8:3. Given its proximity to Nazareth (6 km) and importance in the region, it is notably absent from the New Testament narrative.

Today **Zippori National Park** includes excavations of buildings from different time periods. One important site is the **Roman villa** from around 200 CE, which has a *triclinium* with a mosaic floor featuring scenes from the story of the pagan god Dionysis, and other pagan characters such as Pan and Hercules. This floor also contains a mosaic of a woman's face dubbed the "**Mona Lisa of the Galilee**" for its exquisite artistry down to the faint pink blush across her cheeks. Some scholars theorize that she is a depiction of one of the four seasons, while others think her life-like features are modeled after the lady of the house.

Zippori National Park:
☎04-656-8272;
adult/child 25/13NIS;
8am-4pm winter,
8am-5pm summer

"Mona Lisa of the Galilee" at Zippori

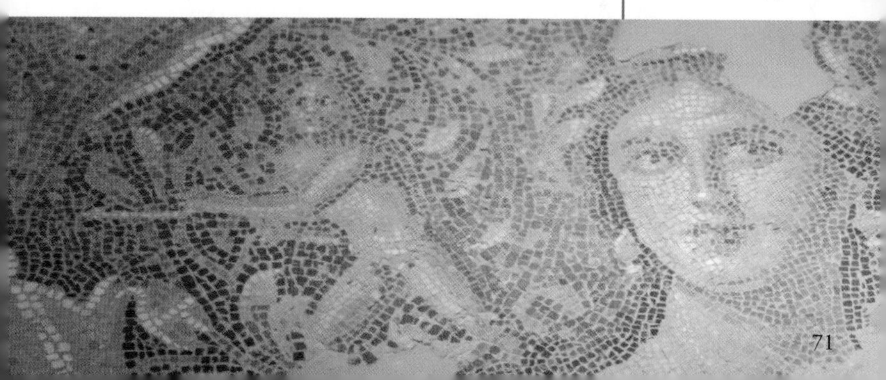

The **Nile House**, a 5th-century public building, houses more unique mosaics and may have been used for public ceremonies. The name derives from a well-preserved mosaic featuring scenes of the Nile. Another nearby mosaic depicts Amazon woman warriors. More mosaics of interest can be found in the **6th-century synagogue.** This mosaic floor is one of several in the region that depicts a zodiac along with biblical and harvest scenes. The mosaics at Sepphoris suggest that wealthy Jews under Roman rule assimilated to Greco-Roman culture in many ways.

Other excavations at the site include a 1st-century CE 4,000-seat **Roman amphitheater**, two **Byzantine churches** and a 12th-century **Crusader fortress**. The fortress houses a small **museum** of artifacts, and views from the roof help to orient you to the surrounding area. Don't miss taking a walk through the cavernous **Roman-era cisterns**.

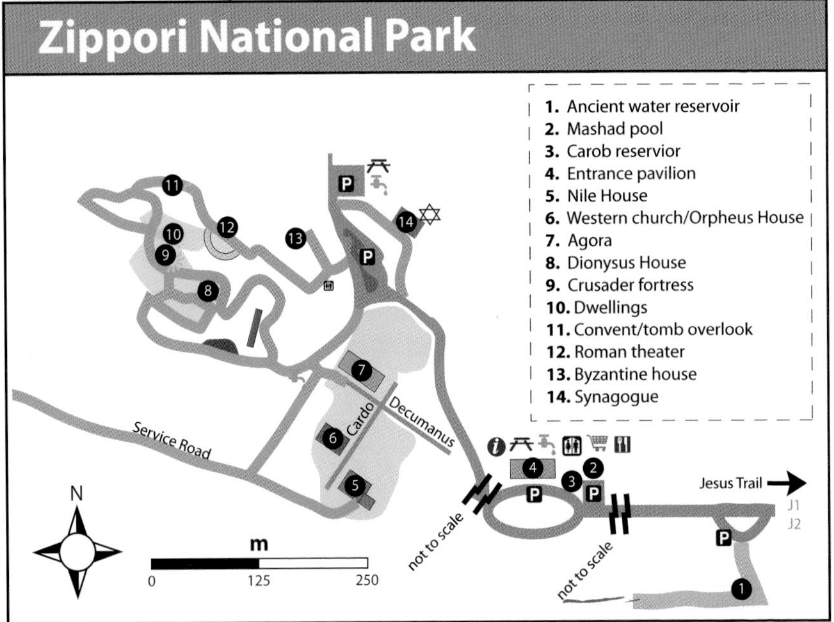

Prickly Pear Cactus

Opuntia monacantha fruit blooms near Zippori National Park.

Scattered throughout the Galilee, particularly in areas that were inhabited by Arabs before 1948, the **prickly pear cactus** is a ubiquitous part of the scenery. This non-native cactus was imported from the southwestern United States in the 19th century and used as a divider between property lines by the Arab inhabitants of the land. Chances are when you see significant clusters of the plant that the area was an Arab village prior to the war in 1948.

While its colorful fruit may look tempting, don't be fooled! The tiny hair-like spines (or technically, glochids) on the surface of the fruit are wicked to remove from your skin. Weeks after touching it, you may still be picking the tiny invisible splinters out of your fingertips.

However, if you are eager to test your hunting and gathering skills, the best way to de-thorn the fruit is to pick one up with paper or thick cloth and roll it in the dirt until the skin is smooth. Then cut the skin lengthwise and peel. Chew carefully, as the fruit is full of hard seeds. Cactus fruit is in season in summer, and at its most tasty when golden yellow in color; red fruits have become overripe in the sun.

The plant is known in Hebrew as *Tsabar,* and a variation of the word, sabra, became widely used as a term for native-born Israelis who were considered "tough on the outside, but sweet on the inside." The name in Arabic is similar, *Sabr*, which means "patience."

The mosaic arts reached their zenith in the Byzantine period (photo opposite).

J2

ZIPPORI TO CANA

Follow an ancient aqueduct, visit Jonah's hometown, renew your wedding vows (with a glass of wine) in Cana

5.6 km
1.5-2 hours

Difficulty:
Gradual ascent from Zippori to Mash'had, descent to Cana.

Admission Fees:
Zippori NP.

Biking Detours:
None.

Transport for Cana:
Small minibuses run regularly from the main street in Cana to Paulus the Sixth St. in Nazareth every day. Buses 431, 24, 25, and 28-31 run between Nazareth and Cana.

Exterior of Cana Wedding Church (above)

From the entrance to Zippori National Park, follow the orange and red blazes through the forest. Note the ancient aqueduct to your right 50 m into the trail. Join the Israel Trail and continue through the town of Mash'had. At the central mosque, bear left and leave the Israel Trail, turning right shortly after the mosque. Continue downhill to exit Mash'had toward Cana through olive groves. The trail ends at the sundial on Church Street, just before the Catholic and Orthodox churches of Cana.

Accommodations:

6 **Cana Wedding B&B:** ☎050-400-7636; dorm 100NIS, double 300NIS

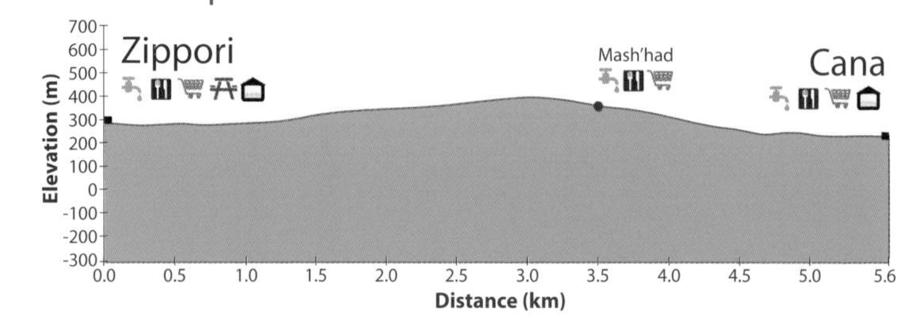

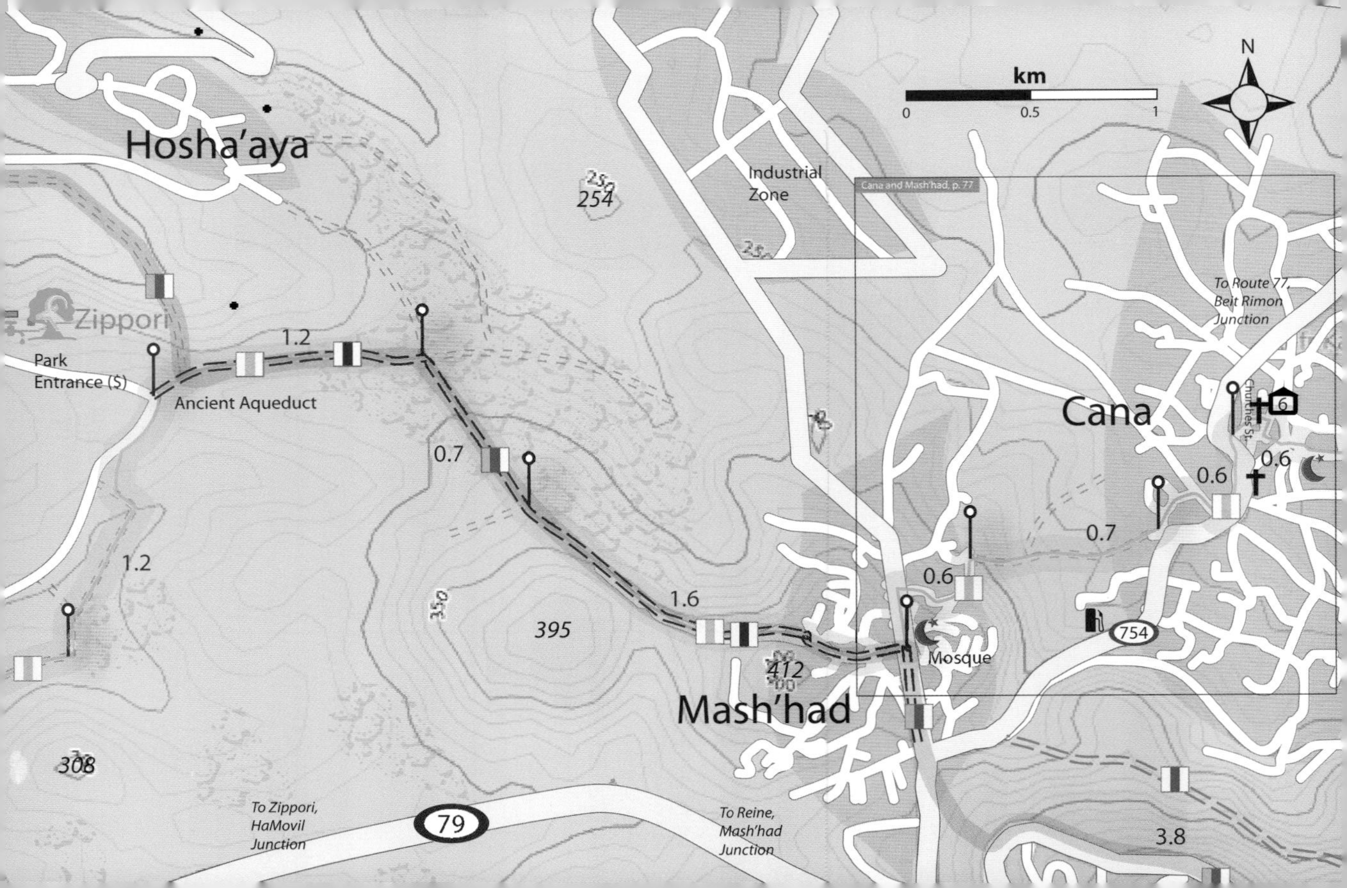

N
km
0
0.5
1
Hosha'aya
Industrial
Zone
254
Cana and Mash'had, p. 77
To Route 77,
Beit Rimon
Junction
Zippori
Park
Entrance ($)
Ancient Aqueduct
1.2
0.7
1.2
Cana
Churches St.
6
0.6
0.6
0.7
0.6
1.6
395
Mosque
754
412
Mash'had
308
3.8
79
To Zippori,
HaMovil
Junction
To Reine,
Mash'had
Junction

Mash'had and Jonah משהד مشهد

The mosque at Mash'had, said to house the tomb of Jonah

For as Jonah was three days and three nights in the belly of a huge fish, so the Son of Man will be three days and three nights in the heart of the earth. Matthew 12:40

Before reaching Cana you will pass through the small town of **Mash'had** with a population of about 6,700 people, mainly Muslim. This town is identified with the Old Testament city of Gath Hepher, whose main claim to fame is being the birthplace of **Jonah** (2 Kings 14:25), the reluctant Old Testament prophet whom Jesus references in both Matthew and Luke when he speaks of the "sign of Jonah" (Matthew 12, Luke 11). One traditional grave of Jonah is located in the Mash'had mosque, though the better-known traditional spot is in Iraq near historical Ninevah.

Cana كفر كنا כפר כנא

This, the first of his miraculous signs, Jesus performed in Cana of Galilee. He thus revealed his glory, and his disciples put their faith in him. John 2:11

Cana is the traditional site of the wedding feast where Jesus performed his first miracle of turning water into wine (John 2:1-11), a passage that has consternated Christian teetotallers for centuries. This unique miracle, only included in John's gospel, bears little resemblance to the healing, feeding, and exorcising miracles described throughout the Synoptic Gospels. Various interpretations of this scripture including viewing the wine as allegorical, or the event as a demonstration of the extravagant generosity of the kingdom of God.

Cana Wedding Church
☎04-651-7011;
Open 8am-noon everyday, 2-6pm Mon-Sat, 2-5pm in winter

Wedding celebrations at that time went on for days, even up to a week, and included all the members of the community. To run out of wine prematurely was a great shame for the family of the groom. In the basement of the **Franciscan Wedding Church** (8am-12pm, 2pm-5pm, entrance free) stone jars are on display, similar to those that held the famous water in its pre-wine stage. Probably larger than you were picturing, each of these stone jars holds approximately 450 liters (120 gallons). When you consider that John's account includes six such jars, you start to see exactly why such a miracle may be seen as scandalous.

The location of historic Cana has been quite controversial and many scholars consider there to be four main candidates. The town of Cana (known as *Kfar Cana* or village of Cana locally) is the most common traditional site for Cana, with pilgrim graffiti dating back to the 4th century. However, many scholars agree that this location had more to do with encouraging pilgrim tourist economics than factual evidence.

Colorful flags adorn the courtyard of the Greek Orthodox Church in Cana.

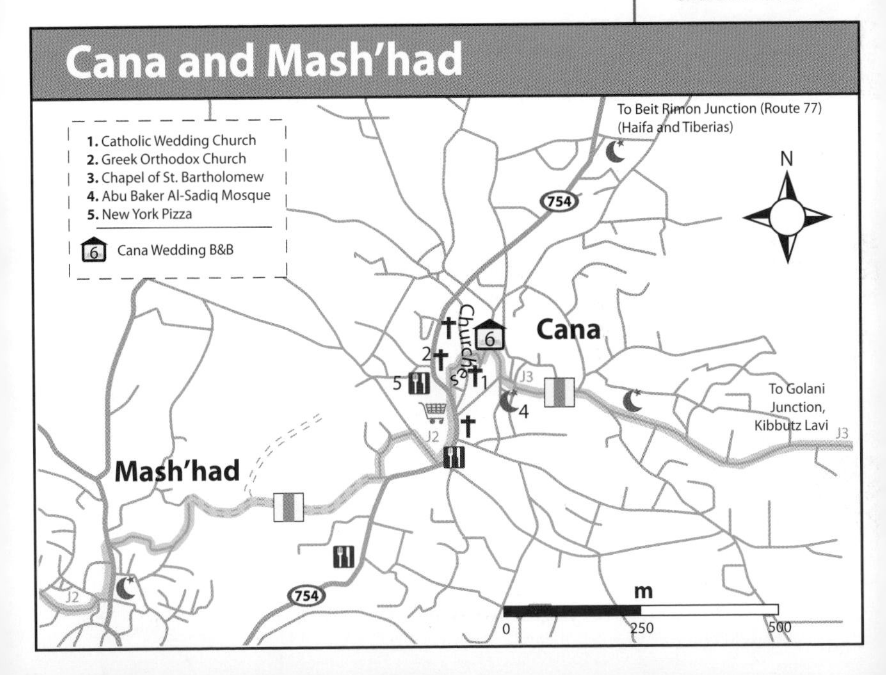

Greek Orthodox Church

Souvenirs in Cana shop

The main criteria for the location of Cana include proximity to Nazareth and main roads, lack of access to running water, as the jars were most likely the way of maintaining water supply in Cana and evidence of a historical village dating to at least the 1st century. See the section on Khirbet Cana (pp. 206-207) for information on the most likely alternate site.

Cana is also mentioned later in John as a place where Jesus heals a royal official's son (John 4:46) and the hometown of the disciple Nathanael (also called Bartholomew) (John 21:2).

The Jesus Trail passes through the modern town of Kfar Cana, which is located at the traditional site of the wedding feast. The **Fransiscan Wedding Church** was built in 1879 over the ruins of earlier Byzantine ruins. Though not as open to visitors, the nearby **Greek Orthodox Church** has a lovely tranquil courtyard and small peaceful sanctuary flanked by its own set of ancient stone jars.

The town of Cana as viewed from Mash'had

Pomegranates

רימון
الرمان

I went down to the grove of nut trees to look at the new growth in the valley, to see if the vines had budded or the pomegranates were in bloom. Song of Solomon 6:11

Ripe pomegranate ready to be harvested

Kfar Cana is known for its delicious **pomegranates**, a fruit made up of brilliant red seeds in an outer casing slightly smaller than a grapefruit. The seeds are pressed into juice, eaten whole or used as an ingredient in various recipes.

Pomegranates have significance to monotheistic traditions as well as Greek mythology. In Jewish tradition, pomegranates are said to have 613 seeds representing the 613 commandments (or *mitzvot*) that Orthodox Jews are to follow. For Christians, the pomegranate is sometimes used as a symbol of the death and resurrection of Jesus. In the Quran, pomegranates are one of the plants flourishing in paradise. In the ancient Greek story of Persephone, the daughter of the goddess of harvest is lured into the underworld where she eats pomegranate seeds that bind her to return each year.

J3

CANA TO LAVI

14.4 km
3.5-5 hours

Difficulty: Gentle grades up the ridge heading east out of Cana, easy descent to valley floor, flat to Golani Junction.

Biking Detours: Stay on the green-blazed road instead of turning off for footpath on red.

Transport for Kibbutz Lavi/ Golani Junction: Buses 431, 28, 28א, 29, 30 and 31 can drop you off or pick you up at Golani Junction, or ask a sherut driver going to Cana to take you to Golani Junction for a few extra shekels.

Enjoy expansive scenery and ridge views, walk on an ancient Roman road, learn about Shabbat observance at a religious kibbutz

From Church Street, the trail weaves up through the town of Cana past an artistically-painted mosque. The trail exits Cana by a dirt road on a ridge with views into the Tur'an Valley and of the town of Tur'an and descends through the Beit Keshet Forest. After skirting an army base, the trail then turns left and continues parallel to Route 65, passes under it, and continues through Lavi Forest crossing under Route 77 via another underpass to Golani Junction. The trail leads to a short section of Roman road 100 m from Golani Junction, then follows dirt paths to Kibbutz Lavi. The route ends at a cemetery and Holocaust memorial in a grove of trees with historic wine presses.

Accommodations:

- 7 **Yarok Az Organic Goat Farm** (Ilaniya +0.5 km off route): ☎054-255-8791; www.yarokaz.co.il; dorm 100NIS, double 300NIS, camping 50NIS
- 8 **Kibbutz Lavi Hotel:** ☎04-679-9450; www.hotel.lavi.co.il; double 400NIS
- ▲ Free **JNF campground** in Lavi Forest. Picnic tables, water and bathrooms (which are sometimes locked).

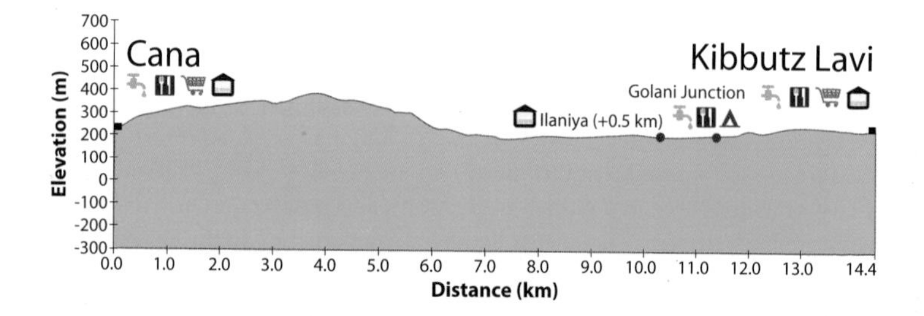

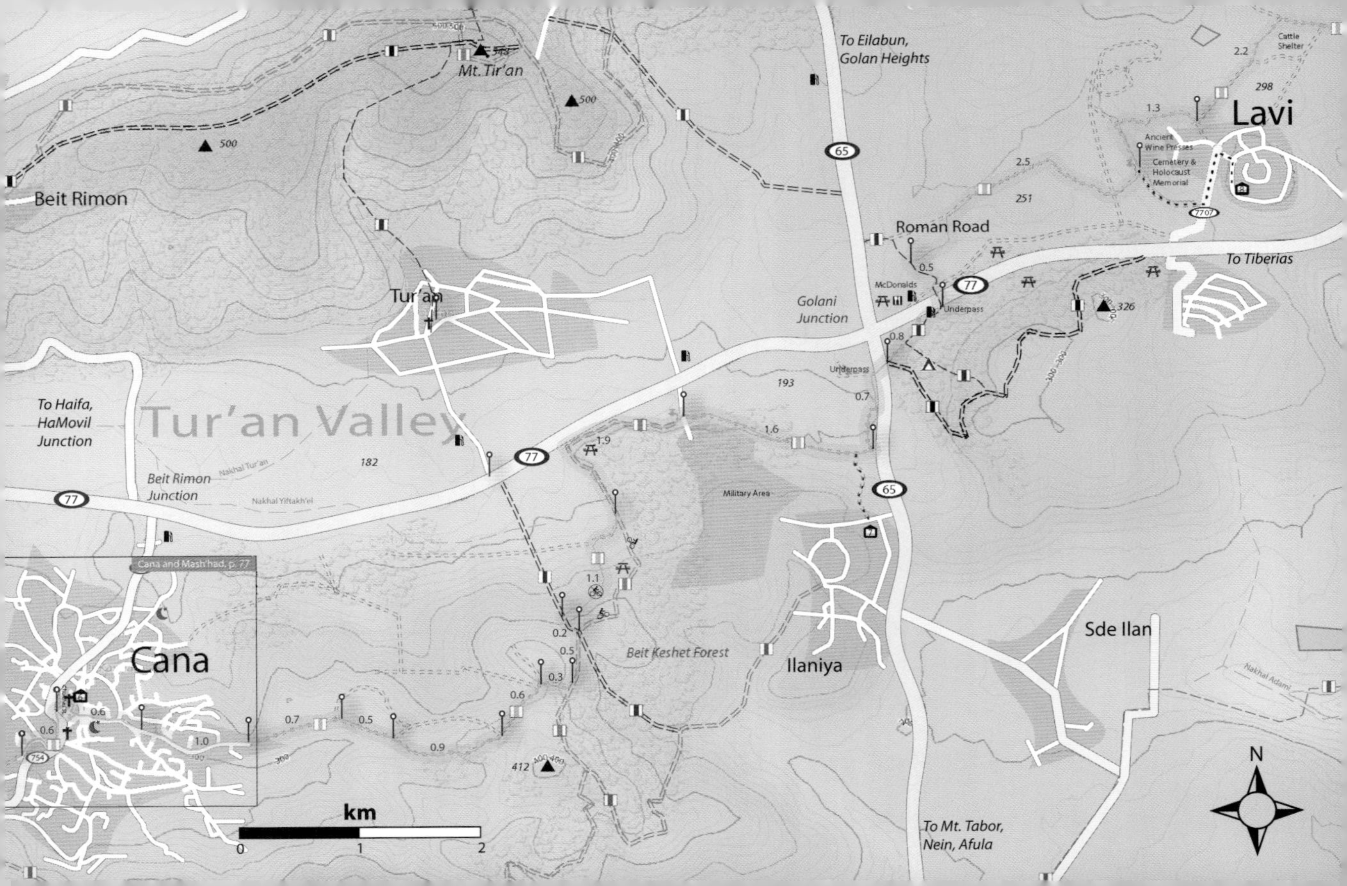
Lavi
Cattle Shelter
Ancient Wine Presses
Cemetery & Holocaust Memorial
To Tiberias
To Eilabun, Golan Heights
Roman Road
McDonalds
Underpass
Golani Junction
Mt. Tir'an
Beit Rimon
Tur'an
Tur'an Valley
To Haifa, HaMovil Junction
Beit Rimon Junction
Nakhal Tur'an
Nakhal Yiftakh'el
Military Area
Beit Keshet Forest
Ilaniya
Sde Ilan
Nakhal Adami
To Mt. Tabor, Nein, Afula
Cana
Cana and Mash'had, p. 77
km
0
1
2
N

Cyclamen persicum in the wild

Cyclamen النبات רקפות

From late fall to early spring, a blush of pink flowers peek their delicate blossoms out of the ground after lying dormant during the dry summer. Sometimes called "the poor man's orchid," **cyclamen** flowers consist of five curving petals that rise springily above their dark green heart-shaped leaves which resemble ivy. There are over 20 species of cyclamen ranging in color across the red-pink spectrum, from deep magenta to an entirely white albino version.

Cyclamen are of the genus *Primulaceae*, related to the primrose. They grow wild in the Mediterranean region, including parts of North Africa and as far east as Iran. The leaves of the flower are edible and included in some traditional Palestinian recipes in which they are boiled and stuffed with rice, ground meat and spices. In Europe, the plant was commonly known as sowbread, as pigs often rooted up the rhizomes from underground to eat. Cyclamen edged out the red poppy-like anemone flower as the flower to represent Israel in a display at the 2008 Olympic Games in Beijing.

Tur'an طرعان טורעאן

The town of **Tur'an** is visible from the trail ridge after leaving Cana, easily recognizable by its golden-domed mosque and the unfortunate chunk of mountain missing due to quarrying. The spring at Tur'an played an important role in the Crusader defeat at Hattin as Crusader forces mysteriously continued on from Tur'an late in the day, allowing the Muslim army to block Crusader access to water. Today the town of 11,000 is mainly Muslim.

Golani Junction

צומת גולני
فترق غولاني

At **Golani Junction**, north-south Route 65 meets east-west Route 77 between Nazareth and Tiberias. It's an easy spot to catch a bus to just about anywhere, and an opportunity to indulge in an ice cream cone or burger in McDonald's (as well as visit the WC). Next to McDonald's, you'll see the Golani Museum featuring displays about the Golani Brigade, a division of the Israeli Army formed in 1948 out of soldiers from the Upper Galilee. The Brigade has been involved in every major war and military operation in Israel since 1948. The unit's symbol is a green tree on a yellow background. Museum displays are primarily in Hebrew.

Golani Brigade Museum
☎ 04-6767215;
adult/child/senior 14/10/10NIS;
Sunday-Thurs 9am-4pm,
Fri 9am-1pm

Author David Landis on the path across from Tur'an

Roman Roads

הדרך הרומית
الطريق الرومانية

Every valley shall be filled in, every mountain and hill made low. The crooked roads shall become straight, the rough ways smooth. Luke 3:5

Omnes viae Romam ducunt. ("All roads lead to Rome.")
—Latin proverb

Section of ancient road near Golani Junction (opposite)

About 100 m past Golani Junction, you will come to a ridge with the remains of an ancient **Roman road** that linked Acre and Tiberias. Jesus likely used this road on his journey from Nazareth to the Sea of Galilee, as it was a major east-west thoroughfare during his time.

Exquisite roads were one of the hallmarks of the Roman Empire. The Romans were the first to create a comprehensive system of paved roads over such a large territory. The roads served the primary purpose of supporting military and trade movement, thereby promoting Rome's political and economic development. The road networks also facilitated the movement of ideas and technology and allowed foods, fashions and other cultural artifacts to spread. You might say this was the beginning of globalization, where the ease of moving ideas and goods contributed to better understanding between separate cultural and religious identities.

The method for constructing roads varied depending on the available materials and type of ground in different regions. The standard method was to first dig a ditch through the earth until hitting bedrock or at least a solid layer of ground. The standard width of a Roman road was supposed to be 2.45 m, however, there are examples of a large variety of widths. The width also depended on whether the road was

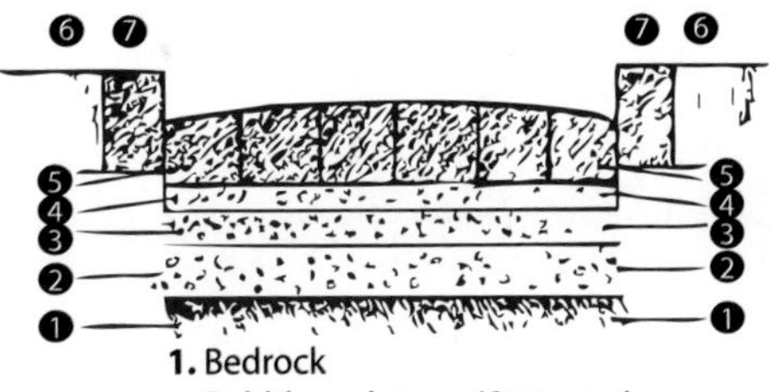

1. Bedrock
2. Rubble and stone (*Statumen*)
3. Gravel (*Pavimentum*)
4. Concrete (*Rudum*)
5. Stones (*Summa crust*)
6. Raised footpath (*Crepido*)
7. Curb stones

Paul on the Road to Damascus

About noon as I came near Damascus, suddenly a bright light from heaven flashed around me. I fell to the ground and heard a voice say to me, 'Saul! Saul! Why do you persecute me?'
Acts 22:6-7

The book of Acts tells of the dramatic conversion of the Apostle Paul, a Roman citizen and self-professed persecutor of Christians, on "the road to Damascus." On his way to persecute the Christians of Damascus, Paul was blinded by a bright light and received a message from Jesus that led him to dedicate his life to Christian ministry. Many of the Epistles (letters) included in the New Testament are traditionally attributed to Paul's authorship.

The Roman road along the Jesus Trail possibly continued to Capernaum and Damascus. Though many Roman roads have not been excavated, and it is difficult to know the exact location of ancient routes, Paul may have been walking this road when he experienced his life-changing encounter with Jesus.

intended as a *via publica* (public road) or *via militara* (military road). After the ditch was dug, it was partially filled in with rubble and stone. A layer of sand was added when available. Next came a layer of fine gravel packed down firmly, known as the *pavimentum*, followed by an approximately 15 cm (6 in) layer of concrete known as *rudum*. Finally, large flat square or polygonal stones were arranged on the top level, known as the *summa crusta*. The edges of the road were lined with larger curb stones. The construction below the surface served as drainage to divert rain water from the road. The cracks between the stones of the *summa crusta* allowed for freezing and thawing without damage to the road.

Distances along the road were counted by mile stones, or *milia passuum* which means "one thousand paces." A Roman mile was approximately 1500 m. The markers varied by region, but generally were circular or rectangular columns weighing up to two tons (1800 kg) placed by the road every Roman mile. These markers often bore the name of rulers who ordered their construction or repair, as well as the distance to the Roman forum from the post and sometimes listed the names of towns and cities found along the road. Maps were rare and expensive in the Roman Empire, but copies of town lists on different roads with distances between them were available, similar to how train lines are depicted in modern transport.

Three types of way stations existed for the convenience and comfort of travelers. Officials could stay at state hostels and restaurants known as *mansiones* located every

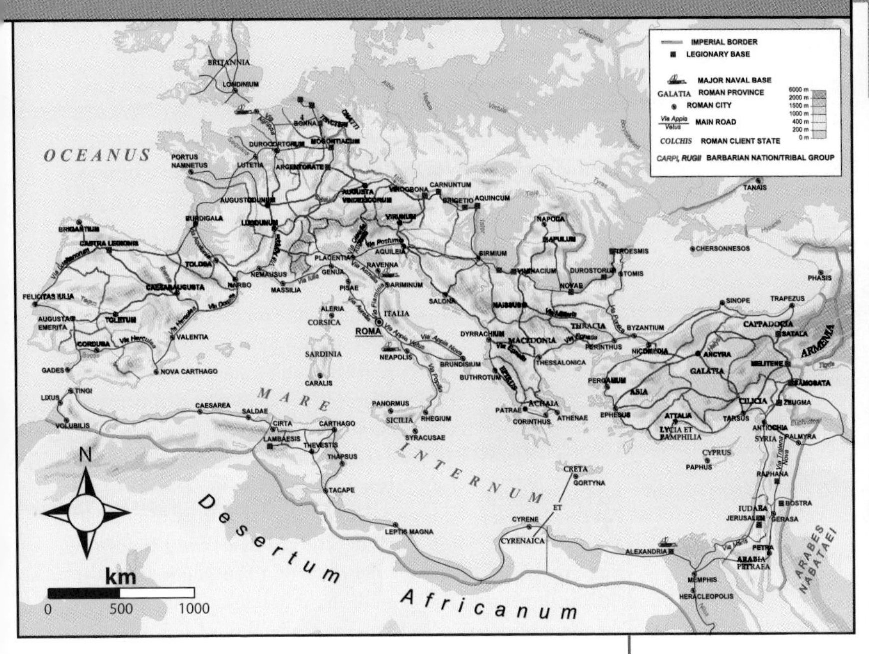

25-30 km, the average distance a man could travel on foot in one day. For non-official travelers, a system of private inns and taverns (like hostels) developed along the road. Finally, for animals and carts used in trade there were changing stations every 20-30 km for carriage repair and veterinary services.

Fifty thousand kilometers of road were built throughout the Roman Empire. One of the most significant was the *Via Maris* which connected the Mediterranean Sea to Damascus and ultimately even farther east to what is now China. This road may have passed through the Jezre'el Valley just by Nazareth and led directly to Zippori. In Roman cities like Zippori, the main roads in the center of town were set up in the pattern of an X with the *cardo* running north-south crossing the *decumanus,* which ran east-west, at a right angle. Roman construction had a predilection for right angles and asserting dominance over, rather than harmony with, nature.

Kibbutz Lavi לביא لفي

Just past Golani Junction the trail continues to **Kibbutz Lavi**, one of the few Orthodox religious kibbutzim (see "What is a Kibbutz?" on p. 160-161). Founded in 1949 by British immigrants, Kibbutz Lavi is the biggest manufacturer of synagogue furniture in the world and is the perfect place to buy a Torah table or new pews (though you may have trouble fitting them in your backpack). The kibbutz also has a large hotel and some small-scale agriculture. Just outside the kibbutz you will pass by a Jewish graveyard and a memorial set up by Lavi residents to remember family members who died in the Holocaust.

Pastoral scenes on the hillside at Kibbutz Lavi

Lavi associates itself with *Pundak Lavi* (Lion's Inn), an ancient inn mentioned in the Talmud. The grounds have a functioning synagogue built over the ruins of a synagogue from the Mishnah period. You can call ahead to book a room or a tour of the grounds or check on the availability of lectures on a variety of topics including the kibbutz movement and Jewish mysticism. As a religious community, Lavi observes Shabbat, including rabbi-approved automated milking machines, a Shabbat elevator (which stops on every floor to ensure no one performs the labor of pressing the button) and a complete ban on driving and using electricity from sundown on Friday to sundown on Saturday.

For a map of Kibbutz Lavi, see p. 91 (J4).

Wine press at Lavi. Grapes were pressed into wine by being trodden underfoot. This gentle system of pressing, as opposed to the millstone used in pressing olives, prevented the grape seeds from being crushed, which would spoil the flavor of the wine.

Olive tree on the hillside of Kibbutz Lavi

J4

LAVI TO NEBI SHU'EIB

6.1 km
1.5-2.5 hours

DIFFICULTY:
Moderate ascent from Lavi to Horns, steep descent to Nebi Shu'eib.

BIKING DETOURS:
Take the black 4x4 trail down the west side of the Horns of Hattin to Nebi Shu'eib.

TRANSPORT FOR NEBI SHU'EIB:
No direct bus route. Taxi from Arbel or Tiberias.

Climb the Horns of Hattin and glimpse the Sea of Galilee framed by Arbel cliffs, visit the Druze shrine of the prophet Jethro

Nebi Shu'eib is tucked in a small valley by the Horns of Hattin (above).

View from Horns of Hattin to Moshav Arbel (opposite)

From the Holocaust memorial and cemetery, the trail passes behind Kibbutz Lavi and around a hill dotted with ruins including a wine press. It continues on dirt roads to the Horns of Hattin and joins black and blue trails to pass up and over the Horns. After descending the Horns on the blue footpath, the trail meets a paved road. Turn left to visit Nebi Shu'eib, or right to continue on J5 to Moshav Arbel.

Accommodations:
No immediate accommodations. Taxi to Arbel or Tiberias.

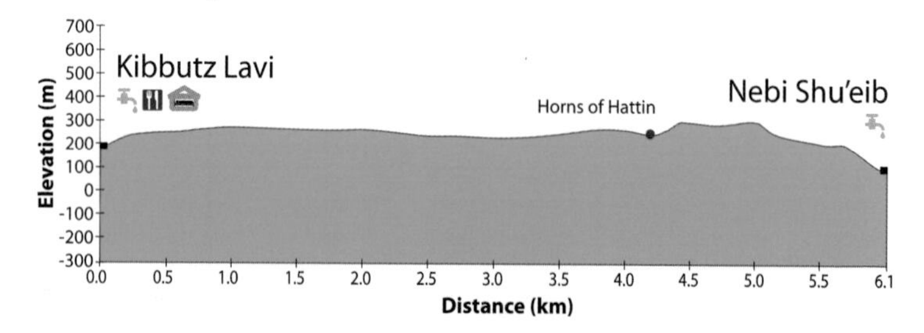

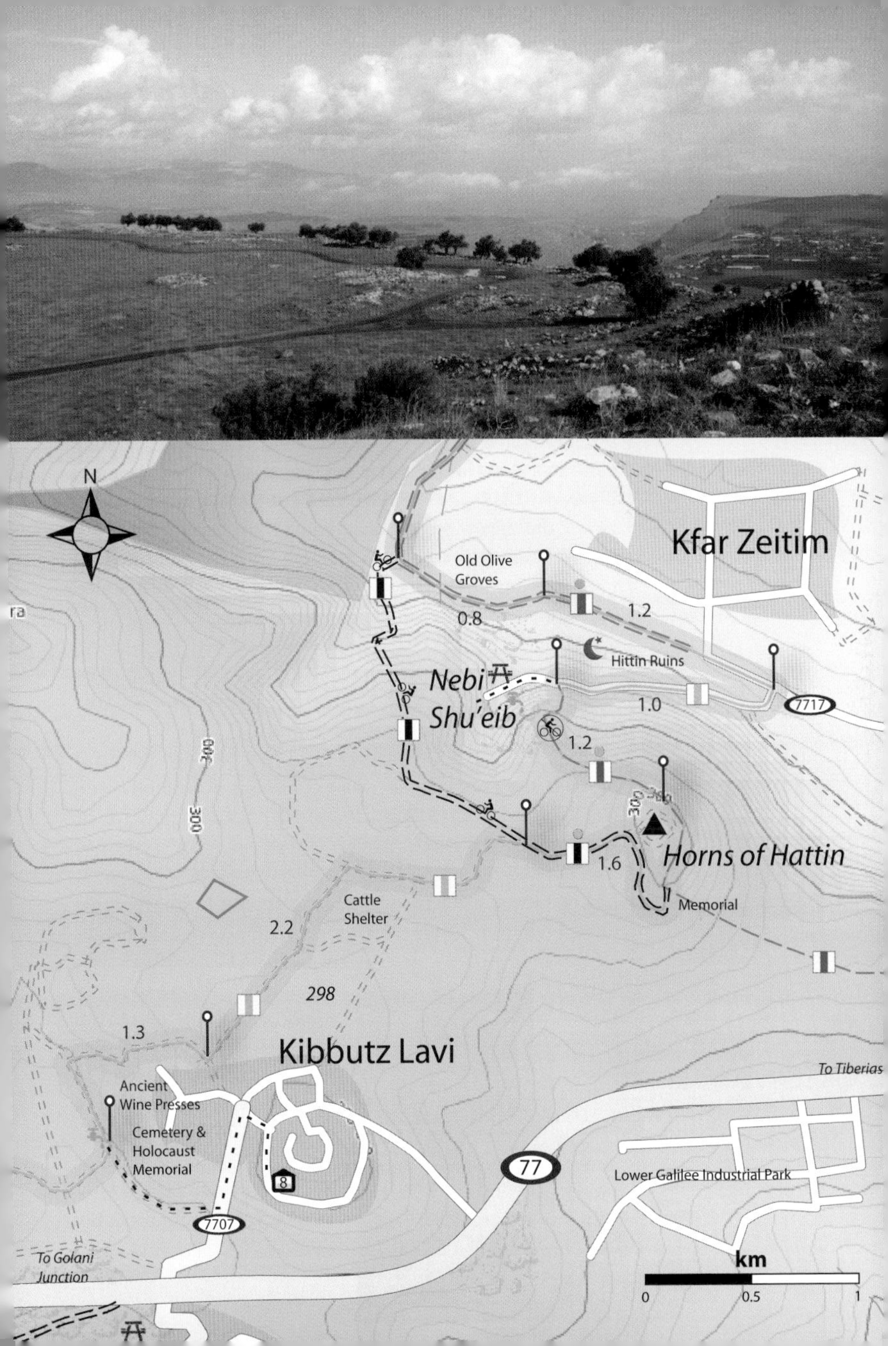

N
Kfar Zeitim
Old Olive
Groves
0.8
1.2
Hittin Ruins
Nebi
Shu'eib
1.0
7717
1.2
300
Horns of Hattin
1.6
Memorial
Cattle
Shelter
2.2
298
1.3
Kibbutz Lavi
Ancient
Wine Presses
Cemetery &
Holocaust
Memorial
8
77
7707
To Tiberias
Lower Galilee Industrial Park
To Golani
Junction
km
0
0.5
1

Horns of Hattin

קרני חיטין
قرون حطين

"They retreated to Mount Hattin to escape the storm of destruction; but on Hattin itself they found themselves encompassed by fatal thunderbolts."

—Muslim chronicler describing the Battle of Hattin in 1187

The **Horns of Hattin** are a double-peaked volcanic formation resembling the horns of a bull. Located 6 km from Tiberias, the formation provides a glorious 360° panoramic view of the entire Jesus Trail route. On a clear day, the view includes the Arbel Cliffs and Sea of Galilee to the east, as far north as Mt. Hermon, and as far west as Nazareth.

Just below the Horns, the decisive Battle of Hattin took place in 1187 between the Frankish Crusader army under King Guy and the Muslim forces under Saladin of the Ayyubid Dynasty. The battle was the culmination of waning Crusader power and the uniting of surrounding Muslim territory under one rule during the Second Crusade. For the first time since the beginning of the First Crusade, Jerusalem was surrounded by a united opposing empire.

Clear days on Hattin yield marvelous views. The word "Hattin" comes from the Hebrew word for "wheat," fitting for this agricultural area of Israel.

The Crusader army gathered in Acre with 1200 knights, over 10,000 foot soldiers and various mercenary fighters. The army carried with it a supposed remnant of the true cross of Christ. To lure the Crusaders from their stronghold, Saladin laid siege on Tiberias where nobleman Raymond's wife was living. The Crusaders fell into the trap and moved their troops east to Sepphoris.

Led by Guy and Raymond, the army set out from Sepphoris toward Tiberias. They passed through the village of Tur'an, which had a natural water source. In what many consider the fatal move, the Crusader army did not stop to camp at the sure water source in Tur'an, but rather pressed on to Tiberias late in the day. Saladin is recorded as saying, "Satan incited Guy to do what ran counter to his purpose."

Path leading to the fateful hill where Crusader forces were defeated in 1187.

After taking Tiberias, Saladin's army moved toward the Crusader army, sending two wing brigades to double behind the Crusaders, thus cutting off their line of retreat and access to the spring of Tur'an. Crusaders were forced to camp on the plateau with no water, supplies or reinforcements, surrounded by the Muslim army.

On the morning of July 4, 1187, the Crusaders awoke blinded by smoke from fires set around their camp. Vicious battle ensued, with some Crusaders defecting to Saladin or fleeing.

After the Crusaders were defeated, Guy and Raymond were taken before Saladin and offered water. King Guy drank thirstily but Raymond refused and told Saladin that if the battle had gone the other way, Raymond would have beheaded Saladin. Enraged, Saladin stabbed Raymond with his sword, cut off his head and sent it to Damascus to be dragged through the streets.

This decisive victory of the Muslim army heralded the downfall of Crusader presence in the region and the end of the Second Crusade. Over the coming weeks almost every Crusader port and stronghold fell. Finally, on October 2 of the same year, Saladin's forces conquered Jerusalem.

Nebi Shu'eib courtyard with Druze and Israeli flags

Nebi Shu'eib

נבי שועייב
النبي شعيب

Now Moses kept the flock of Jethro his father-in-law, the priest of Midian. Exodus 3:1a

Nebi Shu'eib is a huge mosque-like structure nestled at the base of the Horns of Hattin. The building houses the traditional tomb of Jethro, father-in-law of Moses (Exodus 3:1), a prophet in the **Druze** tradition. The Druze religion believes that Jethro passed on rules about justice, righteousness and monotheism to Moses.

Both the Israeli flag and the Druze flag (comprised of five bands of color representing the five major Druze prophets as well as elements in nature) fly over the impressive complex. From the expansive courtyard there is a sweeping view of the Arbel Cliffs and Sea of Galilee. The complex was constructed as a place for Druze to congregate, particularly on April 25 for a special pilgrimage (known as *ziyara*), as well as a place of hospitality for all people.

The chamber housing the tomb-marker dates back to the 3rd century, and travel reports from the 11th century mention the place as a holy site. Some of the current building dates from 1880 but has since been extensively renovated. You might ask to see the impressive chandelier sent from Druze in Damascus in lieu of coming on pilgrimage, as the current political situation makes it impossible for Syrian Druze to visit relatives in Israel.

Photos Opposite: Top of Nebi Shu'eib building (top), Interior of Nebi Shu'eib (middle), Druze from all over Israel flock to Nebi Shu'eib for *ziyara* (bottom).

The Druze religion dates back to 10th-century Egypt as an offshoot of the Ismaeli branch of Islam. While culturally Arab, Druze maintain a separate identity from mainstream Muslim and Christian Arabs in Israel. They are located primarily in southern Syria and northern Israel. They believe in the major prophets of the three monotheisms, incorporate elements of Buddhism into their theology and highly esteem other historical figures including the major Greek philosophers and Alexander the Great.

Outside view of shrine from courtyard (above)

The Druze are non-prosyletizing because of their belief in reincarnation. They believe at some point in history all people had the chance to be Druze, so those that rejected the Druze religion could not accept it in a later reincarnation. They believe that Christianity, Judaism and Islam were corrupted by rituals, and therefore the Druze have no liturgy and virtually no rituals of their own. It is also a secret religion, where certain knowledge is reserved only for religious leaders, a feature thought to be incorporated from Shia Islam.

The Druze are loyal to whichever country they live in, and even fought on the side of Israel in the War of 1948. While other Arab citizens of Israel are exempt from serving in the Israeli military, Druze citizens perform the same military service as Jewish Israelis. Druze are easily recognizable by their distinctive dress—the men wear white turbans and large, puffy Ottoman-style pants, and the women cover their heads with a white cloth.

You will need appropriate clothing in order to enter the complex—pants past the knee and shoulders covered. The tomb is just inside off the expansive patio. As in a mosque, you will need to remove your shoes and cover your head (there are scarves available as well as baseball hats and button-down shirts for modesty) in order to enter the tomb. Photography is not permitted in the tomb. The tomb-marker is covered by a green satin cloth, a color associated with Jethro. By the far wall there is a patch of stone that is said to be the footprint of Jethro. The western wall holds a picture of the Druze leader Sheikh Amin Tarif.

J5

NEBI SHU'EIB TO MOSHAV ARBEL

9.6 km
2.5-4 hours

Difficulty: Fairly flat with moderate ascent at end.

Biking Detours: None. The ascent out of Nakhal Arbel to Moshav Arbel is steep but possible. Riding the road from Nebi Shu'eib to Moshav Arbel saves the climb, but misses the spectacular scenery and great riding of the wadi route.

Transport for Moshav Arbel: No direct transport; taxi from Tiberias or contact accommodations for pick-up.

Ponder recent history at the ruins of a mosque, drink in "Jesus scenery" through the Arbel Valley, visit an ancient synagogue with a spectacular view

From Nebi Shu'eib, follow the road to the ruins of the mosque from the depopulated village of Hittin visible below. The trail joins a blue marked 4x4 trail which follows Nakhal Nimrin and Nakhal Arbel around the scenic Arbel Valley. At an abandoned building, turn right on the blue trail to climb out of the valley. When you reach the paved road, follow it for 100 m, then turn right on a green footpath to an ancient synagogue. Access Moshav Arbel by a footpath leading from the ancient synagogue toward the village.

Shortcut to Wadi Hamam: *If you're short on time or not keen on heights, stay straight at the abandoned building in Nakhal Arbel. You'll soon join the green trail which leads straight to Wadi Hamam, skipping Arbel B&B and J6 (Arbel National Park). However, you'll miss the spectacular views from Mt. Arbel!*

Accommodations:

9 **Arbel B&B (Shavit Family):** ☎04-679-4919; www.4shavit.com; dorm 100NIS, double 350NIS

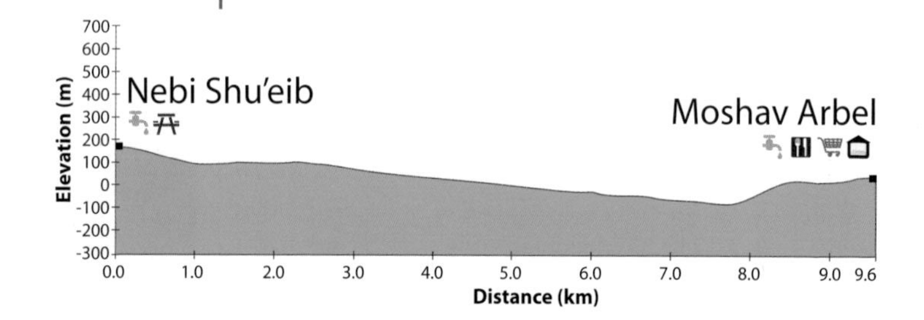

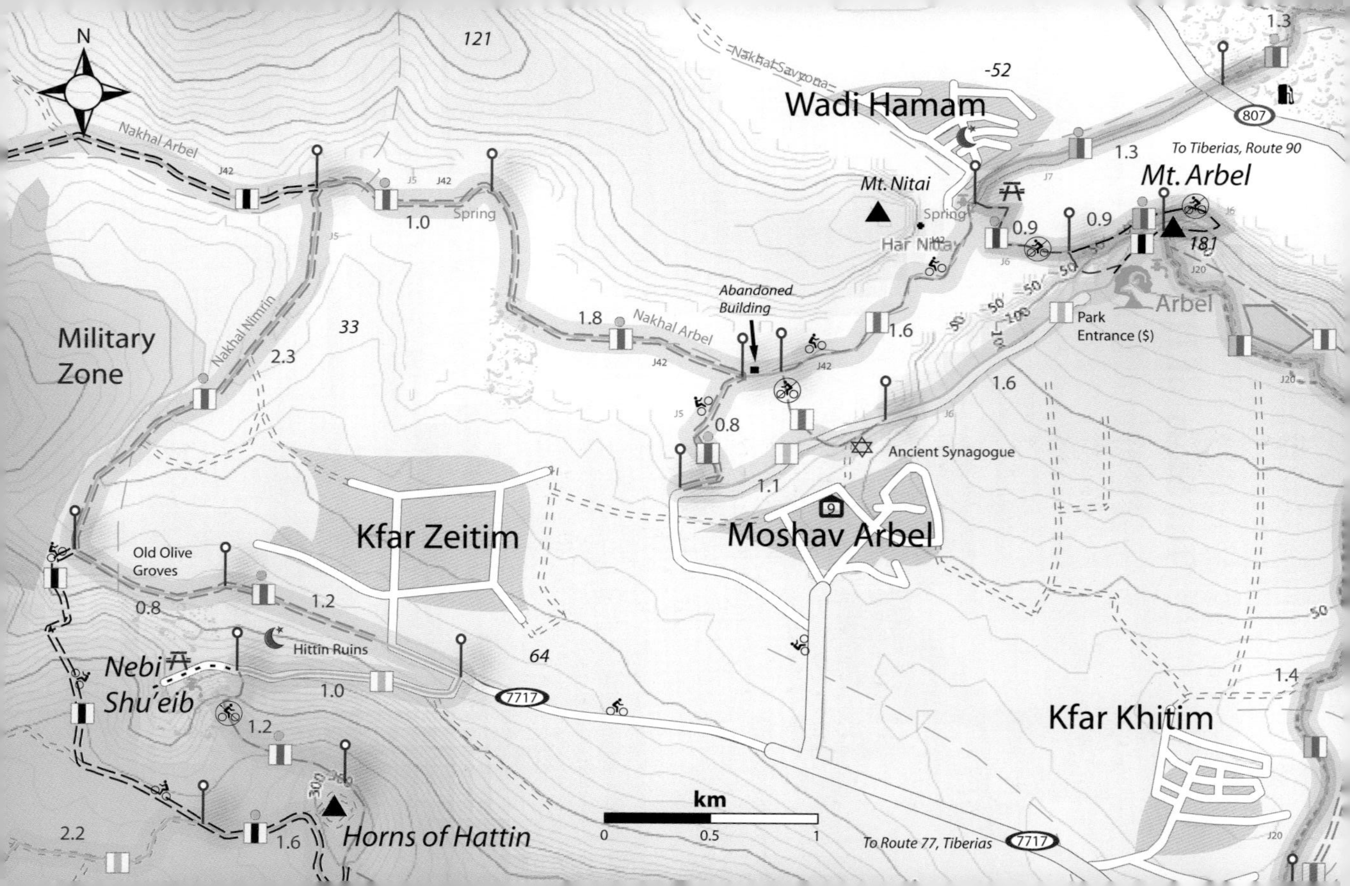

Wadi Hamam
Nakhal Savyona
Mt. Nitai
Har Nitai
Spring
Mt. Arbel
Arbel
To Tiberias, Route 90
Park
Entrance ($)
Abandoned
Building
Nakhal Arbel
Ancient Synagogue
Moshav Arbel
Military
Zone
Nakhal Nimrin
Kfar Zeitim
Old Olive
Groves
Hittin Ruins
Nebi
Shu'eib
Horns of Hattin
Kfar Khitim
km
To Route 77, Tiberias

Depopulated Villages:
The Story of Hittin

חיטין
حطين

"By the end of the 1948 war, hundreds of entire villages had not only been depopulated but obliterated, their houses blown up or bulldozed. While many of the sites are difficult to access, to this day the observant traveller of Israeli roads and highways can see traces of their presence that would escape the notice of the casual passer-by: a fenced-in area, often surmounting a gentle hill, of olive and other fruit trees left untended, of cactus hedges and domesticated plants run wild. Now and then a few crumbled houses are left standing, a neglected mosque or church, collapsing walls along the ghost of a village lane, but in the vast majority of cases, all that remains is a scattering of stones and rubble across a forgotten landscape."

—Walid Khalidi, Palestinian author, *All That Remains*

Ruins of Hittin mosque and village (above and below)

Town of Hittin circa 1934

At the base of Nebi Shu'eib across the new highway, a lone mosque stands to mark the former location of the Arab village of **Hittin**. Hittin was one of over 400 Arab towns and villages in what became Israel that were destroyed or left empty after the war of 1948. Accounts of what happened in these villages vary depending on who tells them. Some villagers say the Israeli army told them to leave and that after the war they could return. Others say they fled out of fear of the war with every intention of returning. Still others say the Arab army fighting against the newly-formed Israeli state instructed villagers to leave until the fighting subsided.

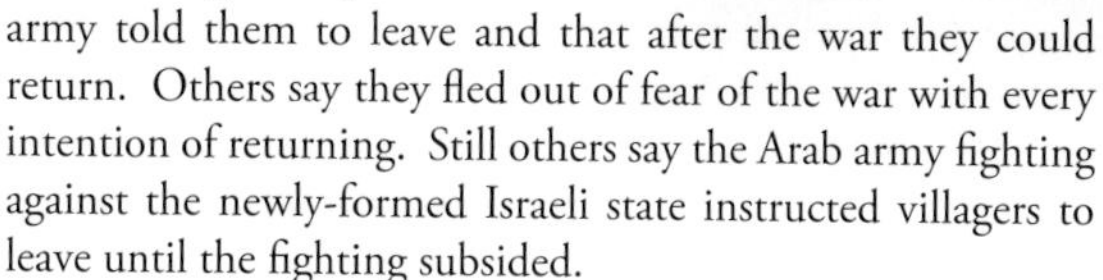

Historians still disagree as to whether this depopulation was part of a prior plan made by the Israeli army to get rid of non-Jewish populations, or an unintended side effect of the war. Regardless, hundreds of thousands of Arab inhabitants fled or were forced to leave their villages and many of them were never allowed to return. Some reside in refugee camps in Syria, Lebanon, or the Palestinian territories; some live in Jordan; some were able to return to live in Arab cities that remained (such as Nazareth) and received Israeli citizenship; some have immigrated abroad.

Small remnants of these villages dot the landscape of Israel and, in some cases, structures still remain as stark reminders and wistful mementos of a culture and people who have lived on the land for generations. The issue of Palestinian refugees and controversy over the legitimacy of the "right of return" (the right of Palestinian refugees to return to their former homes) has been a major point of contention in peace negotiations and is one that, over 60 years later, still has not been resolved.

Hittin has been mentioned as a possible location for Zittim, a fortified Canaanite city mentioned in Joshua 19:35, which

came to be known as Kfar Hattim around the 3rd century BCE. It is then mentioned in records from the Battle of Hattin (see pp. 92-93) as near the location of Saladin's base camp. Early Muslim writers describe Hittin as the birthplace of several prominent Muslim leaders during the Islamic period. Travel records from the Ottoman era describe the town as very fertile and full of olive trees, figs and citrus, well-watered by the spring flowing from Wadi Hamam, and indicate that the town was a popular stopping point for travelers on pilgrimage to Nebi Shu'eib. The population of the town is reported as approximately 600 at the beginning of the Ottoman period and 1300 in 1948.

Olives are harvested in late fall to early winter each year.

Keep an eye out as you walk for evidence of depopulated villages. Many of these buildings were made of stone, often basalt in the Sea of Galilee region (if you take route J10 to Bethsaida you will see many examples of this type of structure). In downtown Tiberias you can see examples of two

Olive trees are exceptionally hearty and can even withstand fire.

mosques from the former Arab inhabitants. Lavi Forest near Golani Junction stands on land that was once part of the Arab city of Lubya, still dotted with village cisterns and fruit trees. So many former residents of Saffuriya (located near and on the ruins of Zippori) now live in Nazareth that there is a city quarter named for them.

For more information about depopulated villages contact **Zochrot**, an Israeli organization that aims to raise awareness among Israelis about the plight of Palestinians. Zochrot organizes visits to depopulated villages with former residents to hear stories of life before 1948 and leave signs identifying the ruins that remain (☎03-695-3155; zochrot@netvision.net.il).

Ruins of the entrance to the Hittin Mosque

Olive Harvest

But I am like an olive tree flourishing in the house of God; I trust in God's unfailing love for ever and ever. Psalm 52:8

The Middle East is well-known for its production of oil in the petroleum sense—black gold, if you will. But long before the advent of fossil fuels, Homer referred to another kind of Middle Eastern oil as "liquid gold:" olive oil. Ninety-five percent of the world's olive oil comes from the Mediterranean region, and olive oil plays an important role in Jewish history as described in the Hebrew Bible, as well as in Palestinian written and oral tradition. The olive tree symbolizes prosperity, beauty and fertility and makes up an ubiquitous part of the landscape. Jesus chooses the garden of Gethsemane, an olive grove, for his final night before crucifixion.

Olives are harvested from mid-October to December every year. Entire families gather out in the field for this time-consuming intergenerational ritual. A tarp is placed under each tree and family members climb a ladder to shake the ripe olives down onto the tarp. Small rakes are used to pull clumps of olives off the tree. The olives are collected from the tarp and sorted into buckets, bagged and sent to market, sometimes on the back of a donkey as in ancient times.

Some of the olives are treated to be sold and eaten. Others are taken to olive oil mills to be made into olive oil. The ancient method of olive oil extraction was first to crush the olives under large circular millstones, usually attached to a donkey that would walk in a circle, pulling the stone over the olive fruit. This was done for 30-40 minutes to thoroughly crush the olives, allow time for the oil to form into large drops and infuse the oil with the taste and aroma of the fruit enzymes.

Approaching the cliffs of Arbel in spring (opposite top)

Fourth-century synagogue with a view (opposite bottom)

From the first crushing stage, the olive paste was pressed using one of several methods. The most common method was the torcular, or lever press. An excellent example of this can be seen at Nazareth Village (p. 12). In this method, the mash was placed in stone holes with a stone plug attached to a heavy beam. The beam rested on the stone plugs, exerting pressure that presses out the olive oil, which ran through channels in the stone into a collecting jar. After pressing the olive oil, the pulp was dried and used as fuel.

Both green and black olives come from the same tree, but are picked at different levels of maturity. It takes around 4.5 kg (10 lbs) of olives to produce 1 L (≈1 qt) of olive oil.

Synagogue of Ancient Arbel

A green trail off to the right from the paved road to Arbel will lead you to a **4th-century synagogue** which was part of the ancient settlement of Arbel. The ancient town was inhabited from the 2nd century BCE to the 8th century CE, and was the hometown of the Jewish sage Nitai. Note the heart-shaped double columns, carved doorway and niche facing Jerusalem that would have held the ark and housed the Torah scrolls. The synagogue affords a great view of Arbel Valley, which one Jewish tradition cites as the place the Messiah will appear. Intact, the synagogue would have had two stories and been lined on three sides by benches.

J6

MOSHAV ARBEL TO WADI HAMAM

3.6 km
2-3 hours

DIFFICULTY:
Steep descents with small sections of rock scrambling.

ADMISSION FEES:
Arbel National Park.

BIKING DETOURS:
Retrace route from Mt. Arbel down to wadi on blue and green trails. Requires walking your bike over loose stones.

TRANSPORT FOR WADI HAMAM:
From Tiberias, take a taxi or bus 841/963 toward Tabgha. Get off at Migdal Junction and walk 1 km on Route 807, turn left at gas station and walk 1 km.

Behold the lay of the land at Mt. Arbel—one of the best views in the country, descend the cliffs to explore ancient caves

From the ancient synagogue parking lot, follow the road to Arbel National Park entrance (fee area). Admire the view of the Sea of Galilee from the lookout at Mt. Arbel, then carefully follow the steep (but manageable) black path down the face of the cliffs. Continue downward on the red trail at the ancient cave fortress and dwellings. Stop for a drink at the Wadi Hamam spring, and finish your route at the parking lot on the outskirts of the Bedouin village of Wadi Hamam.

The Jesus Trail route follows the Israel Trail (orange/blue/white) from the top of Mt. Arbel to the entrance of Nakhal Amud (J7). If you don't want to descend the steep cliff path, follow the biking detour through Nakhal Arbel on the green trail.

Accommodations:
No immediate accommodations. Walk out to Migdal Junction (2 km) to take a bus for overnight in Tiberias or other.

Group at Arbel Cliffs at dusk (photo opposite)

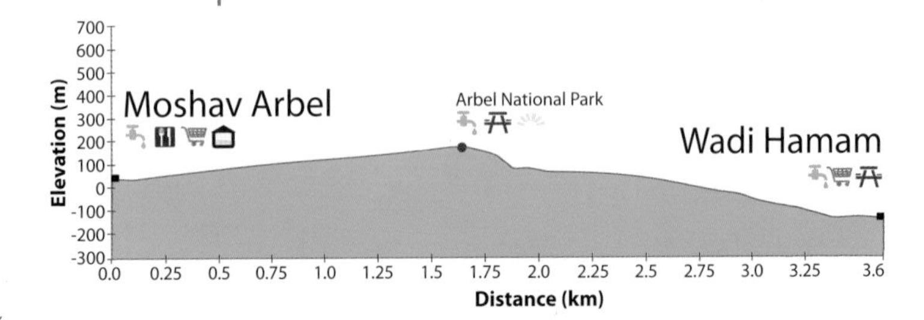

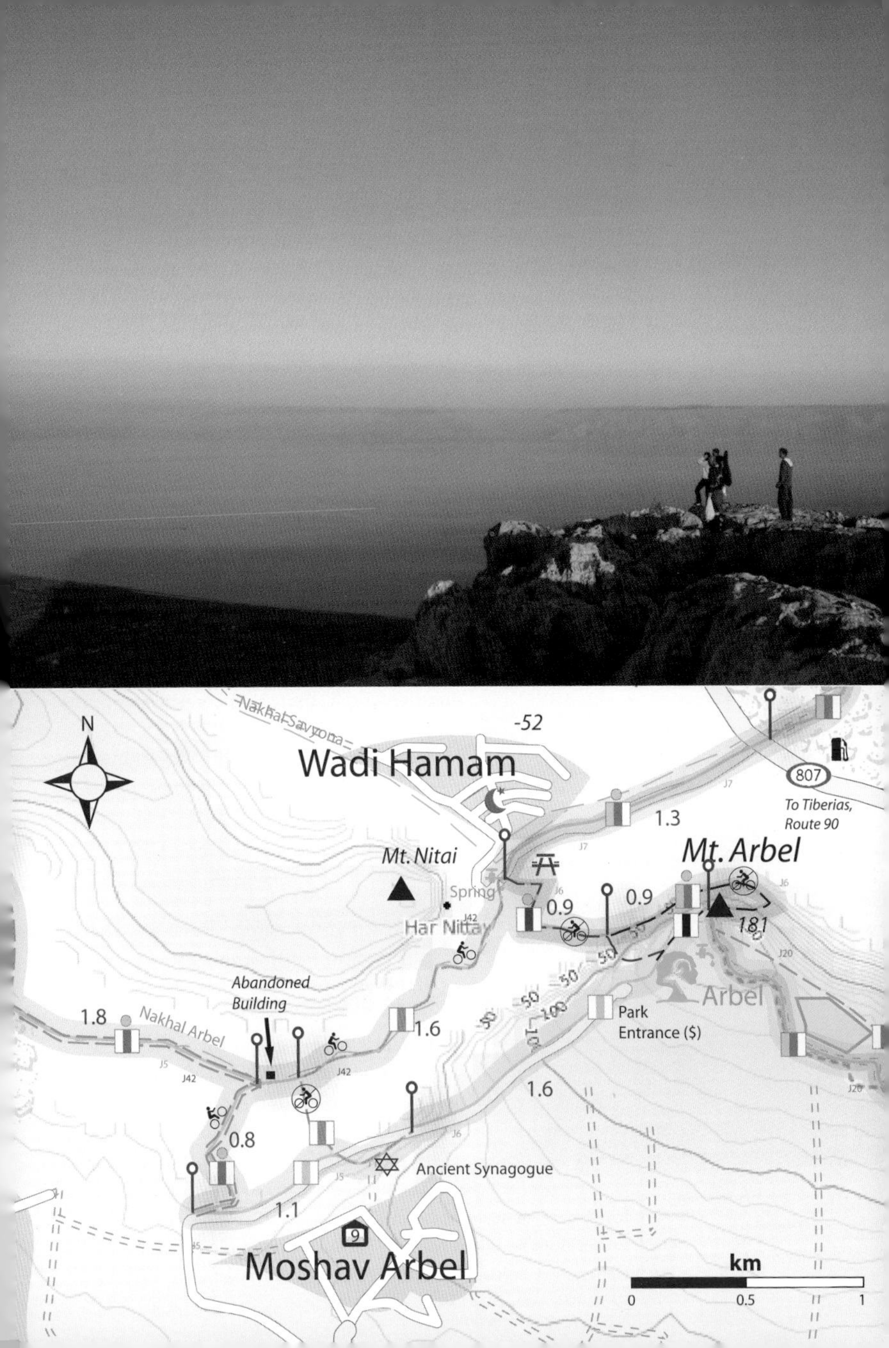

N
Nakhal Savyona
-52
Wadi Hamam
807
To Tiberias,
Route 90
1.3
Mt. Arbel
Mt. Nitai
Spring
Har Nittay
0.9
0.9
181
Arbel
Abandoned
Building
1.8
Nakhal Arbel
1.6
Park
Entrance ($)
1.6
0.8
Ancient Synagogue
1.1
9
Moshav Arbel
km
0
0.5
1

Arbel National Park ארבל اربيل

Arbel National Park
☎04-673-2904;
adult/child 20/9NIS;
8am-5pm summer,
8am-4pm winter,
other hours by request

The most identifiable land formation around the Sea of Galilee is **Mt. Arbel**. Originally a large, continuous hill overlooking the lake, an earthquake in 759 BCE split the mount into two cliff faces—Arbel to the east and Nitai to the west. The cliffs plunge almost 400 m, from 180 m above sea level to 200 m below sea level. On a clear day, the breathtaking view includes the Sea of Galilee, Tiberias, Safed, sites along the northeast shore of the sea and into the Golan, including the snow-capped peak of Mt. Hermon.

Looking west from the Arbel Lookout

The Jesus Trail follows the Israel Trail blazes on a steep but beautiful route down the cliff face. Just off the trail there are numerous caves to explore, some containing *mikvehs* and cisterns. Be careful as you descend. There are metal staples in the rock to assist you on the steepest section, but they can be quite slippery when damp.

The caves have been inhabited by different people groups throughout history. In the late 16th to early 17th century the caves were incorporated into a palace of sorts for the Bedouin sheikh Fakhr al-Din.

The most dramatic story related to Arbel is told by historian Josephus (see p. 205) of the methods employed by Herod the Great to eradicate the threat of Hasmonean rebels hiding out in the caves of Arbel. First, Herod went after the rebels by lowering down his soldiers in large baskets on ropes to pull out the rebels, causing them to fall to their deaths. To finish the job the soldiers set fire to the caves. In typical Josephus style, the noble Hasmonean rebels chose to die rather than be taken captive, and those remaining chose to kill themselves (a Josephus motif also used at Masada and Gamla).

Josephus' account, as recorded in *The Jewish War:*

Arbel Cliffs in springtime

> *Now these caves were in the precipices of craggy mountains, and could not be come at from any side, since they had only some winding pathways, very narrow, by which they got up to them; but the rock that lay on their front had beneath it valleys of a vast depth, and of an almost perpendicular declivity; insomuch that the king was doubtful for a long time what to do, by reason of a kind of impossibility there was of attacking the place. Yet did he at length make use of a contrivance that was subject to the utmost hazard; for he let down the most hardy of his men in chests, and set them at the mouths of the dens.*
>
> *Now these men slew the robbers and their families, and when they made resistance, they sent in fire upon them [and burnt them]; and as Herod was desirous of saving some of them, he had proclamation made, that they should come and deliver themselves up to him; but not one of them came willingly to him; and of those that were compelled to come, many preferred death to captivity.*

Metal handholds to assist in descending Mt. Arbel

Spring flowers blossom near Wadi Hamam.

And here a certain old man, the father of seven children, whose children, together with their mother, desired him to give them leave to go out, upon the assurance and right hand that was offered them, slew them after the following manner: He ordered every one of them to go out, while he stood himself at the cave's mouth, and slew that son of his perpetually who went out.

Herod was near enough to see this sight, and his bowels of compassion were moved at it, and he stretched out his right hand to the old man, and besought him to spare his children; yet did not he relent at all upon what he said, but over and above reproached Herod on the lowness of his descent, and slew his wife as well as his children; and when he had thrown their dead bodies down the precipice, he at last threw himself down after them.

By this means Herod subdued these caves, and the robbers that were in them.

View of Wadi Hamam from Arbel Cliffs

Carob Trees חרוב

Ceratonia siliqua خروب

> *He longed to fill his stomach with the pods that the pigs were eating, but no one gave him anything.* Luke 15:16

From the entrance to Arbel National Park, the trail will take you up to the **Carob Tree Lookout**, with its marvelous view of the plain of Ginosar, the Sea of Galilee and even Mt. Hermon on a clear day.

Carob tree at lookout on Arbel Cliffs

Carob trees are flowering evergreens with edible seedpods, which used to be used for sugar and are now sometimes used as a cocoa substitute. Carob seeds were used in ancient times for weighing precious metals, from which we get the term "carat." Carob trees are very hearty and can withstand drought conditions. Also known as the "locust tree," John the Baptist probably ate carob and honey, rather than the more common translation that he was eating locust insects! Used as animal feed in biblical times, the "pods" fed to the pigs in the parable of the Prodigal Son may well have been carob pods.

Wadi Hamam وادي الحمام ואדי חמאם

The valley between Mt. Nitai and Mt. Migdal, near the base of Mt. Arbel, is known as **Wadi Hamam** or the "Valley of the Doves." The Muslim town of Wadi Hamam lies in this valley. With a population of about 1300, the residents are Bedouin originally from farther north who settled in the valley after being displaced in 1948. Before 1948 there was another village by the same name in its place that was destroyed in the war. The water of Wadi Hamam spring is drinkable.

In 2007, an ancient synagogue and other Roman-era buildings were discovered in the valley on the slopes of Mt. Nitai. Though not yet open to the public, preliminary excavations have returned significant finds such as synagogue floor mosaics and an industrial-sized olive press.

J7

WADI HAMAM TO TABGHA

10.1 km
2-3 hours

Difficulty: Flat farmland, slight ascent near Tabgha.

Biking Detours: None.

Transport for Tabgha: From Tiberias, buses 841 and 963 run regularly to Capernaum (Kfar Nakhum) junction; follow signs to Tabgha (1 km).

Wander through pleasant orchard scenery, visit the Church of the Multiplication of Loaves and Fishes, dip your toes in the Sea of Galilee

From Wadi Hamam parking lot, follow the Israel Trail for 1.3 km to cross Route 807 to the left of the yellow gas station to Route 90 near the entrance of Migdal. Continue through Ginosar Valley past orchards. Split from the Israel Trail just after an Ottoman bridge (remnant of the historic railroad) and turn east when the Israel Trail enters Nakhal Amud. Pass a gas station at the junction of Routes 8077 and 90 and continue to carefully cross Route 90 and descend to Route 87. Walk along the road to the entrance of the Church of the Multiplication of the Loaves and Fishes at Tabgha. Follow the pilgrim sidewalk to other sites.

Accommodations:

- 10 **Beit Bracha Christian Guesthouse** (Migdal): ☎04-679-2338; www.cmj-israel.org; single 180NIS, double 360NIS
- 11 **Ginosar Inn**: ☎04-670-0311; www.ginosar.co.il; double 400+NIS
- 12 **Karei Deshe** (Tabgha): ☎02-594-5631; www.hihostel.com; dorm 120NIS, double 320NIS
- 13 **Pilgerhaus Tabgha:** ☎04-670-0100; double 650+NIS

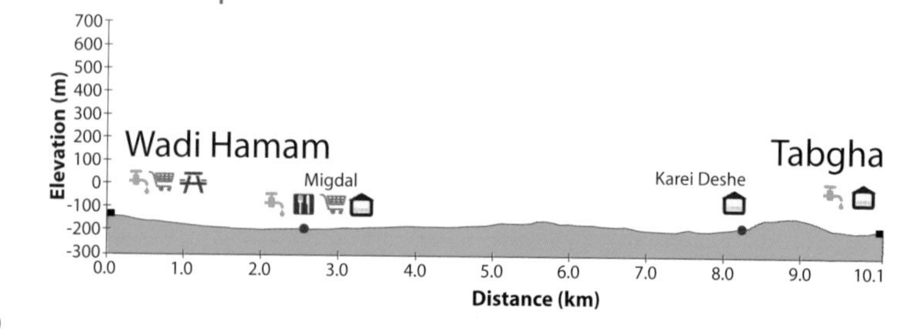

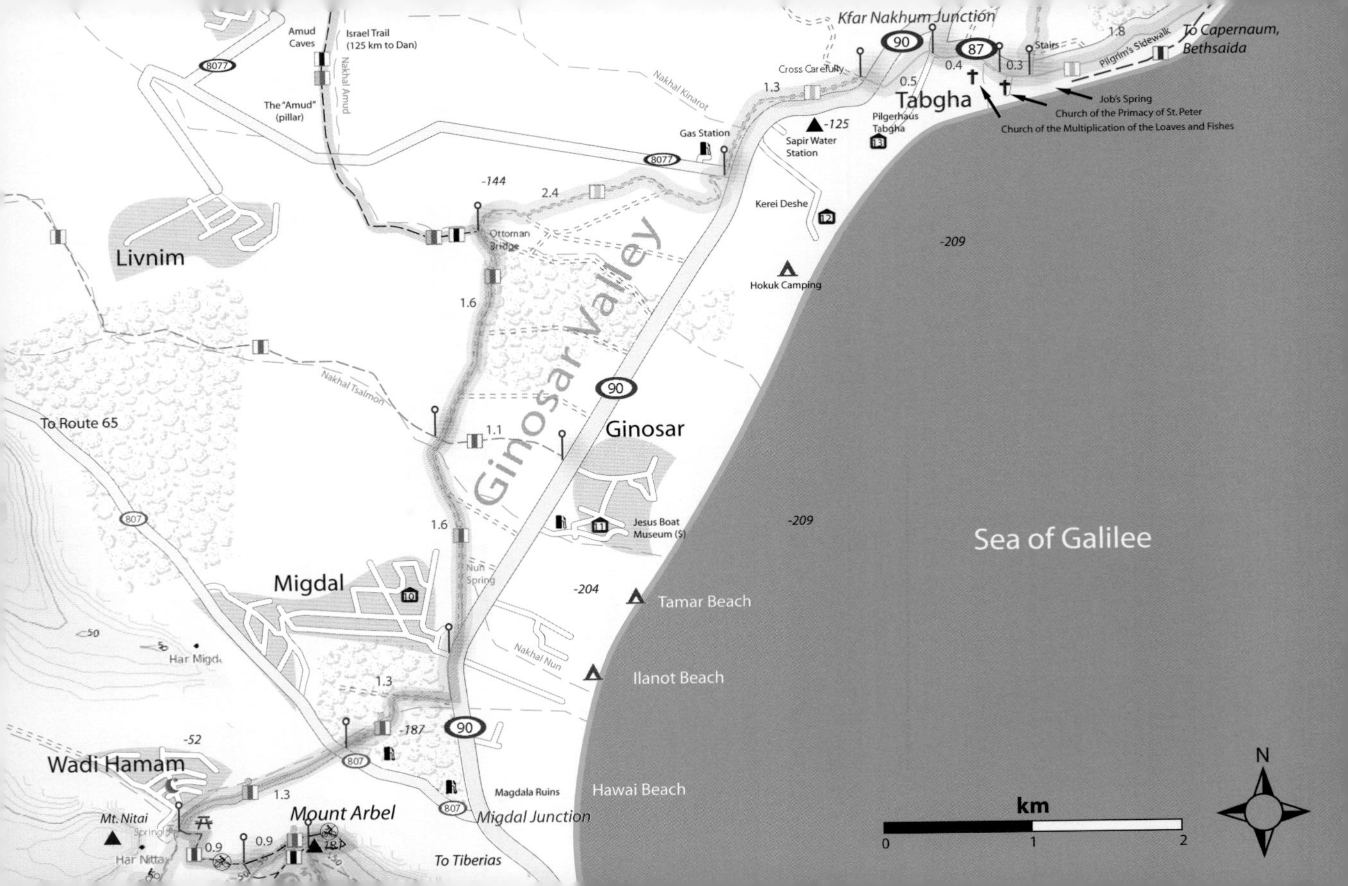

Kfar Nakhum Junction
To Capernaum, Bethsaida
Pilgrim's Sidewalk
Stairs
Job's Spring
Church of the Primacy of St. Peter
Church of the Multiplication of the Loaves and Fishes
Tabgha
Pilgerhaus Tabgha
Cross Carefully
Sapir Water Station
-125
Gas Station
Nakhal Kinarot
Amud Caves
Israel Trail (125 km to Dan)
Nakhal Amud
The "Amud" (pillar)
8077
-144
Ottoman Bridge
Kerei Deshe
Hokuk Camping
-209
Livnim
Ginosar Valley
Nakhal Tsalmon
To Route 65
Ginosar
Jesus Boat Museum ($)
Sea of Galilee
Nun Spring
Migdal
Tamar Beach
-204
Nakhal Nun
Ilanot Beach
Har Migdal
-187
-52
Wadi Hamam
Hawai Beach
Magdala Ruins
Migdal Junction
Mount Arbel
Mt. Nitai
Spring
Har Nitai
To Tiberias
807
90
87
1.8
0.5
0.4
0.3
1.3
2.4
1.6
1.1
0.9
km
0
1
2
N

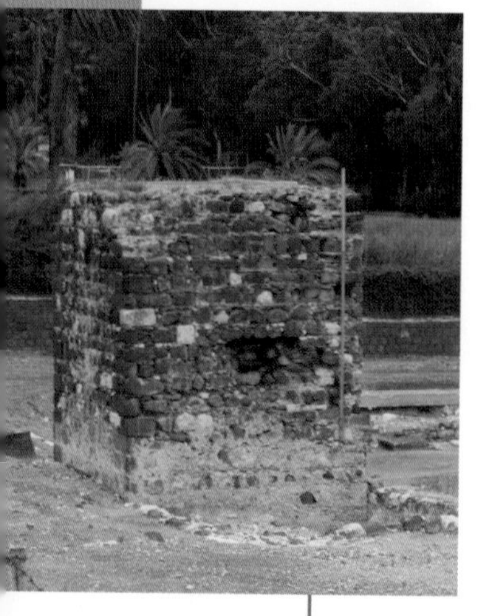

Ruins of an ancient storage tower at Magdala

Magdala מגדל مجدال

When Jesus rose early on the first day of the week, he appeared first to Mary Magdalene, out of whom he had driven seven demons. Mark 16:9

The most famous resident of **Magdala** is undoubtedly Mary Magdalene. She is described as having been healed of seven demons and was the first to see Jesus again after the resurrection. Meaning "tower," Magdala was a small town 6 km north of Tiberias dating back to Roman times. The towers were traditionally thought to be for drying fish caught in the Sea of Galilee. Magdala also went by the Greek name of *Taricheae.*

The Roman-era ruins at Magdala, administrated by the Catholic Church, are not open to the public, but visible through a fence. The ruins include a synagogue and Byzantine church, a mosaic of a fishing boat and ancient perfume vials perhaps similar to the ones an unnamed sinful woman used to anoint the feet of Jesus (Luke 7:38). Today, a small Jewish village named Migdal is located 1 km from the ruins.

Jesus Boat Exhibit
☎04-672-7700;
www.jesusboatmuseum.com;
adult/child 20/15NIS;
8am-5pm Sat-Thu,
8am-1pm Fri

The Jesus Boat ישוע סירה يسوع قارب

Jesus stepped into a boat, crossed over and came to his own town. Matthew 9:1

In 1986, Moshe and Yuval Lufan, fisherman brothers from Kibbutz Ginosar, discovered the remains of a boat that was later dated as being from the 1st century. Dubbed "the **Jesus Boat**," the remnants were carefully extracted and preserved in the **Yigal Allon Center**, along with a recreation of the complete boat. Detour 2 km off the Jesus Trail on a blue trail to visit the museum.

The extraction of the boat from the mud of the lake took 12 days of painstaking work. The boat had been cocooned in mud for about 2000 years, and the majority of the structure of the wood had been replaced by water. To excavate the boat, researchers built a special hanging platform over the boat to avoid any contact with the wood. After clearing the mud, the boat was encapsulated in polyurethane foam and floated out to sea to transport to reconstruction facilities. The further preservation efforts included seven years in a chemical bath that gradually replaced water in the wood with synthetic wax.

The boat was most likely used for fishing and transportation, leading to speculation that it may have been the boat of one of Jesus' disciples and could have served as his transportation as some point during his life. The boat is made up of 12 different types of wood, leading to theories that it was repaired repeatedly before being sunk after it was no longer seaworthy. The boat measures 8.2 m (27 ft) long by 2.3 m (7.5 ft) wide with a height of 1.2 m (4 ft).

Amud Caves الكهوف العامود מערות עמוד

If you have a taste for truly old history, detour just a kilometer or so off the trail to visit **Amud Caves**, three prehistoric caves which contained some of the oldest evidence of human settlement in the region. The caves are located in Nakhal Amud, named for the natural limestone pillar at the entrance to the wadi (*amud* is Arabic and Hebrew for "pillar").

In the main Amud cave, a nearly-complete skeleton of a 25-year-old Neanderthal man was found. A bit further are the Zuttiyeh and Emireh caves, where skeletons found date from the Middle Paleolithic Age (120,000-45,000 BCE), though skull fragments in Zuttiyah cave date even further back, from around 250,000 BCE.

From Amud Cave, looking out into Nakhal Amud

Rocky beach on the Sea of Galilee

Sea of Galilee

ים כנרת
بحيرة طبريا

As you might guess from a cursory glance at a map, the **Sea of Galilee** isn't a sea; it's a lake. In Hebrew it is known as Lake Kinneret, from the Hebrew word for harp, since the flat western shore and curving eastern shore resemble the shape of the instrument. At 8 km wide and 21 km long, it is the largest freshwater lake in Israel. Today, as in antiquity, the main economic activities of the region are agriculture and fishing. Since Byzantine times it has also been a place of pilgrimage and tourism.

Pollution and the Sea of Galilee

The now-famous Zionist dream of "making the desert bloom" has wreaked environmental problems on the Galilee, especially the Sea of Galilee. In recent years the Sea of Galilee has dropped about 5 m (16.5 ft), from -209 m to -214 m. The lake provides 50% of Israel's drinking water, and is piped all over the country. Deep beneath the surface, the lake is fed by salt-water vents, so if the water continues to fall at current levels, it will soon be too saline for drinking and agricultural purposes.

Water, water, everywhere but not a drop to drink?

Israel does have several water desalinization plants in the southern coastal city of Ashkelon that make fresh water from the saline waters of the Mediterranean Sea. The drawback? Each cubic meter of desalinized water costs $.55-$.60, much more expensive than natural fresh water. Officials are discussing importing water from Turkey.

Water is not only over-consumed in homes, but current agricultural trends in the Galilee utilize more water than can be sustainably available. Moisture-guzzling citrus and banana farms surround the sea, and the majority of their produce is exported. Sixty percent of the country's fresh water is used in agriculture, which contributes only about 2% to Israel's GDP. This agricultural practice amounts to the economic equivalent of exporting drinking water from a country already strapped for water.

Climate change also affects the region, with drought-level rainfall for the past four years in a row. Israel received only 65% of their average yearly rainfall in 2008. While Israelis have long paved the way in irrigation practices such as drip irrigation, it may now be time to expand into water conservation and desalinization.

The receding waters of the Sea of Galilee present problems to local businesses, particularly tourism and fishing. In the past, houses on the lake were built on stilts to accommodate times of flood. Now waterfront property that may once have boasted deck-side views directly onto the water are sometimes 300 m from the shore, where dazzling views can only be seen via binoculars. The business of local fisherman has also suffered. With fewer and fewer catches, some are barely able to cover their own expenses. The aesthetics of the lake suffer as well, which threatens to adversely affect the tourism industry.

Fisherman at sunset on the Sea of Galilee

St. Peter's Fish

> *...Go to the lake and throw out your line. Take the first fish you catch; open its mouth and you will find a four-drachma coin. Take it and give it to them for my tax and yours.* Matthew 17:27b

As soon as you set foot on the shores of the Sea of Galilee you will most likely see restaurants touting **St. Peter's fish**, more commonly known as tilapia. The term "St. Peter" references a New Testament story in which Jesus instructs Peter to pay the temple tax with a coin from the mouth of a fish. While the story does not name the species of fish, tilapia has been fished from the Sea of Galilee for thousands of years and is traditionally associated with the fish of the story.

Fishing was an important industry at the time of Jesus, and 15 harbors from his time period have been discovered.

With Jesus in the Boat

Matthew 14:22-32
Jesus walks on water out to a boat.

Mark 4:35-41
Jesus calms the storm from a boat.

Mark 4:38
Jesus sleeps on a boat.

Luke 5:1-11
Simon, James and John leave their fishing boat to follow Jesus.

Tabgha

الطابغة עין שבע

Jesus then took the loaves, gave thanks, and distributed to those who were seated as much as they wanted. He did the same with the fish. John 6:11

Fourth-century pilgrim Egeria:

"In the same place (not far from Capernaum) facing the Sea of Galilee is a well watered land in which lush grasses grow, with numerous trees and palms. Nearby are seven springs which provide abundant water. In this fruitful garden Jesus fed five thousand people with five loaves of bread and two fish."

In the region of Tabgha, on the northern shore of the Sea of Galilee, lies the **Church of the Multiplication of Loaves and Fishes**, the traditional site of the food multiplication story found in all four gospels (Matthew 14:13-21, Mark 6:31-44, Luke 9:10-17, John 6:5-15). It is also where Jesus appeared to his disciples after his resurrection (John 21:1-17).

The first church on the site was constructed in the mid-3rd century. The mosaic of the loaves and fishes was excavated next to a large rock, perhaps where Jesus blessed the food before multiplication. Part of the rock can be seen under the altar behind the mosaic. Under glass to the right of the altar you can see remains of the earlier 4th-century foundation. To the right is an inscription naming Patriarch Martyrios of Jerusalem as the church's founder.

Fish pond at Church of the Multiplication of Loaves and Fishes

The large monastery and expanded church were added in the 5th century and soon after destroyed, most likely by the Persians when they invaded in 614. The Byzantine structures and mosaics were excavated in 1932 by German archeologists. In 1982 the current reconstruction was added. The mosaics depict water birds and plants, ecology of the marshy swamps typical of the local area.

The name Tabgha is a variation on its ancient Greek name, *Heptapegon*, meaning seven springs. Some of these springs were warm and so Tabgha was rich in fish who came to feed in the warmer waters. Six of these springs have been identified in modern times (see Job's Spring on p. 121).

Courtyard of church at Tabgha

Pilgerhaus Tabgha

Pilgerhaus Tabgha

This German guesthouse on the shore of the Sea of Galilee was founded in 1889 (even before the ruins at Tabgha were excavated) to house visiting pilgrims and provide education to local Bedouin. After the war in 1948, the guesthouse was confiscated to be used as an Israeli youth hostel, not to be returned to its German caretakers until the 1990s. It reopened in its current form in 2002.

J8 TABGHA TO CAPERNAUM

2.3 km
30-45 min

DIFFICULTY: Flat sidewalk.

BIKING DETOURS: None.

ADMISSION FEES: Capernaum historic site.

TRANSPORT FOR CAPERNAUM: Take a taxi or walk from Capernaum (Kfar Nakhum) Junction.

Entrance sign to Capernaum (opposite)

Contemplate rich Sea of Galilee views at the Church of the Primacy of St. Peter, visit Capernaum—the town of Jesus

The trail follows the pilgrim sidewalk connecting the Church of Multiplication of Loaves and Fishes to the Church of the Primacy of St. Peter and Capernaum. Note: At the time of printing, this section is not yet marked with paint blazes.

Accommodations:

14 **Vered HaGalil** (Korazin, +4 km off route): ☎04-693-5785; www.veredhagalil.com; cabins from 480NIS

15 **Frenkel's B&B** (Korazin, +4 km off route): ☎04-680-1686; www.thefrenkels.com; double 500NIS

16 **Sea of Galilee Guest House** (Almagor, free pick-up): ☎04-693-0063; www.seaofgalileeguesthouse.com; dorm 100NIS, double 450NIS

See **Karei Deshe** near Tabgha (p. 110) or take a bus back to Tiberias, see Tiberias accommodations p. 150.

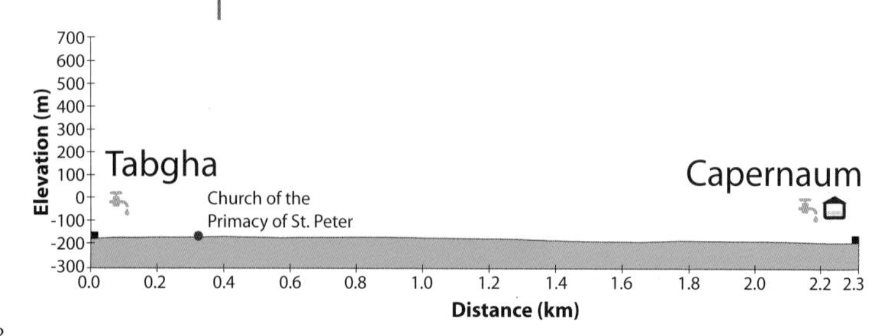

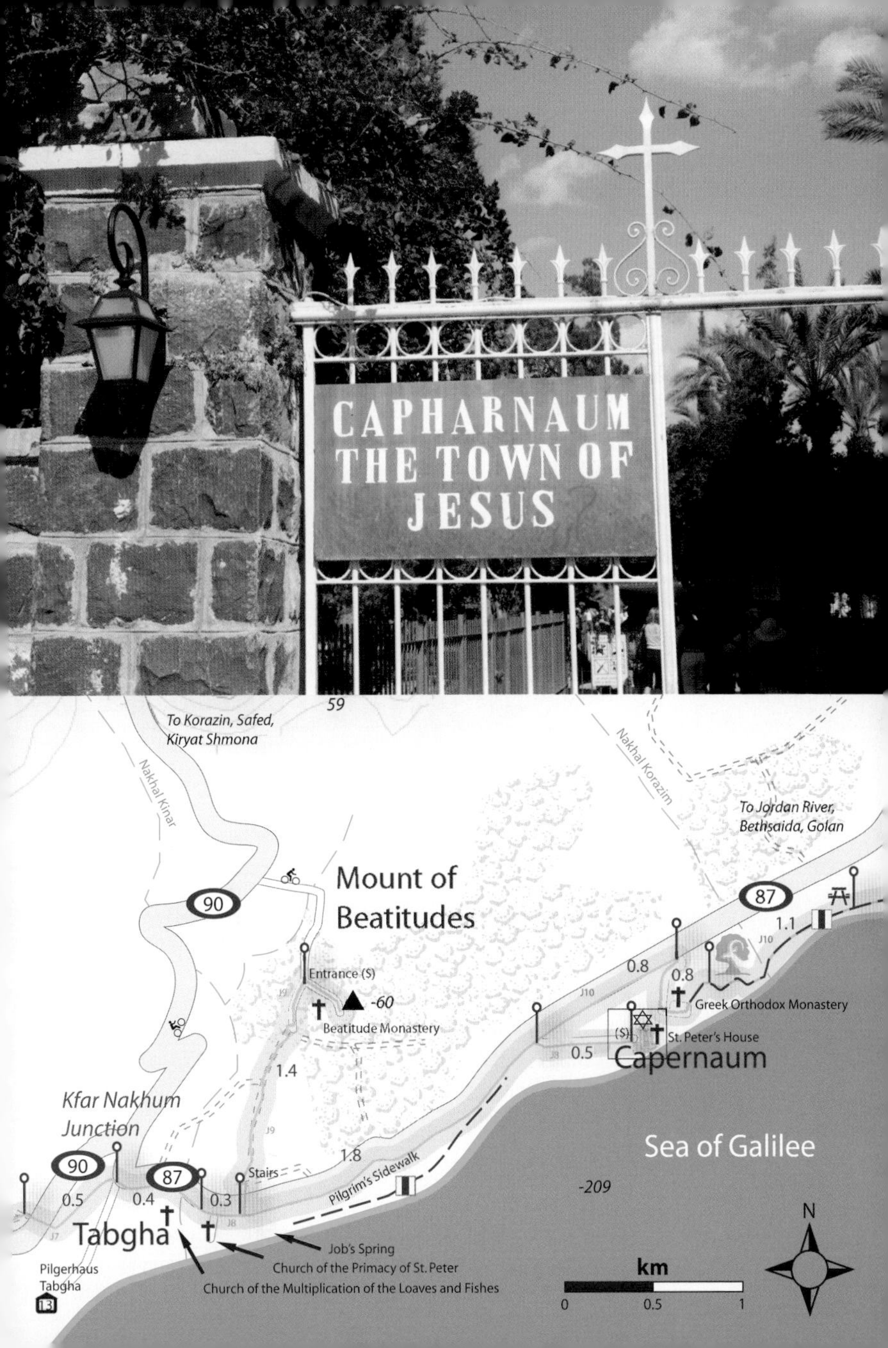
CAPHARNAUM
THE TOWN OF
JESUS
59
To Korazin, Safed,
Kiryat Shmona
Nakhal Kinar
Nakhal Korazim
To Jordan River,
Bethsaida, Golan
Mount of
Beatitudes
90
87
1.1
J10
0.8
0.8
Entrance ($)
-60
Greek Orthodox Monastery
Beatitude Monastery
($)
St. Peter's House
0.5
Capernaum
1.4
Kfar Nakhum
Junction
Sea of Galilee
1.8
Stairs
Pilgrim's Sidewalk
-209
0.5
0.4
0.3
N
Tabgha
Job's Spring
Church of the Primacy of St. Peter
Church of the Multiplication of the Loaves and Fishes
Pilgerhaus
Tabgha
13
km
0
0.5
1

Peaceful tranquility prevails at the Church of the Primacy of St. Peter.

Church of the Primacy of St. Peter

הכנסייה של פיטר
كنيسة بيتر

> *"Simon son of John, do you love me?" Peter was hurt because Jesus asked him the third time, "Do you love me?" He said, "Lord, you know all things; you know that I love you." Jesus said, "Feed my sheep."* John 21:17

Also in the region of Tabgha, the **Church of the Primacy of St. Peter** was built by Franciscans in 1933 to remember the place where Jesus bestowed church leadership on Peter in Matthew 16:18.

The church is built over a flat rock that Byzantine pilgrims believed was the *Mensa Christi* where Jesus ate fish with his disciples after the resurrection. The quaint basalt church building connects to a peaceful rocky beach with a relaxing view of the sea and perhaps a few fishing boats. Less impressive than the more elaborate churches in the area, this is nonetheless a meditative space to connect with the simple origins of the Christian story.

The current church is partially built over the ruins of a 4th-century structure. The steps hewn into the rock on the shore side of the church date from the 2nd or 3rd century and are mentioned by the 4th-century pilgrim Egeria.

The concept of the "primacy of Peter" is a Catholic doctrine stating that Peter was the first Bishop of Rome and therefore the first Pope, given the "keys to the kingdom" and called the foundation of the church in Matthew 16:18-19, where Jesus says:

> *"And I tell you that you are Peter, and on this rock I will build my church, and the gates of Hades will not overcome it. I will give you the keys of the kingdom of heaven; whatever you bind on earth will be bound in heaven, and whatever you loose on earth will be loosed in heaven."*

Job's Spring gushes into the Sea of Galilee.

Job's Spring (Ein Ayub)

עין איוב
عين أيوب

> *So Satan went out from the presence of the Lord and afflicted Job with painful sores from the soles of his feet to the top of his head. Then Job took a piece of broken pottery and scraped himself with it as he sat among the ashes.* Job 2:7-8

Shortly after the Church of the Primacy of St. Peter, a metal staircase to the right leads down to **Job's Spring**, a warm sulfuric spring that gushes into the Sea of Galilee. There is a local tradition that Job lived in a nearby cave and treated his sores in the healing water of this spring.

Ruins of the synagogue at Capernaum

Capernaum كفر ناحوم כפר נחום

And you, Capernaum, will you be lifted up to the skies?
Matthew 11:23a

Capernaum Historic Site
Adult 3NIS;
8am-4:40pm Mon-Sat

Note:
Capernaum National Park (entrance free) is a natural area 1 km east of the historic site and churches (see J10).

Capernaum (Kfar Nakhum) served as Jesus' home base during his ministry in the Galilee. There are numerous references to Capernaum in the New Testament including the healing of the centurion's servant (Matthew 8:5-13), driving out of a demon (Mark 1:21-26), healing of a paralytic (Mark 2:1-12) and Jesus preaching in the synagogue (Mark 1:21).

The city of Capernaum dates back to the 2nd century BCE, the time of the Hasmonean Dynasty. At the time of Jesus, Capernaum was a city of approximately 15,000, much larger than the small hamlet of Nazareth which may have had a population of only 400 people. Capernaum was also in close proximity to other Jewish towns and was conveniently close to the international trade route linking Damascus to the Mediterranean, the *Via Maris* (see p. 22) as evidenced by the marble 2nd-century Roman milestone featured at the site (See Roman roads pp. 85-87).

The ruins of Capernaum were discovered in 1838 by an American explorer. Later in the 19th century, the Franciscans took over custodianship of the site, planting eucalyptus and palms and building a harbor to create an oasis for visitors. Excavations revealing the synagogue and octagonal church began in 1905.

The synagogue dates from the 5th century and is unusually large and ornate, leading scholars to two main interpretations. One, since Capernaum was most likely a mixed city of Jews, Gentiles and Christians, perhaps the synagogue was enhanced as a kind of "one-upmanship" to maintain Jewish identity over and against the Christian presence. An alternate interpretation—perhaps the synagogue was built by Christians as a place for Christian pilgrims to remember the synagogue where Jesus preached.

Statue of Peter with the "keys to the kingdom" at Capernaum

Recently excavations resumed and unearthed the living quarters currently visible by the synagogue. Among these small houses is the one traditionally known as **Peter's house**. As early as the second half of the 1st century, this one particular house appears to have been treated differently than other dwellings. The floors were plastered, the walls were refinished and inscribed with religious graffiti. Normal domestic ceramics are not found at this house, but rather a large number of oil lamps, suggesting that soon after the life of Jesus the house was used for religious purposes, perhaps as a house church for early Christians.

In the 4th century again this room was updated with plaster and an archway and higher walls were added. Finally, in the 5th century an **octagonal church** was built over the room. This peculiar history leads many to claim that the room is from the dwelling of Peter, the disciple of Jesus. A contemporary **Catholic church**

with an uncanny resemblance to a UFO was built over Peter's house in 1990. The glass floor lends a bird's eye view to the octagonal church below.

From the 2nd to 4th century there is evidence of a thriving Christian community in Capernaum. After the Arab conquest around 700, the town was destroyed and no longer inhabited. The synagogue and house of St. Peter have been restored and made into a museum.

The pink-domed church east of the ruins is the site of the **Orthodox Church of Capernaum,** a charming little chapel with a peaceful garden. Continue on J10 for 1.1 km to visit this church, as well as to enter Capernaum National Park.

Visit the brightly-colored Greek Orthodox Church of Capernaum to view the beautifully-painted interior.

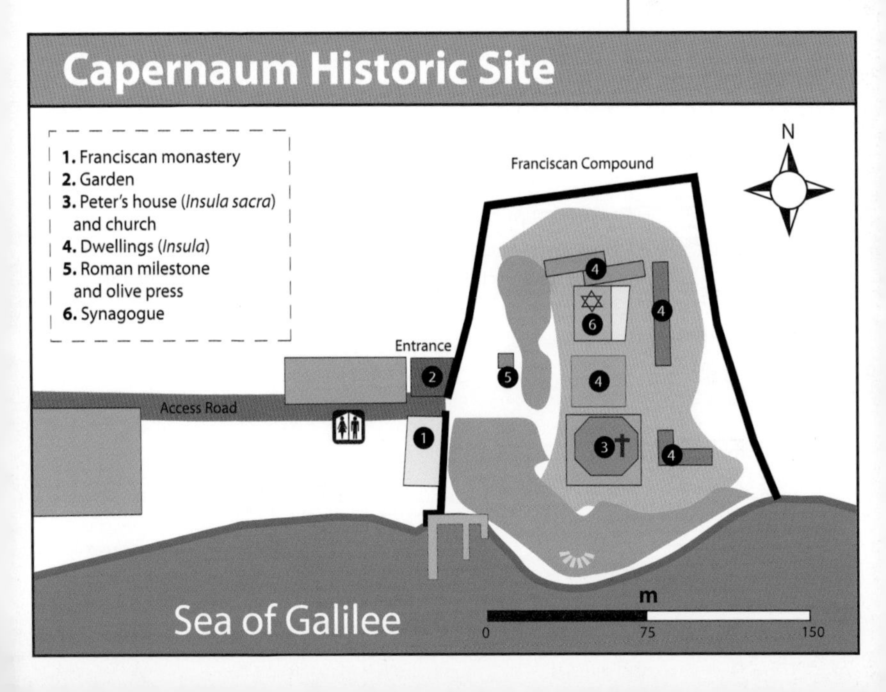

J9

TABGHA TO MT. OF BEATITUDES

1.4 km
20-30 min
each way

DIFFICULTY:
Short uphill walk on wide stable path.

ADMISSION FEES:
5NIS per person.

BIKING DETOURS:
You will probably need to walk your bike up the first 150 m or take Route 90.

TRANSPORT FOR MT. OF BEATITUDES:
Take bus 841 to Mount of Beatitudes branching. Walk the road 1 km to entrance.

Savor sweeping hillcrest views, peaceful gardens and space for reflection

Soon after the Church of the Primacy of St. Peter, the unmarked trail to the Mount of Beatitudes begins by going up a short metal staircase on the north side of Route 87. The trail continues on a dirt path which later meets a paved road near the entrance to the site. The paved road curves clockwise around the hill and leads to the gated church complex entrance. ***Map on p. 119.***

ACCOMMODATIONS:
There are pilgrim accommodations at the Mount of Beatitudes but only for large tour groups.
See accommodations under Tabgha (J7), Capernaum (J8) and Tiberias (J20).

Mount of the Beatitudes

הר האושר
جبل التطويبات

The **Mount of the Beatitudes** is the traditional site of the Sermon on the Mount (Matthew 5-7), which contains a passage known as the Beatitudes. The term "beatitude" comes from the Latin word *beati,* which means "blessed," as can be seen in the Latin renderings of these verses in stained glass inside the present church.

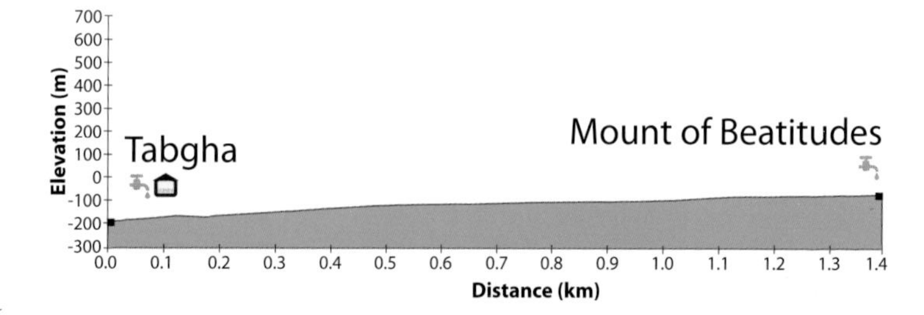

Trail leading to the church at Mt. of Beatitudes

Today the site consists of a **Franciscan church** with a tranquil garden (5NIS per car; 8am-11:30am, 2:30pm-4:40pm Mon-Sat). The church, built in 1938, features the eight beatitudes in stained glass and provides a good vantage point to view the Sea of Galilee. Remains of a small chapel dating from the 4th century can be seen down the hill from the church. In 381, the Spanish pilgrim Egeria wrote of Tabgha, "Near there on a mountain is the cave to which the Savior climbed and spoke the Beatitudes."

While there is no direct evidence that this mount is *the* mount from the sermon, its proximity to Capernaum and the plain of Genneserat (where listening crowds may have congregated) make it a good possibility. Other mounts that have been considered as possible sites of the sermon are Mt. Arbel and the Horns of Hattin. Luke's gospel contains a shorter sermon commonly known as the Sermon on the Plain. These could very well be two takes on the same sermon, with Jesus on the mount and the crowds gathering on the plain below.

The Beatitudes

"Blessed are the poor in spirit,
for theirs is the kingdom of heaven.

Blessed are those who mourn,
for they will be comforted.

Blessed are the meek,
for they will inherit the earth.

Blessed are those who hunger
and thirst for righteousness,
for they will be filled.

Blessed are the merciful,
for they will be shown mercy.

Blessed are the pure in heart,
for they will see God.

Blessed are the peacemakers,
for they will be called sons of God.

Blessed are those who are persecuted
because of righteousness,
for theirs is the kingdom of heaven.

Matthew 5:3-10

J10

CAPERNAUM TO BETHSAIDA

12.4 km
3-5 hours

Difficulty: ▬□□
Very little elevation change.

Biking Detours:
None.

Admission Fees:
Bethsaida/Jordan River Park (if with car).

Transport for Bethsaida:
Take bus 15 from Tiberias to Yehudiya Junction, which is 2.5 km from the park entrance.

Walk a Roman street at Bethsaida where Jesus likely walked, cool off by (or in!) the Jordan River

Walk east on the pilgrim sidewalk along the road outside of the Capernaum historic site. Turn right at the sign for Orthodox Capernaum. Follow signs to the Orthodox church and continue east through Capernaum National Park to meet a bike trail, which you will follow until you pass mobile military bridges near the Jordan River. Cross Arik Bridge and turn right on a red 4x4 trail, followed by a left on a green 4x4 trail. Cut back to the road on an unmarked 4x4 path to join the red trail to Route 87. Walk north along Route 888 from the Bethsaida Junction to enter the Jordan River Park and historic area.

Accommodations:

▲ **Jordan River Park** (Camping)**:** ☎04-692-3422; free if entering by foot; bathrooms, showers, snack stand

Also see Capernaum (J8), p. 118.

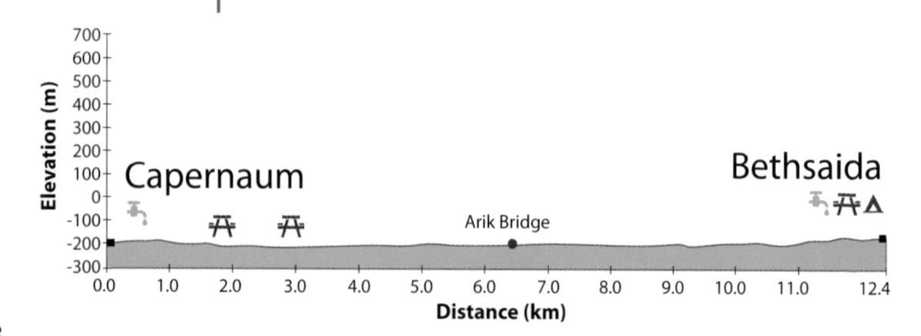

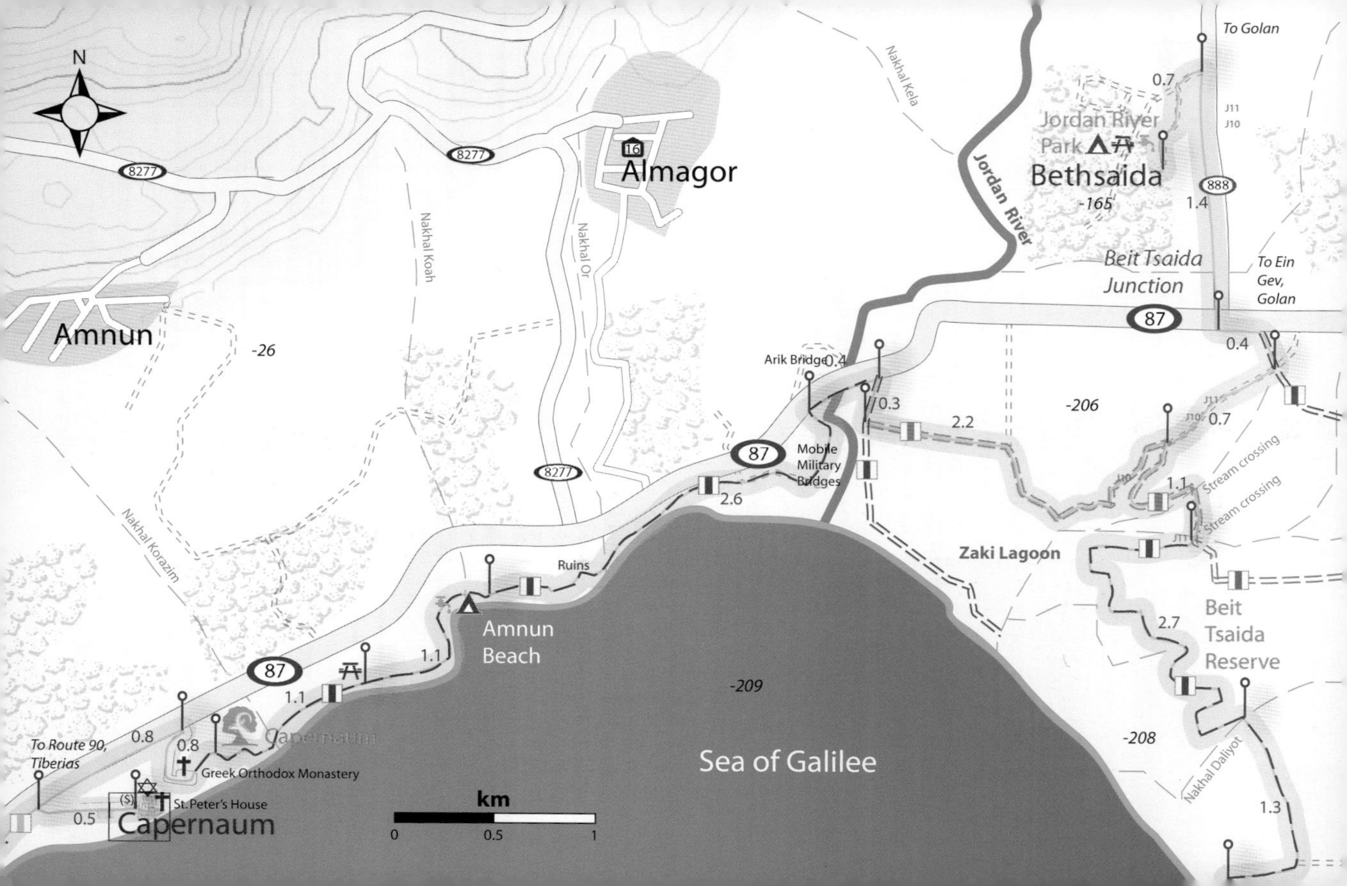
N
Almagor
16
8277
Amnun
-26
Nakhal Koah
Nakhal Or
Nakhal Kela
Nakhal Korazim
Jordan River
Jordan River Park
Bethsaida
-165
To Golan
888
1.4
0.7
J11
J10
Beit Tsaida Junction
To Ein Gev, Golan
87
0.4
-206
2.2
0.7
Stream crossing
Stream crossing
1.1
Arik Bridge
0.4
0.3
Mobile Military Bridges
2.6
Zaki Lagoon
Beit Tsaida Reserve
2.7
-208
Nakhal Daliyot
1.3
Ruins
Amnun Beach
1.1
1.1
-209
Sea of Galilee
To Route 90, Tiberias
0.8
0.8
0.5
Greek Orthodox Monastery
St. Peter's House
Capernaum
km
0
0.5
1

The Jordan River north of the Sea of Galilee

Jordan River

נהר הירדן
نهر الأردن

Confessing their sins, they were baptized by him in the Jordan River. Matthew 3:6

The **Jordan River** stretches 250 km from its waterheads at the base of Mt. Hermon to its final resting place in the no-outlet Dead Sea, dropping 700 m of elevation in the journey. The Jordan River Valley runs the length of the country, serving as its eastern border, as part of the Syrian-African Rift.

Considered one of the world's sacred rivers, the Jordan is mentioned frequently in both the Old and New Testaments as an important landmark. The significance of "crossing over Jordan" in the Exodus story symbolized the movement from slavery in Egypt to entering the promised land, a motif in many contemporary spiritual songs. In the New Testament, the Jordan is given additional significance as the baptismal place of both Jesus and John as well as other followers of Jesus. Today the Jordan River is still a popular place to renew baptismal vows.

You can rent kayaks or inner tubes at **Abu Kayak** ☎04-692-1078; 9am-5pm Apr-Nov

The river is also a source of controversy in regards to water rights, particularly between Israel and Jordan. Since both countries siphon off some of the water for their own use, the river is considerably smaller than it would have been at the time of Jesus, in some places little more than a muddy creek.

Near historic Bethsaida is the **Jordan River Park,** a well-maintained recreation area with a variety of outdoor activities including hiking trails, bird-watching areas and the opportunity to take a kayak or inner tube out on the Jordan River.

Mobile military bridges left over from 1967 war

Two nature trails begin from the flour mill, left over from when an Arab village was located in the area. The park also features picnic areas, a snack bar, camping, swimming and clean bathrooms. Cabin accommodations are in the works for 2010.

Bethsaida

بيت صيدا בית צידה

Woe to you, Korazin! Woe to you, Bethsaida! If the miracles that were performed in you had been performed in Tyre and Sidon, they would have repented long ago in sackcloth and ashes. Matthew 11:21

Bethsaida and Jordan River Park
☎04-692-3422;
entrance free to walkers, 55/70NIS per vehicle for day/overnight use

Bethsaida is one of only three towns on the Sea of Galilee mentioned in the Bible (Bethsaida, Korazin, and Capernaum—all of whom are accused of lacking faith). The gospels relay Bethsaida as the hometown of Simon Peter, Andrew and Philip. The current archeological site is fairly new and still in the process of excavation. The site of Bethsaida has been a subject of exploration and controversy for hundreds of years.

While many New Testament site locations were solidified by the 4th century, this site of Bethsaida was not discovered until the 1980s. Some doubted that this could be the site due to its distance from the Sea of Galilee (2 km) and higher elevation. However, geological evidence suggests that a major earthquake in 363 CE may have drastically changed the geography of the area with floods shifting the shoreline south and elevating Bethsaida.

Path through the ruins at Bethsaida

Excavations show that the city was inhabited starting in the 3rd millennium BCE and was part of the Gesher kingdom in the 1st millennium BCE. In 734 BCE it was conquered by the Assyrians and its inhabitants deported. Bethsaida was not reinhabited until the late 2nd century BCE. It then came under the control of Herod the Great, who gave it to his son Philip, who renamed the city Julias after the wife of Caesar or the mother of Tiberius. In the time of Jesus, Bethsaida was a Hellenistic city. Andrew and Philip are both Hellenized names and the gospels indicate that they spoke Greek (John 12:20).

Today the main features of the site are the Iron Age city wall, the **House of the Winegrower** (a dwelling where intact wine jars were found) and the **House of the Fishermen**, which was scattered with fishing paraphernalia such as anchors and hooks.

Korazin כורזים كورزين

Korazin National Park
☎04-693-4982;
adult/child 20/9NIS;
8am-4pm Oct-Mar,
8am-5pm Apr-Sept

Completing the trio of cities cursed by Jesus, **Korazin** is located about 4.5 km from the Sea of Galilee. As of printing of this book, no walking route exists to Korazin other than paved driving roads. There are a variety of obstacles between Capernaum and Korazin, including fences and private land, but park rangers are still hoping to develop a path along Nakhal Korazin in the near future. Call the Korazin National Park office for updates. The site is still worth a visit by taxi or car.

View from Bethsaida

Korazin synagogue made from dark, volcanic basalt limestone

The town of Korazin dates back to the 1st century, though the majority of the ruins visible at the archeological site date from the 3rd and 4th centuries. The main building material was volcanic basalt, readily available in the region. Described by New Testament scholar Jerome Murphy-O'Connor as, "Capernaum with a view," the Korazin synagogue retains the same Galilean style as the Capernaum synagogue, though in basalt instead of limestone.

Behind the ticket office is the grave of Bedouin Sheikh Ramadan from the Mamluk period, who is remembered as one of Saladin's generals. To the east of Korazin are large basalt stones, some of which are dolmens—crude megalithic stone tables from prehistoric times probably used as grave markers.

J11

BETHSAIDA TO KURSI

15.8 km
4-6 hours

Difficulty:
Several stream crossings and occasional loose sand.

Admission Fees:
Kursi National Park.

Biking Detours:
None. Some sandy and overgrown sections.

Transport for Kursi:
Take buses 15, 18, 19 or 22 from Tiberias.

Stroll along the beach, wade through remote bird-filled estuaries, imagine herds of swine hurtling into the sea at Kursi

From historic Bethsaida, follow Route 888 south to Bethsaida Junction, then enter the Beit Tsaida Nature Reserve on a red trail. After 400 m turn right on an unmarked trail to a junction with a green trail where you will turn left. There are two stream crossings on the green trail, which vary from ankle to knee-deep water, depending on the season. (If the area appears to be too wet, you can take the longer detour on the red, green and blue trails). After the second crossing, you will see a hanging green sign (photo below).

Continue straight for 100 m on a blue trail to meet the purple trail which you will follow to a series of beaches with water and basic services. Shortly after Dugit Beach you will pass Tel Hadar and then continue past Tse'elon Beach. When you see a large sign with the shape of the Sea of Galilee, turn left toward Route 92, cross through an underpass and follow parallel dirt roads until the junction with Route 789. Arrive at Kursi National Park.

Accommodations:

▲ Some of the beaches near Kursi have camping areas that include bathrooms (no toilet paper), showers and picnic tables. These private beaches charge campers entering by car, but normally don't charge those who walk in.

For other accommodations, take a bus, taxi or hotel pick up to Tiberias, Ein Gev or other nearby accommodations.

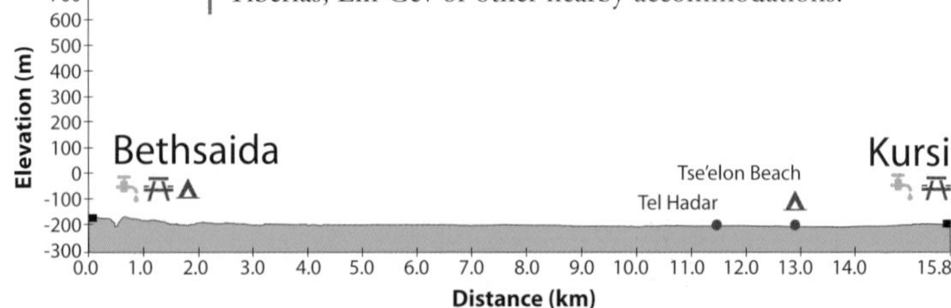

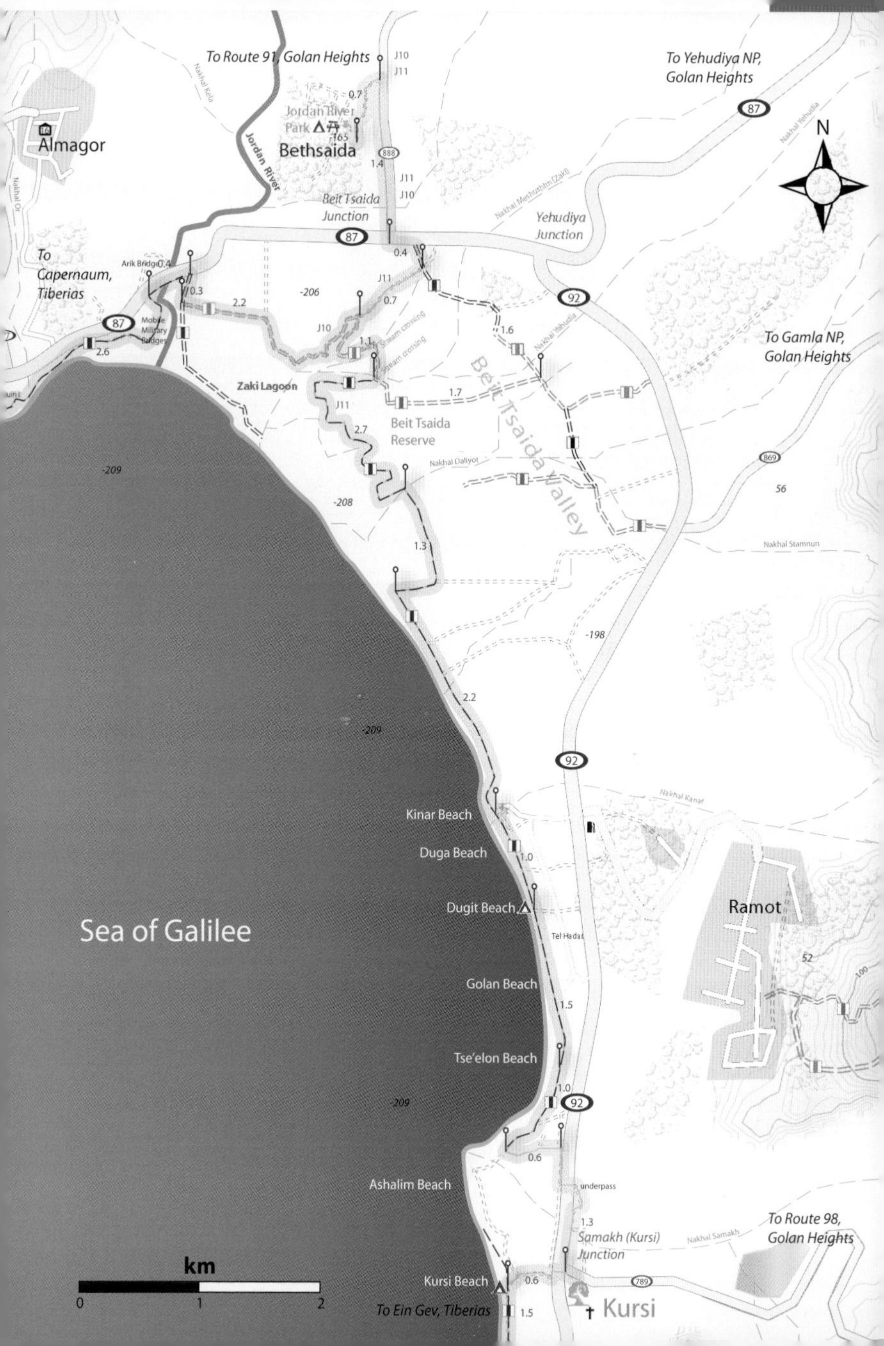

To Route 91, Golan Heights
To Yehudiya NP, Golan Heights
Almagor
Jordan River Park
Bethsaida
Jordan River
Beit Tsaida Junction
Yehudiya Junction
To Capernaum, Tiberias
Arik Bridge
Mobile Military Bridges
Zaki Lagoon
Beit Tsaida Reserve
Beit Tsaida Valley
To Gamla NP, Golan Heights
Nakhal Daliyot
Nakhal Stamnun
Nakhal Kanaf
Kinar Beach
Duga Beach
Dugit Beach
Tel Hadar
Sea of Galilee
Golan Beach
Tse'elon Beach
Ramot
Ashalim Beach
underpass
Samakh (Kursi) Junction
Nakhal Samakh
To Route 98, Golan Heights
Kursi Beach
To Ein Gev, Tiberias
Kursi
km
0
1
2
N

The ruins at Kursi include the largest Byzantine monastery in Israel.

Kursi National Park الكرسي כורסי

The demons begged Jesus, "If you drive us out, send us into the herd of pigs." Matthew 8:31

Kursi is the traditional site of the exorcism story in which Jesus casts multiple demons out of a man living among tombs and into a herd of pigs. The story is found in all three Synoptic Gospels (Matthew 8:28-34, Mark 5:1-20, Luke 8:26-39). The stories in Mark and Luke are the most similar, with Matthew reporting two demon-possessed men and providing less detail.

The name of the biblical site is commonly known as Gergasa, however scholars do not agree on the location or name of this site. Earliest copies of Matthew name the place of this exorcism as "in the region of the Gadarenes," while Mark and Luke write, "in the country of the Gerasenes." Gedara and Gerasa were both Gentile cities located near the Sea of Galilee, east and south, respectively, of the sea. Neither of these sites are directly on the sea. Later manuscripts of Matthew list the place as "the region of the Gergasenes."

Kursi National Park
☎04-673-1983;
adult/child 13/7NIS;
8am-5pm Apr–Sept,
8am-4pm Oct-Mar

Many commentators have noted that the location must have been a Gentile area, as were both Gadara and Gerasa, considering there were pigs nearby. The story can be interpreted as a veiled condemnation of the Roman Empire in which the pigs, representing the Gentile Roman military "legions," drown in the sea (the demon identifies itself by the name of "Legion"). To 1st-century ears this may have conjured up images of the hated Roman military presence retreating to the Mediterranean Sea.

Biblical criticism aside, excavation of the area of Kursi shows Christian veneration from as far back as the 5th century, when a monastery was built on the spot. It was the largest Byzantine monastery in Israel, measuring 115 x 130 m (375 x 435 ft). There is also a bathhouse nearby, an unusual combination. Damaged during the Persian invasion in 614 CE, the monastery was repaired and in use until the 8th century, when it was destroyed by an earthquake.

Tel Hadar תל הדר تل هدار

A small hill on the eastern shore of the Sea of Galilee, **Tel Hadar** is identified as a possible alternate location to Tabgha for Jesus' feeding miracles. Some historians believe Tel Hadar to be the only geographically suitable hill given the route that Jesus was walking in the larger context of the story. In the late 1990s a two-ton rock inscribed with Bible verses and images was placed on the site. Ruins from as far back as the Bronze Age have been found in excavations of the tel (see "tels" p. 167).

Twentieth-century excavations revealed impressive Byzantine mosaics depicting flora and fauna. The mosaics also depict baskets of bread, perhaps a reference to feeding stories traditionally remembered at nearby Tabgha. Climb the steps to a small chapel believed to be the spot where the demon-possessed man was freed of his bondage, which affords expansive views of the site and the Sea of Galilee.

Today, the basalt ruins of the monastery and delicate mosaic-work are impressive to behold.

These wild pigs near Kursi do not appear to be demon possessed.

J12

KURSI TO EIN GEV

5.8 km
1.5-2.5 hours

DIFFICULTY: ▬□□
Flat walk along the shoreline.

ADMISSION FEES:
Kursi National Park.

BIKING DETOURS:
None. You may have to walk through some sandy and overgrown sections.

TRANSPORT FOR EIN GEV:
Buses 15, 18, 19 and 22 run to Ein Gev from Tiberias.

Stroll along peaceful shoreline, take a moonlit swim in the Sea of Galilee, enjoy a dinner of local fish

From Kursi NP, cross Route 92 back toward the Sea of Galilee. Turn toward the sea at the sign for Kursi Beach. Follow the lakeshore south either by walking along the beach or intermittent sidewalks. When you arrive at the fence for Ein Gev, turn left and walk back out through the beach entrance to the main road. Enter Kibbutz Ein Gev or cross Route 92 to ascend to Susita.

ACCOMMODATIONS:

- **Ein Gev Holiday Homes:** ☎04-665-9800; www.eingev.com; double 535NIS
- **Gofra Beach Camping:** ☎04-673-1942
- **Susita Beach Camping:** ☎04-665-8030; bathrooms, showers, picnic tables

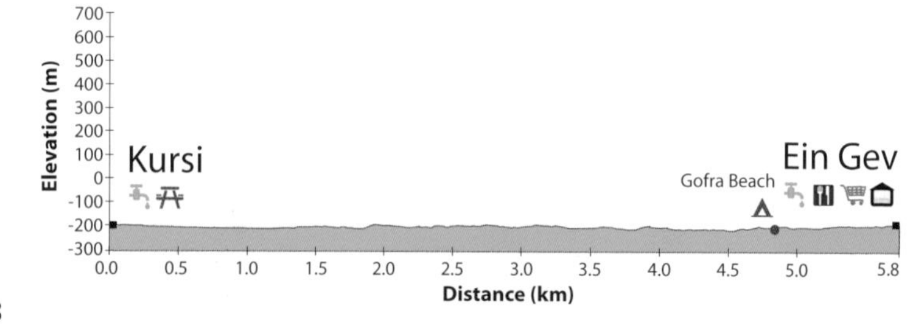

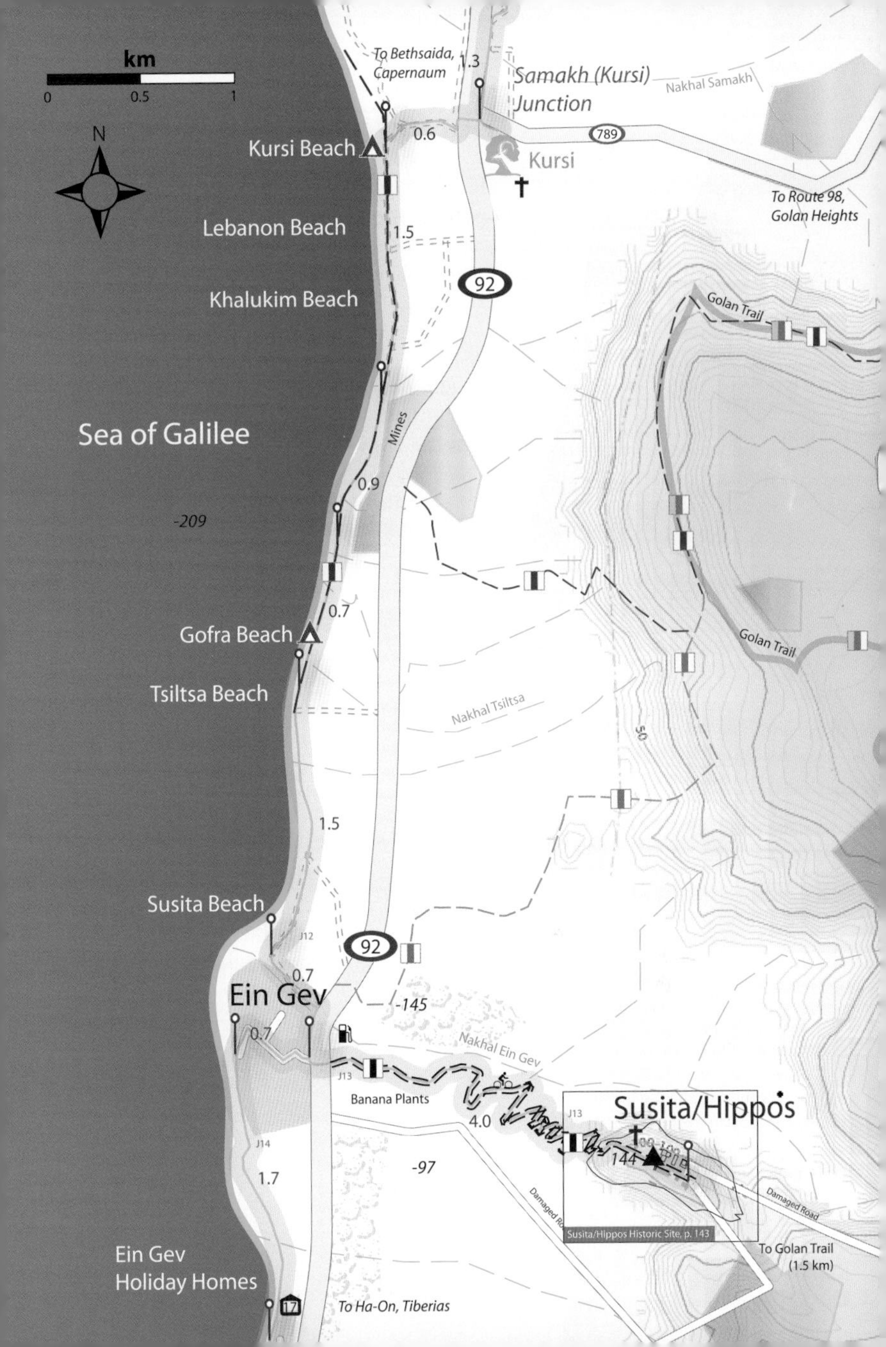

km
0
0.5
1
N
To Bethsaida, Capernaum
1.3
Samakh (Kursi) Junction
Nakhal Samakh
0.6
789
Kursi Beach
Kursi
To Route 98, Golan Heights
Lebanon Beach
1.5
92
Khalukim Beach
Golan Trail
Mines
Sea of Galilee
0.9
-209
0.7
Gofra Beach
Golan Trail
Tsiltsa Beach
Nakhal Tsiltsa
50
1.5
Susita Beach
J12
92
0.7
Ein Gev
-145
0.7
Nakhal Ein Gev
J13
Banana Plants
Susita/Hippos
J13
4.0
144
J14
-97
1.7
Damaged Road
Damaged Road
Susita/Hippos Historic Site, p. 143
To Golan Trail (1.5 km)
Ein Gev Holiday Homes
17
To Ha-On, Tiberias

Author Anna Dintaman walks the shoreline.

Ein Gev עין גב عين جيب

On the eastern shore of the Sea of Galilee lies one of the most famous kibbutzim in Israel, and a favorite vacation spot for Israelis and foreigners alike. Kibbutz **Ein Gev**, meaning "spring of the cistern," was built in 1936 as a tower and stockade settlement that served an important military role for Israel due to its strategic location at the foot of the Golan Heights.

Tower and stockade settlements were Jewish communities built during the Arab Revolt from 1936-39. The British had restricted new Jewish settlements but allowed existing ones to stay, so new settlements were built covertly during the night starting with a guard tower built from partially preassembled materials, then encircled with a fence. The fence and tower were often constructed in just one night to avoid detection. These settlements became important in creating facts on the ground that helped to determine which land would be given to the Jewish partition when the state was established.

Today the site is best known for its tourism facilities, including the largest restaurant in Israel (☎04-665-8035), featuring St. Peter's Fish and a range of high-quality accommodations. Stop by for a kibbutz tour on a mini-train (16NIS) or a visit to the **House of Anchors** fishing museum. The restaurant and cafe overlook a pleasant private beach. In April of each year, the kibbutz hosts a large music festival featuring world-class musicians. The kibbutz runs a sailing company, so it may be possible to catch a boat back to Tiberias from Ein Gev, but call ahead to check availability. In addition to tourism, the kibbutz has different types of agriculture including bananas and ostriches. Ein Gev is home to about 500 residents.

If you're interested in a **boat ride on the Sea of Galilee**, contact these companies. They cater mainly to groups, but if the timing is right independent travelers can usually ride along as well.

Holy Land Sailing
☎04-672-3006;
holylandsailing@012.net.il

Kinneret Sailing
☎04-665-8008

Minefields الألغام الأرضية מוקשים

Around the eastern shores of the Sea of Galilee, further south near Beit She'an and north of Hittin ruins you may see some disconcerting trilingual signs warning of **minefields**. It's important to stick to well-worn paths in these areas and not venture across fences. Both Israel and Syria scattered hundreds of thousands of land mines throughout the Golan Heights and down into the Galilee. Israel captured the Golan in the Six-Day War of 1967 and annexed the territory in 1981. Despite UN peacekeeper de-mining efforts, the occasional device explodes wounding or killing residents or hapless hikers wandering off the beaten path. But don't worry, the trail steers clear of any danger zones.

Minefield areas are fenced off and clearly marked.

Peaceful evening on the Sea of Galilee

J13

EIN GEV TO SUSITA/HIPPOS

AND RETURN TO EIN GEV

8.0 km
3-5 hours
(round trip)

Difficulty: Sustained uphill.

Biking Detours: None. It's possible, but very steep!

Transport for Susita: None; you must walk from Ein Gev (see J12).

Climb to remote Roman ruins, walk the well-preserved *decumanus* and savor broad views of the Sea of Galilee

Cross Route 92 from the entrance to Kibbutz Ein Gev to ascend to Susita via a black marked trail which begins at the gas station near banana trees. Ascend over 300 m on serpentine switchbacks as you pass basalt huts sporadically along the way and a war memorial near the top. Continue east and join the decumanus of the ancient city of Susita. Return by the same path. ***The biking map from Ein Gev to Susita is included in J12 on p. 139.***

Accommodations:
No accommodations at Susita other than camping (no water). Backtrack to Ein Gev for other accommodations.

Susita (Hippos) سوسيتا סוסיתא

The remote ruins at Susita afford broad views of the Sea of Galilee (opposite).

Tucked away on a steep hillside above Kibbutz Ein Gev, the ancient Roman city of **Susita** (entrance free, no set hours) is still in the process of being excavated. While not mentioned explicitly in the New Testament, Susita, known as Hippos in Greek, formed one of the ten cities of the Decapolis. Susita had control over a fortified hill, some of the surrounding land and a small port on the Sea of Galilee. The name Susita comes

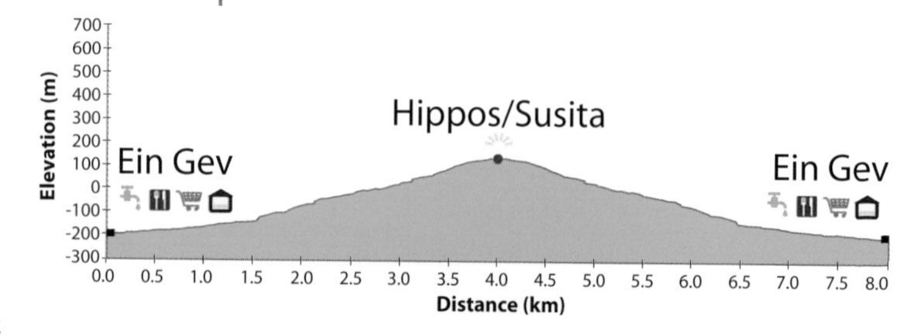

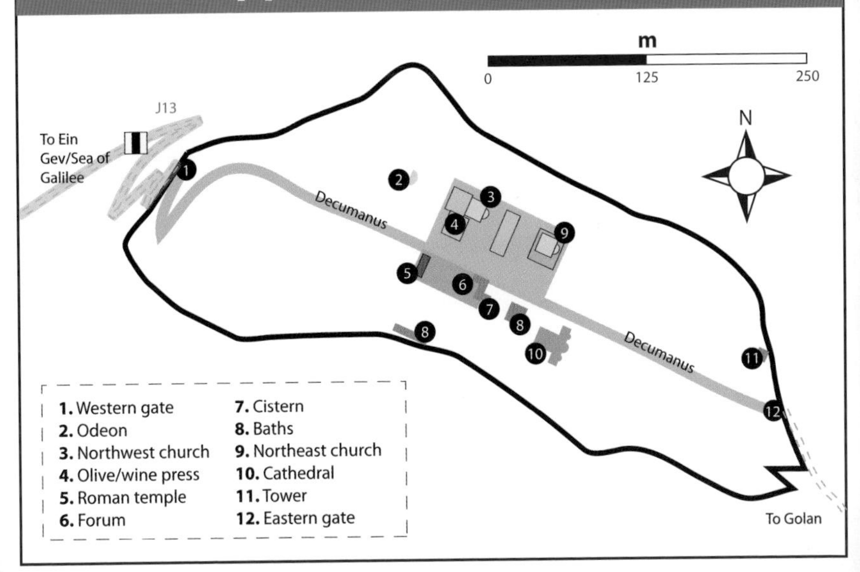

Susita/Hippos Historic Site
m
0
125
250
N
J13
To Ein Gev/Sea of Galilee
Decumanus
Decumanus
To Golan
1. Western gate
2. Odeon
3. Northwest church
4. Olive/wine press
5. Roman temple
6. Forum
7. Cistern
8. Baths
9. Northeast church
10. Cathedral
11. Tower
12. Eastern gate

Roman *decumanus* at ruins of Susita in springtime

from the Aramaic word for "horse," because the hill vaguely resembles the head and neck of a horse from above. The Greek name, Hippos, also means "horse."

The city was founded by Greek colonists in the 2nd century BCE and most likely served as a border fortress for the Seleucid empire. It developed into a full-fledged Greek *polis*, complete with temple, shopping area, public buildings and cisterns for water collection. After the Maccabean Revolt in 142 BCE, the land fell briefly under the Hasmonean Jewish dynasty. A Hasmonean attack under Alexander Jannaeus conquered Hippos around 80 BCE and, according to Josephus, forced the inhabitants to be circumcised.

After the Romans conquered the region in 63 BCE, Susita became an autonomous city that even minted its own coins with the image of a horse. As a pagan city, sources cite it as an enemy of the Jewish city of Tiberias just across the lake. Apparently Susita had some Jews, as it is recorded that after the Great Jewish Revolt Susita began to persecute their Jews. The city came under Christian control in the 4th century and Umayyad control in the 7th century. The city was flattened in an earthquake in 749 CE, never to be rebuilt.

Decapolis

So the man went away and began to tell in the Decapolis how much Jesus had done for him. And all the people were amazed. Mark 5:20

The **Decapolis** (Greek: *Deka-* "ten", *polis-* "city") was a group of 10 or more Greek cities in the region of present-day Jordan, Israel and Syria that shared cultural, political and economic

The path switchbacking up to Susita

ties. This federation of cities was set up after Pompey's successful campaign (64-63 BCE), and the cities were bastions of Greek culture in the sea of Semitic culture surrounding them. Each city was autonomous (most minted their own coins) and controlled an area of land in its vicinity. After the Roman conquest, the cities were given a Roman facelift, including organizing the city with a central *cardo* (north-south road and economic center) and *decumanus* (east-west secondary road).

The Decapolis is first referred to as such by Pliny, who includes Scythopolis (Beit She'an, p. 192) and Susita (Hippos), both accessible by trails in this book. Other noteworthy Decapolis cities are Philadelphia (Amman, Jordan) and Damascus (Syria).

Recently archeologists have uncovered the sandal-print of a Roman soldier at Susita, only the second of its kind in the world. Soldiers wore special hobnailed sandals which left specific imprints. Excavation is still underway at Susita, and at last visit there was no entrance fee, just a steep switchbacking ascent, lending the site a more remote and unspoiled feel. The view of the sea is magnificent, and the ruins are well-preserved and impressive.

J14

EIN GEV TO YARDENIT

14.5 km
3-5 hours

Difficulty:
Flat walk along the lakeshore.

Biking detours:
None.

Transport for Yardenit:
From Tiberias, take bus 15, 18, 19, 22 or 24. The journey takes 10-15 minutes.

Collect seashells and watch fishermen along the lakeshore, visit an ostrich farm, get (re)baptized in the Jordan River

From Ein Gev, continue to walk along the seashore. Follow intermittent purple trail markings. After several kilometers walk on the bike path to the right of the main road. Upon entering town, walk along sidewalk. Follows signs to Yardenit.

Accommodations:

18 **Ohalo Manor Hotel** (500 m from Yardenit)**:** ☎04-667-5526; www.ohalo.com/english; double 380NIS

19 **Miki's Place** (Kinneret Moshava)**:** ☎052-247-9057; dorm 100NIS

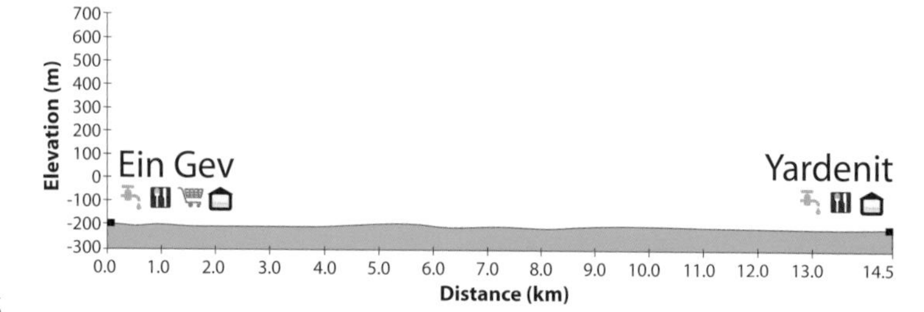

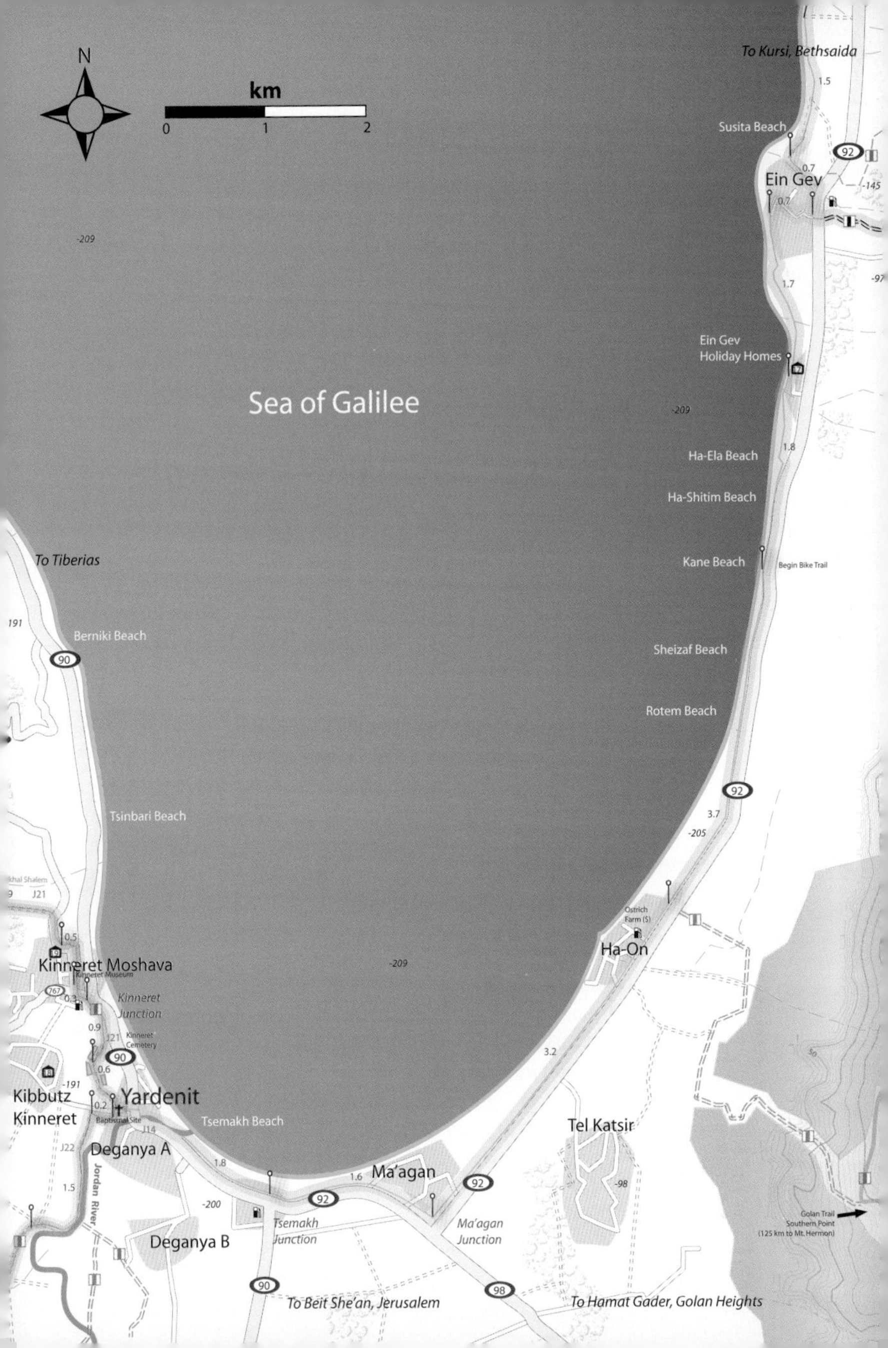

N
km
0
1
2
Sea of Galilee
To Kursi, Bethsaida
Susita Beach
Ein Gev
Ein Gev Holiday Homes
Ha-Ela Beach
Ha-Shitim Beach
Kane Beach
Begin Bike Trail
Sheizaf Beach
Rotem Beach
To Tiberias
Berniki Beach
Tsinbari Beach
Ostrich Farm ($)
Ha-On
Kinneret Moshava
Kinneret Museum
Kinneret Junction
Kinneret Cemetery
Kibbutz Kinneret
Yardenit
Baptismal Site
Tsemakh Beach
Deganya A
Jordan River
Ma'agan
Tel Katsir
Tsemakh Junction
Ma'agan Junction
Deganya B
Golan Trail Southern Point (125 km to Mt. Hermon)
To Beit She'an, Jerusalem
To Hamat Gader, Golan Heights
-209
-205
-200
-191
-145
-98
-97

Ha-On Ostrich Farm

Ha-On Ostrich Farm
www.haon.co.il;
adult/child 10/10NIS;
10am-1pm Sun-Thurs

Ostrich farming became relatively popular in Israel in the 1990s. Ostrich eggs were imported from South Africa and the birds were raised for their skin, used in high-end fashion accessories. Only later did Israelis learn that ostrich meat is exceptionally lean and, though it resembles red meat, has a taste similar to chicken. At **Ha-On Farm**, visitors can view a film about ostrich life cycles, get up close and personal with the birds and create art projects out of ostrich shells.

Yardenit Baptismal Site ירדנית

At that time Jesus came from Nazareth in Galilee and was baptized by John in the Jordan. As Jesus was coming up out of the water, he saw heaven being torn open and the Spirit descending on him like a dove. And a voice came from heaven: "You are my Son, whom I love; with you I am well pleased." Mark 1:9-11

Yardenit
☎04-675-9111;
www.yardenit.com;
8am-6pm Mar-Nov,
8am-5pm Dec-Feb

Open every day. Closes one hour earlier on Fridays and the eve of national holidays. Baptism hours end one hour before closing time.

The **Yardenit** baptismal site is located along the shores of the Jordan River near where the waters of the Sea of Galilee exit to the south. The traditional site of Jesus' baptism by John is further south near Jericho but not easily accessible. Many Christian pilgrim groups pass through the Yardenit baptismal compound and descend into the murky Jordan River to be baptized. Groups can rent or buy white robes for the event.

The complex includes a restaurant and huge store with all manner of souvenirs and a wide selection of books. Walls around the complex are lined with tiles depicting Mark 1:9-11 in many different languages including Hawaiian Pidgin. Over 400,000 tourists visit the area per year. Even if you can't catch a silent contemplative moment, it is a convenient place for a dirty hiker to catch a shower. Five shekels gives you rights to the sparkling clean shower and changing area.

The site is run by Kibbutz Kinneret, founded by Eastern European immigrants in 1913, the second oldest kibbutz in Israel.

Baptismal service in the Jordan River at Yardenit

Route Extensions:
To continue to Tiberias, see J21 and walk the route in reverse (13.1 km). To continue to Nazareth, take the Israel Trail using routes J22-25 (47km).

What is Baptism?

The gospel narratives tell of people coming to John the Baptist at the Jordan River to be covered with water after the confession of their sins. Jesus also came to John to be baptized. This ritual of submerging, pouring or sprinkling water over the head has become a part of Christian practice.

Water **baptism** is a Christian sacrament that represents inclusion in the Christian community, receiving life by believing in Jesus and cleansing from sin. Some Christians, including Catholics, practice infant baptism. Other Christians, such as Baptists and Pentecostals, practice adult baptism in which the act also serves as a public confession of faith in Jesus and acceptance of church membership.

J20 MT. ARBEL TO TIBERIAS

6.1 km
1.5-2.5 hours

Difficulty:
Rolling ascents and descents.

Biking Detours:
None, but you may need to walk your bike on a few short, steep sections of footpaths.

Admission Fees:
Arbel National Park.

Transport for Tiberias:
Bus 431 runs to/from Nazareth. Regular *sheruts* to Tel Aviv leave from the Tiberias bus station, and frequent bus service runs to Jerusalem and Tel Aviv.

Walk rolling hills with peaceful sea scenery, explore ancient history and modern spas in Tiberias

This route follows the Israel Trail markings for the J20 section. From Arbel National Park, follow Israel Trail markings away from the cliff toward the water reservoir. The trail skirts agricultural fields and passes a Jewish cemetery, dips into a valley to cross the road and ascends through the town of Mitspe to upper Tiberias. Take a city bus or walk the road to downtown Tiberias (2 km).

Accommodations in Tiberias:

- 20 **Tiberias Hostel:** ☎04-679-2611; www.tiberiashostel.com; dorm 75-85NIS, double 350NIS wifi CC P
- 21 **Aviv Hostel:** ☎04-671-2272; www.avivhostel.com; dorm 70NIS, double 250-300NIS wifi CC P
- 22 **Scots Hotel**: ☎04-671-0710; www.scotshotels.co.il; double 1100+NIS CC P
- 23 **Tiberias YMCA:** ☎04-672-0685; www.ymca-galilee.co.il; double 450NIS; camping 120NIS; private beach wifi CC P

View of Tiberias from Bereniki (opposite)

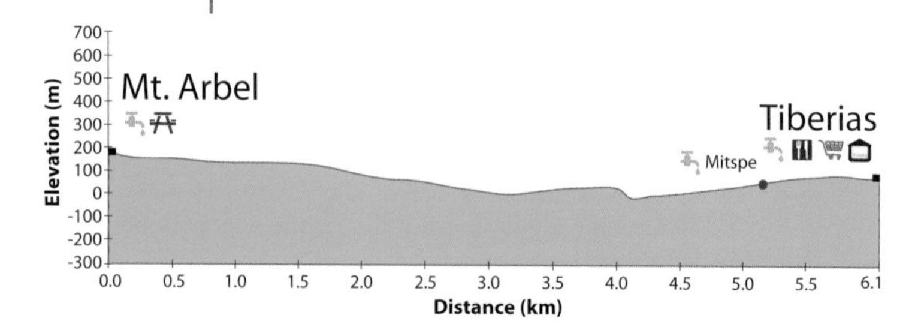

Mt. Nitai
Har Nitai
Mt. Arbel
Arbel
Magdala Ruins
Migdal Junction
Hawai Beach
Recital Beach
km
0
0.5
1
N
Park Entrance ($)
Ancient Synagogue
Moshav Arbel
Sea of Galilee
Arbel Beach
Jewish Cemetery
Kfar Khitim
Nakhal Rakat
Ha-Shaket Beach
Mitspe
Tiberias Downtown, p. 153
To Golani Junction, Nazareth
Mizpa
Tiberias
To Kinneret, Yardenit

The Tiberias pier shows the receding waters of the Sea of Galilee.

Tiberias

طبرية טבריה

Afterward Jesus appeared again to his disciples, by the Sea of Tiberias. John 21:1a

The city of **Tiberias**, named for the Roman emperor Tiberius, is one of four holy cities in Judaism. The series of hot springs in the region first attracted Roman notice in the 1st century and led Herod Antipas to build his own Galilee capital, replete with a grand *cardo*, stadium, gold-roofed palace and great synagogue. Following the Bar Kokhba Revolt in the 2nd century when Jews were exiled from Jerusalem, Tiberias became the center of Jewish life in Israel. Rabbinical academies were established and Jewish scholars and sages were drawn to Tiberias. The *Gemara* was completed in Tiberias, which together with the *Mishnah* comprises what is known as the Palestinian (or Jerusalem) *Talmud,* a central Jewish book. The Sanhedrin also convened in Tiberias for a time in the 2nd century.

Hamat Tiberias National Park
☎04-672-5287;
adult/child 13/7NIS;
8am-5pm Apr-Sept,
8am-4pm Oct-Mar

Though the Gospel of John refers to the Sea of Galilee as the "Sea of Tiberias," the gospels do not mention Jesus ever going to Tiberias. No Christian sites were found there until the 6th century, when Justinian built a church at the high point of the city and extended the city walls. Tiberias was destroyed by an earthquake in 1033, conquered by Crusaders in 1099 and subsequently captured by Saladin in 1187 in prelude to the Battle of Hattin.

Mosaic synagogue floor at Hamat Tiberias National Park

The ancient city is located 2.5 km south of the modern city. The ruins include a basilica, baths, a theater and *cardo* but are largely overgrown. Plans for a maintained archeological park are underway. A bit further south, **Hamat Tiberias National Park** houses the Ernest Lehman/Hamam Suleiman Museum of regional artifacts.

The park also features an ancient synagogue with the oldest known mosaics in Israel. The mosaic floor features a zodiac similar to that found at Beit Alpha, with Helios the sun god in the center and Jewish symbols (such as the Ark of the Covenant and menorahs) in the background. The park is near the 17 hot springs that have been used for therapeutic purposes for two millennia. You can

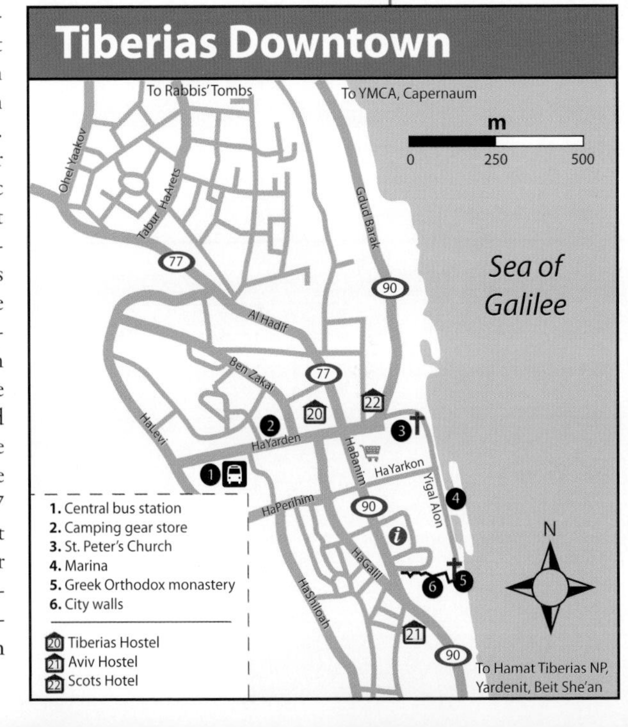

Downtown Tiberias by night (above)

St. Peter's Church in Tiberias was designed to resemble the shape of an upside-down boat (below).

stop by just up the street at the Tiberias Spa if you wish to test the rumored therapeutic nature of the springs.

Today you can visit many tombs of great Jewish *tsadiks* (scholars) such as Rabbi Moshe Ben Maimon (also known as Maimonides or Rambam), Rabbi Meir Ba'al Hanes, who helped to compile the *Mishnah,* and Rabbi Akiva, who was killed for his role in the Bar Kokhba Revolt. The tourist information office is located on HaBanim Street in the midst of Roman ruins. Remains of basalt Ottoman ruins can be seen scattered through the new city.

Tiberias Tourist Information Center
☎04-672-5666;
9am-4pm Sun-Thurs,
9am-12:30pm Fri

Tucked away in an alley, **St. Peter's Church** is worth a wander. The small apse was built to resemble an overturned boat, with narrow windows and a tapered altar to complete the illusion. The church walls were built by Crusaders around 1100. The building was first reconstructed by Franciscans in 1757 with several later renovations.

Two decrepit **mosques** stand near the waterfront. Out of use since 1948, the structures have not been maintained and the entrances are locked.

Access to the Sea of Galilee in Tiberias is limited to a **waterfront promenade** and private hotels or restaurants. The waterfront has numerous restaurants offering St. Peter's fish and other tourist fare.

Modern Tiberias is a convenient place to find a variety of accommodations and services, but suffers from a lack of character with the ambiance of a tacky beach town. If you prefer more peaceful surroundings, you may wish to look for accommodations outside of the city.

Unique historical accommodations can be found at the **Scots Hotel,** a boutique hotel and former hospital dating back to 1884. The YMCA near Tiberias also features historic buildings including a 1920s-era house which was built for the General Secretary of the Jerusalem YMCA.

Relax at a Tiberias resort.

J21

TIBERIAS TO YARDENIT

13.1 km
3-5 hours

Difficulty:
Gentle flat grade with moderately steep descent near end of segment.

Biking Detours:
None, but some sections are steep.

Transport for Yardenit:
From Tiberias, take bus 15, 18, 19, 22 or 24 for 10-15 minutes. From Nazareth, take bus 31.

Relish sea views and pleasant shady forests, visit one of the first kibbutzim in Israel, relax on the tree-dappled banks of the Jordan River

The route follows the Israel Trail markings for the J21 section. Follow the Israel Trail along Sapir Boulevard in upper Tiberias and turn left on a dirt path when the road switches back uphill. Continue south on an elevated dirt path through the Swiss Forest. Descend to Kinneret Moshava by way of Poriya spring, passing the historic settlement buildings. Turn left on Route 767 to the Kinneret Junction with Route 90. Follow dirt paths through palm orchards and fishing pools to arrive at Yardenit.

Accommodations:
See J14 Yardenit accommodations, p. 146.

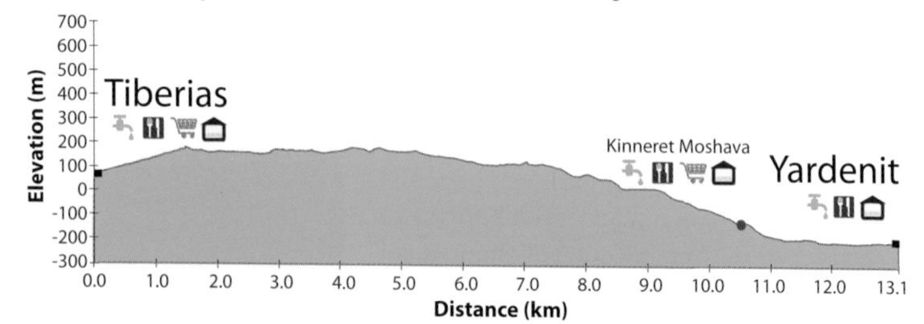

Tiberias Downtown, p. 153
To Wadi Hamam, Ginosar, Capernaum
N
km
0
0.5
1
Mitspe
Mizpa
Tiberias
Gai Beach
Sironit Beach
Municipal Beach
Sea of Galilee
Mt. Bereniki
Swiss Forest
Nakhal Beronika
Tiberias Hot Springs
Shikmim Beach
Swiss Forest
Mt. Menorim
Nakhal Menorim
Nakhal Menora
Nakhal Si'a
Nakhal Osh
Bereniki Beach
Ha-Zor'im
Poriya Plateau
Poriya (Neve Oved)
Tsinbari Beach
Poriya Ilit
Poriya Spring
Nakhal Shalem
Nof HaKinneret Junction
Kinneret Moshava
Kinneret Museum
Kinneret Junction
Kinneret Cemetery
Poriya (Kfar Avoda)
Kibbutz Kinneret
Yardenit
Baptismal Site
Alumot Junction
Alumot
Deganya A
To Route 65, Kfar Tavor
Jordan River
Deganya B
Yavne'el

Ruins of the "Anchor Church" at Mt. Bereniki overlook the Sea of Galilee.

Mount Bereniki

הר ברניקי
جبل برنيس

The next day Agrippa and Bernice came with great pomp and entered the audience room with the high ranking officers and the leading men of the city. Acts 25:23a

Towering above Tiberias, **Mt. Bereniki** features the ruins of a Byzantine church built by Justinian along with dizzying views of the surrounding area. The mount is named after Queen Bernice, great-granddaughter to Herod the Great and sister to Agrippa II, with whom she governed the Galilee in the late 1st century. She is perhaps best known as the lover of the Roman emperor Titus, a romance that has been the subject of many historical novels and plays. According to the book of Acts, the Apostle Paul appeared before Bernice and her brother to plead his case when imprisoned.

Side Route:
Mt. Bereniki is a 2-km detour off of J21 via a black marked trail to the east.

The church on this site has been nicknamed the "Anchor Church," for the huge rock resembling an anchor discovered under the altar. Too large to be an actual anchor, the rock is believed to have carried symbolic meaning for early Christians. Excavations continue at a 2nd to 3rd-century theater on the hillside below the ruins, with the hopes of finding the palace and fort of Herod Antipas.

Swiss Forest יער שוויצרי الغابات السويسرية

Enjoy the shade of the **Swiss Forest**, a beautiful area planted in 1938 to combat erosion from flooding. While not exactly comparable to the Alps, the views of the lake are superb.

Kinneret Moshava כנרת كنيرت

Kinneret Moshava was founded in 1908 as part of the Second *Aliyah* (wave of Jewish immigration). Originally a kibbutz, the community later shifted to private ownership. The cooperative farm features a museum about life in the early kibbutz movement with buildings, photographs and displays in Hebrew. About 550 people live in Kinneret Moshava. The name comes from the Hebrew word for the Sea of Galilee and means "harp," after the shape of the body of water. Modern Kibbutz Kinneret is a separate location, (see map on p. 157).

Kinneret Cemetery בית הקברות כנרת كنيرت مقبرة

After walking through Kinneret Moshava, the trail follows on the right side of Route 90. Just across the road is Kinneret Cemetery, final resting place of some famous Israelis including the beloved poetess Rachel Bluwstein (better known simply as Rahel) and songwriter Naomi Shemer. To the left of Rahel's grave sits a small bench with a box containing a book of her poetry in Hebrew. You can refill water at the fountain.

Land of mine, I have never sung to you nor glorified your name with heroic deeds or the spoils of battle. All I have done is plant a tree on the silent shores of the Jordan.

—Rachel Bluwstein (1890-1931)

Yardenit Baptismal Site

For information on this site, see J14, p. 148.

What is a Kibbutz? كيبوتز הקיבוץ

Plural: *kibbutzim*
A person who lives there: *kibbutznik*

A **kibbutz** is a collective community, traditionally centered around agriculture, which combines Zionism, socialism and utopian ideals into a pleasing mix that anyone of a remotely Bohemian persuasion is sure to find irresistible. The first kibbutzim were established in the early 20th century during what was known as the Second *Aliyah*. To "make *Aliyah*" (literally "to go up") is still the term today for a Jewish person immigrating to Israel. These early kibbutzim used Jewish National Fund money to purchase land, primarily in the Jordan River Valley. Here kibbutz pioneers set up utopian agricultural communities in which all community members worked and received equal compensation in the form of housing, food and other necessities.

Early kibbutzniks fled persecution in Russia and Eastern Europe and, though secular, sought hope and redemption for the Jewish people through physical labor in the land of their heritage. They sought to contradict the racist stereotypes of the helpless, weak and bookish Jew and replace it with the image of a strong, capable workman. They came with little experience and faced challenging conditions, particularly malaria and other diseases as well as general lawlessness and unrest in the region under the loose control of the Ottoman empire. They pressed on, presumably inflamed with Zionist fervor.

In the 1930s, the kibbutzim took on additional military and strategic importance. Many were issued rifles and helped in weapons production and in defending the land in their vicinity. Their placement on the periphery of the region helped to determine the location of the Jewish state. Many early Israeli leaders were part of the kibbutz movement, including the first prime minister, David Ben Gurion, and the fourth prime minister, Golda Meir. In the 1960s and 1970s, volunteering on kibbutzim became a popular activity for young Europeans and Americans who received food, a place to stay and a healthy dose of utopian ideology in exchange for their labor.

Feel the pulse of the early kibbutz movement at the Kibbutz Museum at Moshav Kinneret.

Kibbutzim have seen a decline in recent years and have moved gradually away from agricultural work and purist communal practices in order to keep up with the changing economy. Kibbutzim expanded into other industries, particularly tourism and manufacturing. Many have become privatized with differential wage for members with different skills and experience. Kibbutzim now make up less than 5% of the Israeli economy. There are 256 kibbutzim in Israel, home to 106,000 people. Of those kibbutzim, only 16 are religious, while the rest are secular.

Kibbutzim still accept international volunteers, though not on the same scale as previous decades and with more regulation. Travelers ages 18-35 can still work on a kibbutz, receiving room, board and a small stipend in exchange for eight-hour days six days a week. Most require a minimum commitment of two to six months. For more information or to apply to volunteer see www.kibbutz.org.il/volunteers or call ☎ 03-524-6154/6.

J22

YARDENIT TO KFAR KISH

19.4 km
6-8 hours

Difficulty:
Steep terrain without water refill.

Biking Detours:
None, but there are difficult sections on the black trail from Wadi Yavne'el until the Elot lookout, some of which require walking or carrying the bike. The route is preferable in reverse (downhill).

Transport for Kfar Kish:
No direct transport. From Afula, buses 442, 830, 835 and 841 go to the Gazit Junction, 4 km from Kfar Kish.

Climb out of the Rift Valley for stunning views of the Jordan River and Sea of Galilee, feel the pulse of history at Tel Rekhesh

The route follows the Israel Trail markings for the entire J22 section. From Yardenit, the trail follows the Jordan River and other canals emerging into agricultural fields. It then climbs through and above Wadi Yavne'el and continues to ascend via dirt 4x4s, crossing a red trail where it is possible to exit to Yavne'el for supplies (+3 km). The trail crests the hill at the Elot viewpoint and descends through agricultural fields on 4x4 tracks with Mt. Tabor in the distance. Pass Tel Rekhesh at the junction of the black and red trails, and continue to where the dirt trail meets the paved road. Turn right to enter Kfar Kish or left to continue to Mt. Tabor.

Accommodations:

- 24 **Land of Galilee Home Stay** (Kfar Kish, +1.5 km off route): ☎052-860-6311; www.landofgalilee.com; dorm 100NIS
- 25 **Mount Tabor Inn:** ☎04-662-0124; www.mount-tabor-inn.co.il; double 450NIS
- 26 **Hooha Cyclist's House** (Kfar Tavor, +1 km off route): ☎077-708-0524; www.hooha.co.il; dorm 150NIS, double 480NIS

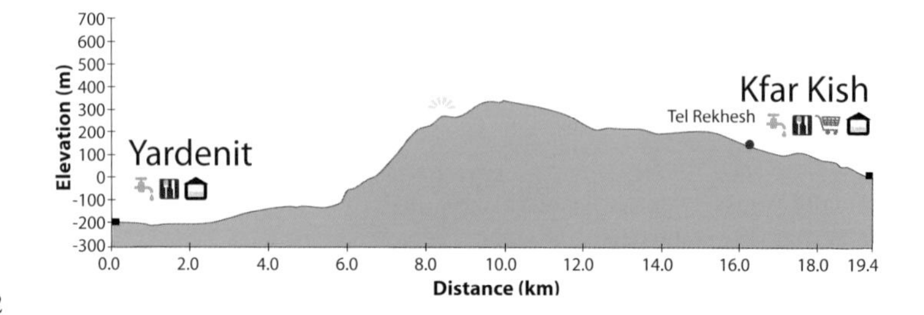

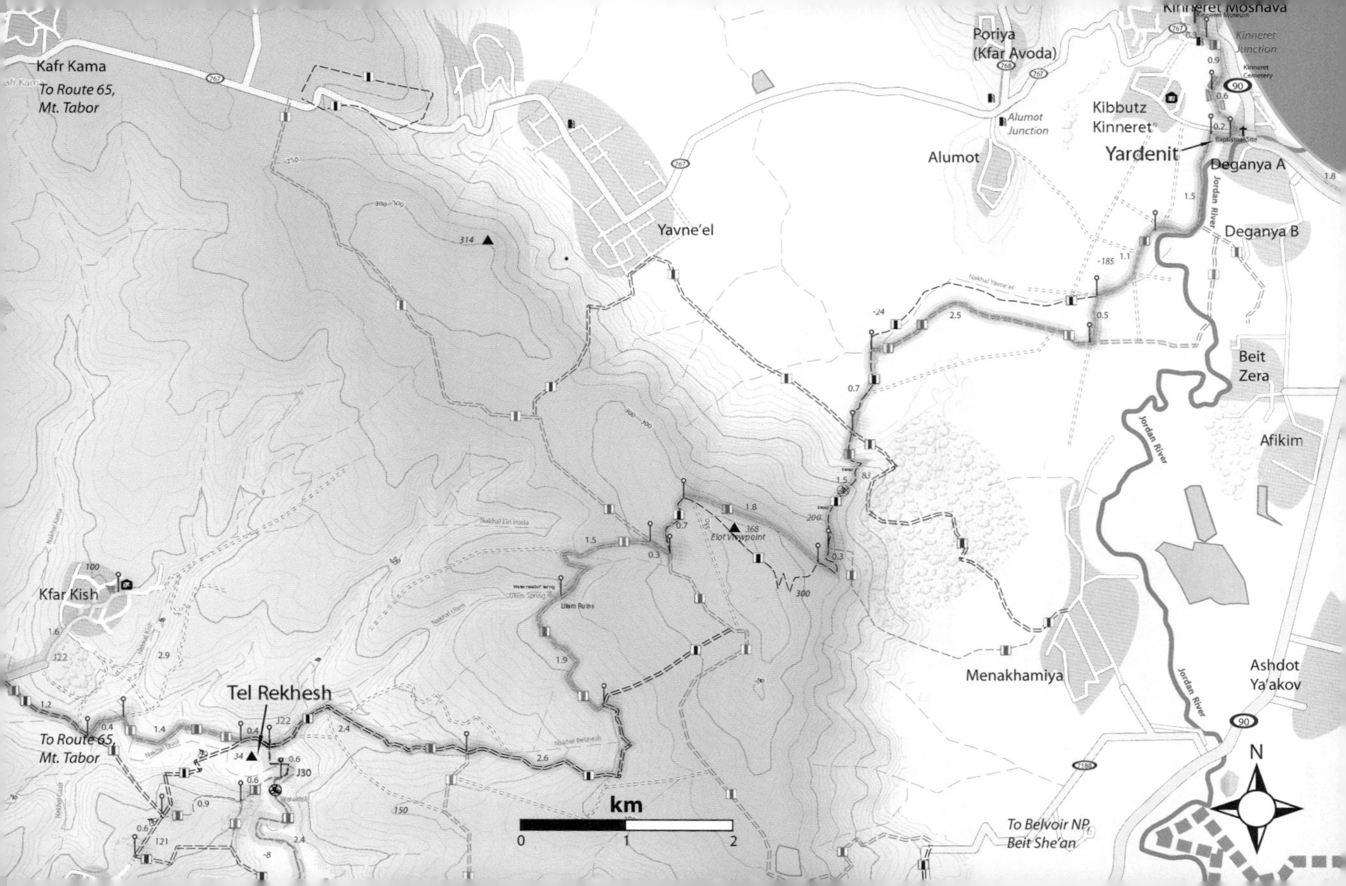
Kinneret Moshava
Kinneret Museum
Kinneret Junction
Kinneret Cemetery
Poriya (Kfar Avoda)
Alumot Junction
Alumot
Kibbutz Kinneret
Baptismal Site
Yardenit
Deganya A
Deganya B
Jordan River
Beit Zera
Afikim
Ashdot Ya'akov
N
Kafr Kama
To Route 65, Mt. Tabor
Yavne'el
Nakhal Yavne'el
314
Eliot Viewpoint
368
Nakhal Ein Hada
Ulam Spring
Ulam Ruins
Nakhal Ulam
Nakhal Rekhesh
Menakhamiya
Kfar Kish
Tel Rekhesh
J22
J30
Nakhal Tabor
To Route 65, Mt. Tabor
To Belvoir NP, Beit She'an
km
0
1
2

Ziziphus spina-christi

Christ's Thorn Jujube Tree עץ שיזף شجرة العناب

The soldiers twisted together a crown of thorns and put it on his head.
John 19:2a

Wadi Yavne'el and other lowland areas are dotted with large shrubby trees with small apple-like fruit known as **Christ's Thorn Jujube**, a tropical evergreen with sacred significance in the Middle East. The edible fruit resembles a small mealy apple and has numerous traditional medicinal uses including treating headaches, aiding weight loss and encouraging pregnancy. The name comes from Christian tradition which associates the branches of the tree with the thorns used to make a crown for Jesus at his crucifixion.

The Quran also mentions this tree as the "lote-tree" which Muhammad encounters in the seventh heaven. Local folklore considers the tree lucky to sleep under and useful for various healing rituals, many of which include hanging lights and cloth from its branches. Local holy men were said to sit under the tree, imparting some of their holiness into the tree's branches.

Ulam Spring עין אלום عين عولم

Stop for a rest at **Ulam spring**, a pleasant shady clearing with a cement holding container of fresh spring water. Since cows also drink from this water, you probably want to filter it before drinking. Locals often cool off by wading in the shallow water. Keep your eyes (and ears) open for the Christ's Thorn Jujube tree (see right), often buzzing with bees in the warmer months.

This spring is almost all that is left of the former Palestinian village of Ulam, whose name is associated with previous Roman and Crusader cities in the area. Before being depopulated in 1948, the town had about 720 inhabitants.

Views of the Jordan River Valley in spring (top) and summer (bottom)

First-century cookware at Nazareth Village

What would Jesus Eat?

Contributed by Anita Rhodes Clymer

While Jesus was having dinner at Levi's house, many tax collectors and "sinners" were eating with him and his disciples, for there were many who followed him. Mark 2:15

Archaeological research shows that the kind of cooking vessels used in the Galilee region in the 1st century were mostly large stew pots. You may imagine the family gathered to eat on a floor mat or at a low table. Each person would share food out of a common bowl, dipping with spoons or using bread to scoop up their stew.

Legumes such as lentils, chickpeas and fava beans would have formed the base of a "1st-century food pyramid" along with grains (wheat, barley and millet). Bread, a simple stew and whatever fruits were in season (or could be dried) would have formed the basic diet of the majority of people in Roman Palestine at the time of Jesus.

The author of Deuteronomy describes the land as being plentiful in olives, grapes, pomegranates, figs and dates (Deuteronomy 8:8). Edible by-products of these fruits would have included fruit leathers, olive oil, wine, vinegar, syrup and honey (or fruit pastes). Other available foods were butter, soft cheese, yogurt, fish (especially by the Sea of Galilee), poultry, lamb (probably only eaten at special events such as the Passover feast, a wedding or a bar mitzvah), wild game (such as deer or ibex), herbs (mint, dill and cumin being common) and some imported spices. The farther a food had to travel, however, the less access common people would have to it.

The lentil soup recipe in the sidebar uses foods and spices available in the Galilee at the time of Jesus, and is a dish that Mary may have served to Jesus, Joseph and other family members in their Nazareth home.

Simple Lentil Soup

Ingredients:

- 30 mL (2 Tbsp) olive oil
- 1 med. onion, diced
- 2 cloves minced garlic
- 5 mL (1tsp) dried dill
- 5 mL (1 tsp) cumin
- 500 mL (2 cups) lentils
- Water
- Salt

Directions:

Sauté onion and garlic in the olive oil until onion is translucent. Add dill, cumin, and lentils and cover with hot water. Cook until lentils are soft (30-45 min). Add more water depending on desired thickness of soup. Serves 6-8.

Tel Rekhesh

תל
רכש

Excavations at Tel Rekhesh

Tel Rekhesh (also known as Tel el Mukharkhash) is an archeological site being excavated by a Japanese team. Little is known about the site thus far save that it has an acropolis, Bronze Age wall, southern terraces and eastern fortification.

The site has been identified with the ancient Israelite settlement of Anaharath, allotted to Issachar in Joshua 19:19 and mentioned in a list by Thutmose III in the 15th century BCE. A model shrine dating from the Iron Age was found here, similar to Israelite shrines found at Tel Dan and Tirzah.

Go Tel it on the Mountain

תל تل

You may notice a common denominator in many of the historical sites in Israel—they begin with the word "tel" (as in Tel Aviv, Tel Rekhesh, Tel Dan). A **tel** (also spelled "tell") is a large mound of earth made by successive settlements. Like a landfill, the rubble of one settlement was built upon by a later population, whose rubble was built on by a later group, on and on until the settlement became a hill. You can see how after 10-20 layers the area of the settlements would be higher than the land around. There are over 50,000 tels spanning the Middle East, each containing archeological artifacts from multiple civilizations.

Tels conceal layers of ancient history.

J23

KFAR KISH TO MT. TABOR

11.0 km
3-5 hours

Difficulty: Steep ascent of Tabor.

Biking Detours: Climb Mt. Tabor via the steep paved road with switchbacks on northwest face.

Transport for Mt. Tabor: From Nazareth, take bus 823 to Afula, and catch bus 350 to Deburiya/Shibli. From there take a taxi to the top or walk the steep 3 km up the road. To climb via the footpath on the southeastern slope, bus to the Gazit Junction.

Climb rugged Mt. Tabor, drink in the view of the Jezre'el from the traditional place of Jesus' Transfiguration

The route follows the Israel Trail markings for the J23 section. From Kfar Kish, the trail parallels the road to Gazit Junction, then crosses Route 65 into the Tavor Nature Reserve and climbs steeply up Mt. Tabor via a well-marked footpath. We recommend descending Mt. Tabor on the switchbacking road for more secure footing and clear views.

Accommodations:

27 **Rashad Family Stay** (Deburiya): ☎050-730-9578; dorm 100NIS, double 400NIS

No accommodations on Mt. Tabor other than unofficial wild camping. Descend 3 km by foot or taxi to sleep in Deburiya.

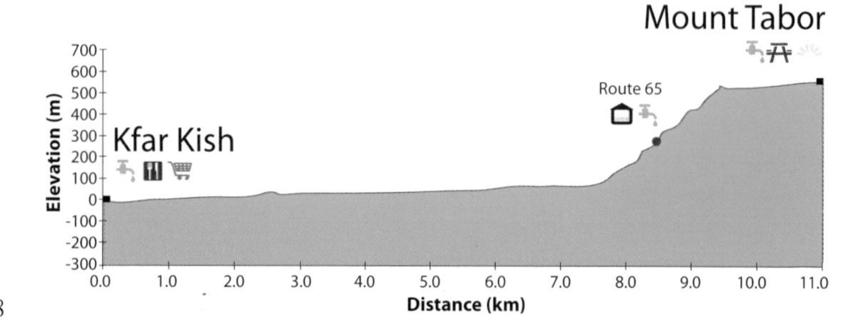

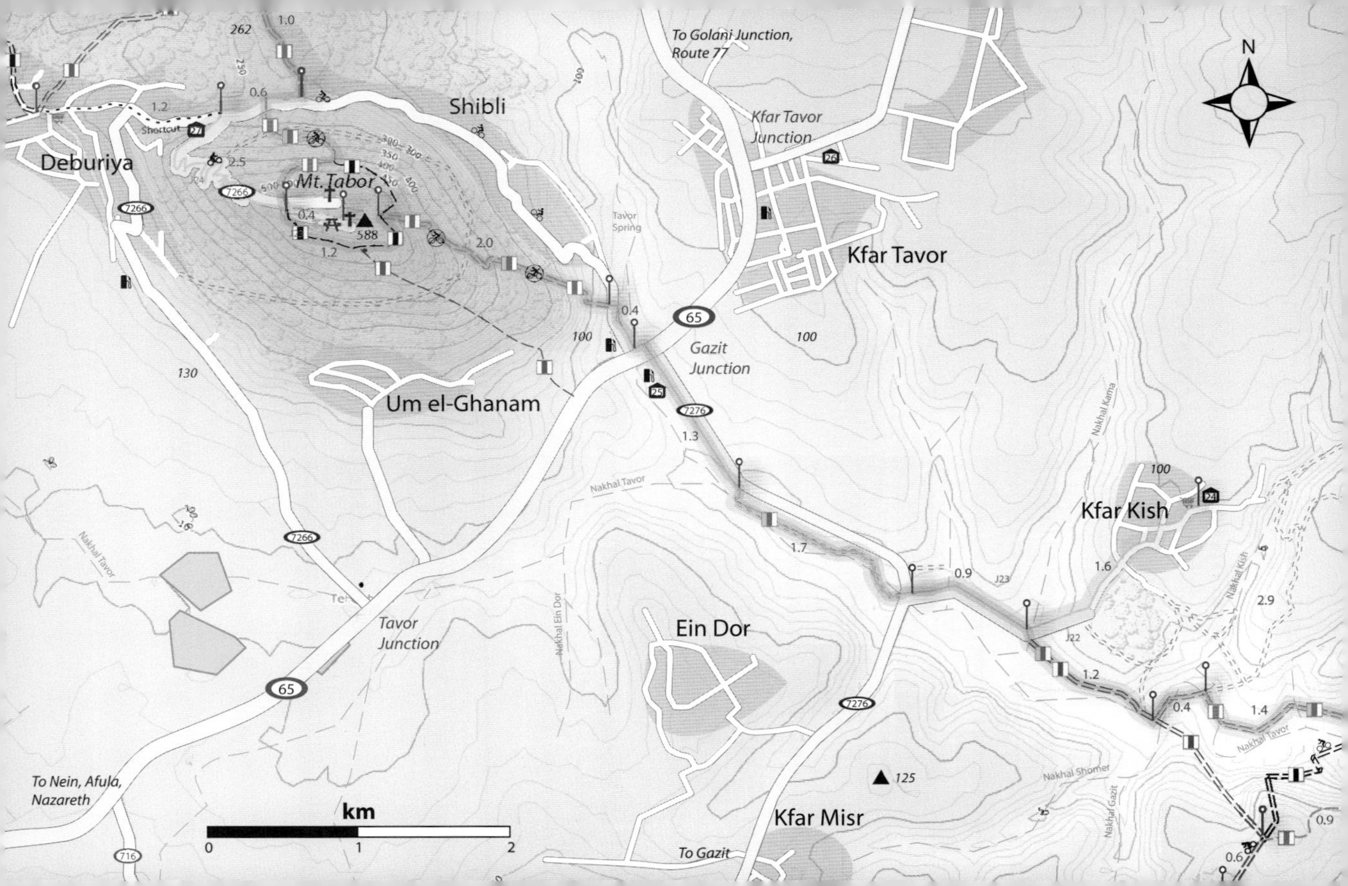
N
To Golani Junction, Route 77
Kfar Tavor Junction
Kfar Tavor
Shibli
Deburiya
Shortcut
Mt. Tabor
588
Tavor Spring
65
Gazit Junction
7276
7266
Um el-Ghanam
Nakhal Tavor
Nakhal Kama
Kfar Kish
Nakhal Kish
Nakhal Ein Dor
Tavor Junction
Ein Dor
Nakhal Shomer
Nakhal Gazit
125
Kfar Misr
To Gazit
To Nein, Afula, Nazareth
716
km
0
1
2

Mount Tabor جبل طابور הר תבור

"As surely as I live," declares the King, whose name is the LORD Almighty, "one will come who is like Tabor among the mountains, like Carmel by the sea." Jeremiah 46:18

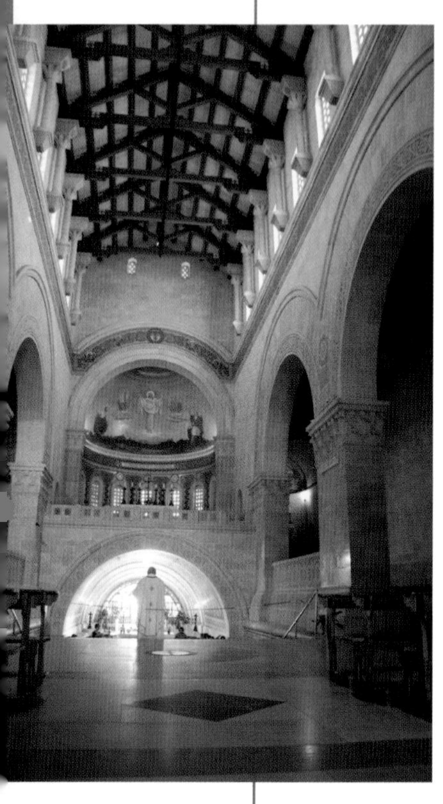

A priest conducts Mass in the Franciscan Church on Mt. Tabor.

Mt. Tabor rises 575 m above sea level in the eastern edge of the Jezre'el Valley. Also known as the Mount of Transfiguration, it is the traditional site of the Transfiguration described in the Synoptic Gospels when Jesus became radiant, spoke with Moses and Elijah and was called "Son" by God (Matthew 17:1-9, Mark 9:1-8, Luke 9:28-36).

The first source citing this as the site of transfiguration was Origen in the 3rd century, followed by St. Cyril and St. Jerome in the 4th century. The mountain became a place of pilgrimage from the 4th century on, with pilgrim records indicating several churches and a monastery on the mount.

In 1099 Benedictine monks were installed at the church on Mt. Tabor by the Crusaders. They were later massacred by a Turkish attack in 1113 but returned to rebuild. Their church monastery survived an 1183 attack by Saladin's army but did not survive long afterthe Crusader defeat at the Horns of Hattin in 1187.

A Muslim fortress was subsequently built on the mountain, precipitating the Fifth Crusade to take back the holy place. While the Crusader siege failed, the fortress was dismantled to stop any further provocation. The walls and gate around the current Franciscan compound are a restoration of the 13th -century fortress walls.

Two churches on top of the mountain commemorate the transfiguration—an impressive **Franciscan church** built on the ruins of Byzantine and Crusader churches, and a modest **Greek Orthodox church** named for the prophet Elijah. Before the churches and just inside the wall, there is an iron door leading to the Cave of Melchisidek (according to Byzantine tradition). The key to the cave can be obtained in the church.

The Franciscan complex is entered through a restoration of the Gate of the Wind, part of the defensive walls of the earlier Arab fortress. On the south side of the grounds is a small chapel built over Byzantine ruins recalling the conversation between Jesus and his disciples after the transfiguration. Straight ahead is the Benedictine monastery built in 1924, with the medieval church ruins to the north.

As impressive as the ruins, the view from Mt. Tabor is especially gratifying at dawn or dusk, with Mt. Hermon, Hattin and the Sea of Galilee to the northeast, Nazareth to the west and Mt. Gilboa to the south. On a clear day you can see the mountains of Jordan, Syria and Lebanon in the distance.

The basilica is open from 8am-12pm and 2-5pm every day but Saturday. The monastery supposedly has pilgrim housing, but we have not been able to confirm availability of accommodations. Picnic tables and a water faucet are located outside the gate to the Franciscan church.

Enter the Franciscan Church on Mt. Tabor through the iron gate (above).

Author Anna Dintaman walks on Mt. Tabor in the morning mist (below).

J24

MT. TABOR TO MT. DEBORAH

13.1 km
Shortcut: 8.8 km
3-5 hours
Shortcut: 2-3 hrs

Difficulty:
Steep descent of Mt. Tabor, gradual ascent of Mt. Deborah.

Biking Detours:
Descend Mt. Tabor on the paved road. Descend Mt. Deborah on the black 4x4 rather than the blue footpath.

Tranport for Mt. Deborah:
Take a taxi from Nazareth or walk in via the paved scenic drive from Nazareth Ilit (J25).

Come face to face with domestic camels, witness everyday Bedouin village life, hike through quiet pine forests

The route follows the Israel Trail markings for the entire J23 section, except for the descent of Mt. Tabor. Starting at the top of Mt. Tabor, take a slight detour from the Israel Trail and walk down the winding road for 3 km until reaching a T on the outskirts of Deburiya. Continue right to enter the town of Shibli just past a tourist rest area. Join the Israel Trail to exit the town and enter the Beit Keshet forest. Walk a series of 4x4 tracks to reach Mt. Deborah, where a picnic area is located on top. Finish the route at the junction of the Israel Trail, black, blue and red trails on Mt. Deborah.

Optional shortcut: From the base of Mt. Tabor on the paved road, turn left to enter Deburiya and continue down through town to find the black 4x4 track climbing up toward Mt. Deborah. This option saves 4.3 km.

Accommodations:
No immediate accommodations. Taxi or bus to Nazareth (p. 58) or Deburiya (p. 168).

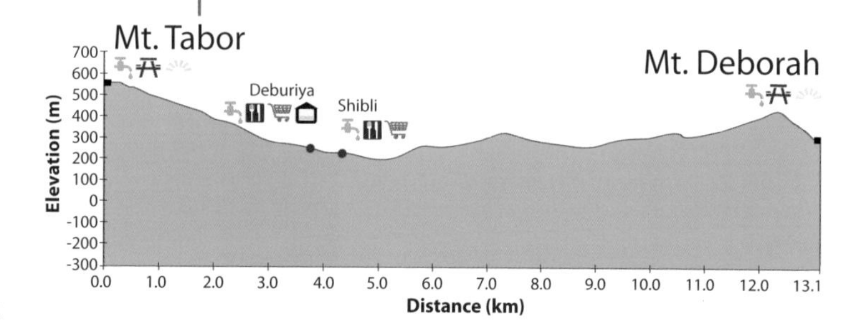

N
Beit Keshet
429
2.4
0.5
1.8
3.1
Nakhal Deborah
262
0.5
0.8
437
Mt. Deborah
0.8
To Nazareth Ilit
1.2
Shortcut
2.0
262
1.0
250
0.6
Shibli
Shortcut
1.2
27
Shortcut
200
151
Deburiya
2.5
7266
Mt. Tabor
300
350
400
450
500
0.4
588
1.2
2.0
To Gazit Junction, Route 65
To Tavor Junction, Route 65
km
0
0.5
1

The town of Deburiya is recognizable by its distinct blue mosque.

Deburiya דבוריה دبورية

Named for the prophetess Deborah, **Deburiya** is a small Arab village of about 8,500 at the foot of Mt. Tabor. Its distinct blue mosque dome makes it easily recognizable from a distance. Though not mentioned in the Bible, oral tradition cites it as the place of a healing miracle of Jesus.

Arabic Coffee קפה ערבי القهوة العربية

You can't travel long in the Middle East before becoming acquainted with **Arabic coffee**. The bitter drink is prepared with finely ground coffee spiced with cardamom and served in very small cups without handles. More than a shot of caffeine, Arabic coffee also symbolizes hospitality and friendship. While most Westerners would find it odd to sit down to a cappuccino in the midst of a hot weather hike, Galilean locals almost always carry Arabic coffee fixings on a walk for an afternoon break (or two). Locals will likely invite you to share coffee with them at some point on your hike. When possible, graciously accept hospitality. If you're low on time, feel free to decline but be sure to express gratitude and regret upon declining.

Shibli שבלי الشبلي

Shibli is a Bedouin town with approximately 4,500 inhabitants, one of about 16 recognized Bedouin towns in the Galilee. The inhabitants are said to be from a wave of immigration from Iraq 400 years ago, but intermarriage has all but eliminated the ethnic distinction.

Mount Deborah הר דבורה جبل ديبورا

Deborah, a prophetess, the wife of Lappidoth, was leading Israel at that time. Judges 4:4

Pre-monarchic Israel was ruled by a system of judges, including the **prophetess Deborah**, the only female judge. Chapters 4 and 5 of the book of Judges recount the story of a battle near Mt. Tabor between the Israelites, led by Deborah, and the Canaanites, led by Sisera. The Israelites won the battle, but Sisera fled and hid in the tent of a supposed ally, Jael, the wife of Heber the Kenite. While Sisera slept, Jael pounded a tent peg through Sisera's temple and killed him, helping to secure the Israelite victory and forty years of peace.

Judges chapter 5 recounts Deborah's song, extolling the goodness of God and attributing the victory to God's faithfulness.

The mount bearing Deborah's name stands 437 m (1433 ft) high, with pleasant views back to Mt. Tabor. Churchill Forest and picnic area provide a pleasant place to rest.

Domestic camel in Deburiya (top)
Olive tree (middle)
Bedouin tent in Shibli (bottom)

J25

MT. DEBORAH TO NAZARETH

7.4 km
2-3 hours

DIFFICULTY: Gradual ups and down.

BIKING DETOURS: Descend Mt. Deborah on dirt 4x4.

TRANSPORT OPTIONS: Local buses can cut the last 3.6 km from Nazareth Ilit to downtown Nazareth.

ACCOMMODATIONS: See Nazareth Old City (J0, p. 58).

Enjoy pleasant forest walking with views of Mt. Tabor, imagine ancient battles on the fertile valley floor below

From the Mt. Deborah trail junction, follow the only paved road west upward to Nazareth Ilit. After entering the outskirts of Nazareth Ilit, either catch a local bus or walk the final 3.6 km to the historic downtown area.

Jezre'el Valley

עמק יזרעאל
مرج ابن عامر

Now all the Midianites, Amalekites and other eastern peoples joined forces and crossed over the Jordan and camped in the Valley of Jezreel. Judges 6:33

The wide and flat **Jezre'el Valley** stretches across the lower Galilee from the Mediterranean coast north of the Carmel mountain range, between the highlands of Samaria (Mt. Gilboa ridge) and Nazareth. The name comes from the Bible and means "God sows," appropriate to this fertile agricultural valley, watered by the Kishon River and Harod spring.

Several battles from the Hebrew Bible took place in the Jezre'el Valley, including the Israelite victory led by Gideon (Judges 6) and the defeat of the Israelites under King Saul by the Philistines (1 Samuel 29). Jezre'el is also the place that Jezebel was devoured by dogs (2 Kings 9).

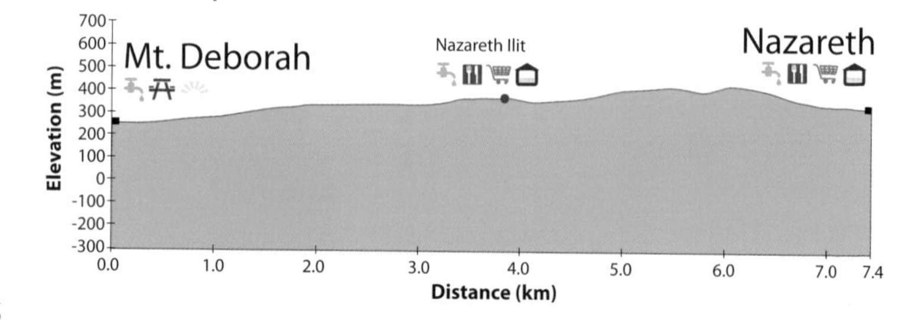

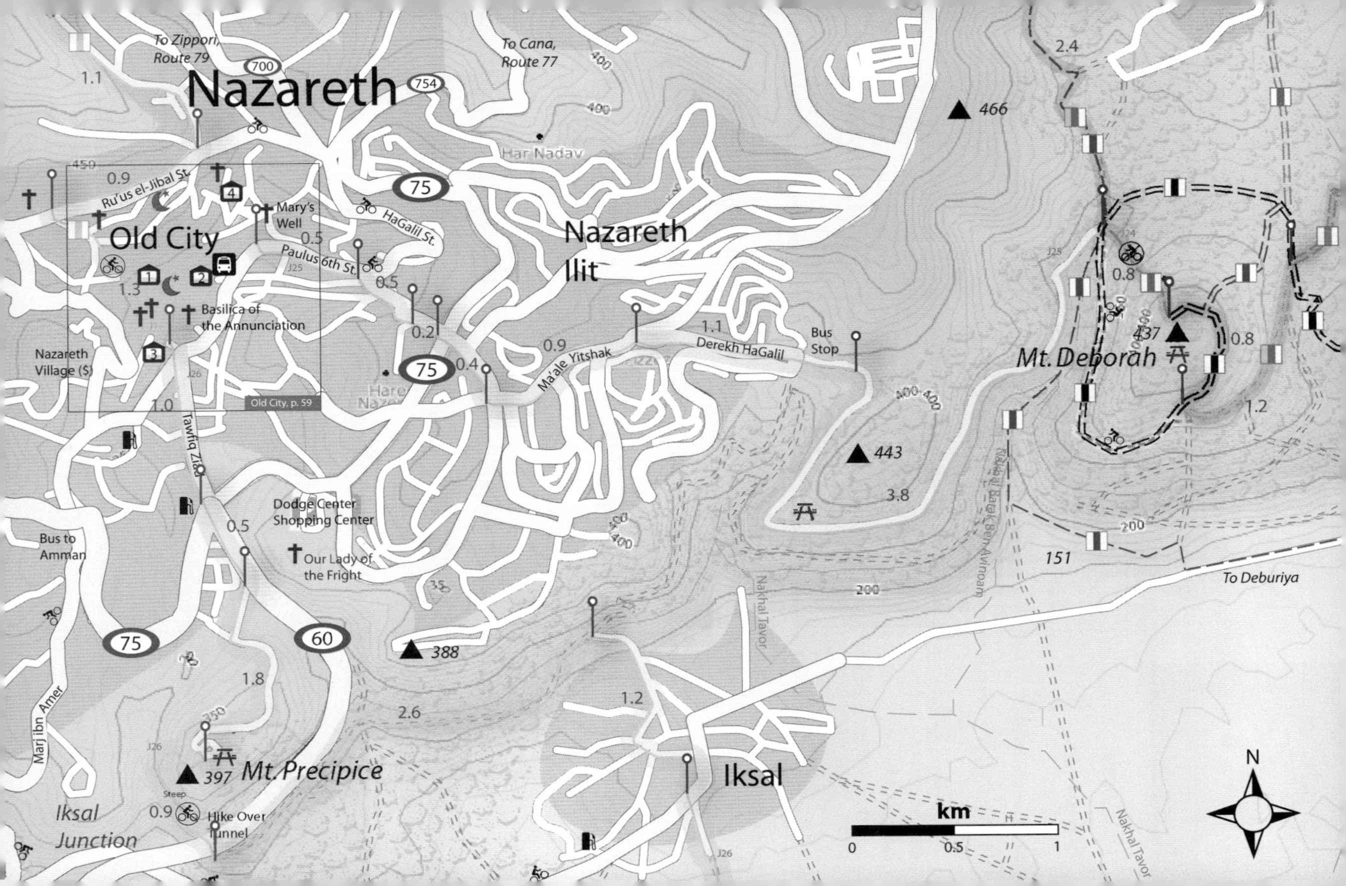

To Zippori, Route 79
700
Nazareth
754
To Cana, Route 77
466
Har Nadav
75
Ru'us el-Jibal St.
Mary's Well
HaGalil St.
Old City
Paulus 6th St.
Nazareth Ilit
Basilica of the Annunciation
Nazareth Village ($)
Old City, p. 59
75
Ma'ale Yitshak
Derekh HaGalil
Bus Stop
Mt. Deborah
437
443
Tawfiq Ziad
Dodge Center Shopping Center
Our Lady of the Fright
Bus to Amman
Nakhal Barak Ben Avinoam
151
To Deburiya
Nakhal Tavor
75
60
388
Marj ibn Amer
Mt. Precipice
397
Steep
Hike Over Tunnel
Iksal Junction
Iksal
km
0
0.5
1
N

J26

NAZARETH TO NEIN

15.1 km
4-6 hours

Difficulty:
Be careful on the steep descent from Mt. Precipice. Unmarked path requires navigational skills.

Biking Detours:
Carefully descend out of Nazareth via Marj ibn Amer Street and continue east to Iksal at the base of the mountain.

Transport for Nein:
From Nazareth, take bus 823 to Afula. From Afula take bus 442, 830, 835 or 841.

Accommodations:
No accommodations exist in Nein. Bus to Nazareth or Deburiya.

Admire the view from Mt. Precipice, visit the off-the-beaten-track church in Nein—site of a healing miracle of Jesus

Unmarked—GPS or good navigation skills recommended.

Start at the Basilica of the Annunciation in Nazareth. From the traffic circle on the main road, walk downhill. At the stoplight continue straight. Follow the sign to the right to Mt. Precipice. From the lookout, follow the shepherd's path around the side of the mount heading east. Pass over the traffic tunnel on the steep downhill side of the highway. Follow the dirt road toward Iksal.

In Iksal, at the Y in the road with an orange building, stay right. Turn right again after a metal gate. Turn left toward the mosque. At the mosque, cross a parking lot and plaza to left of the mosque. Turn left after the huge olive tree across from the bus stop. Turn right across from the grocery store after the butcher, straight out of town along the power line. At the Y, turn left staying to the right of the cell phone tower. At the next Y, walk to the right of the trees. Continue to the gas station and climb up to cross the street.

Follow signs to Nein and the Widow's Son. Arrive in Nein and walk across roundabout plaza to left. Walk uphill toward the mosque on a dirt road. Turn left before the mosque on an asphalt road. The church is straight ahead. Ask for a key to the church from the neighbor living next door.

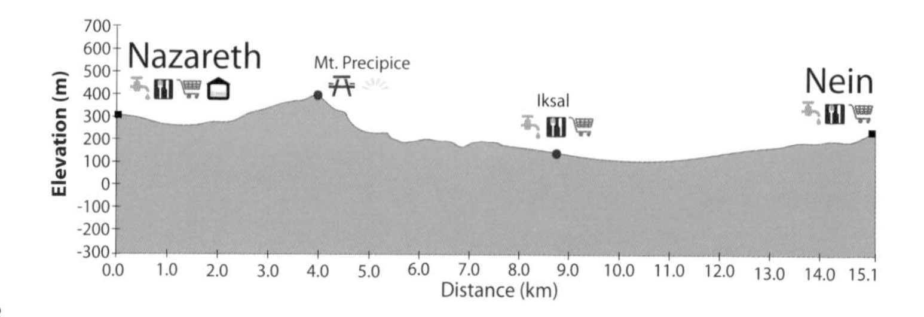

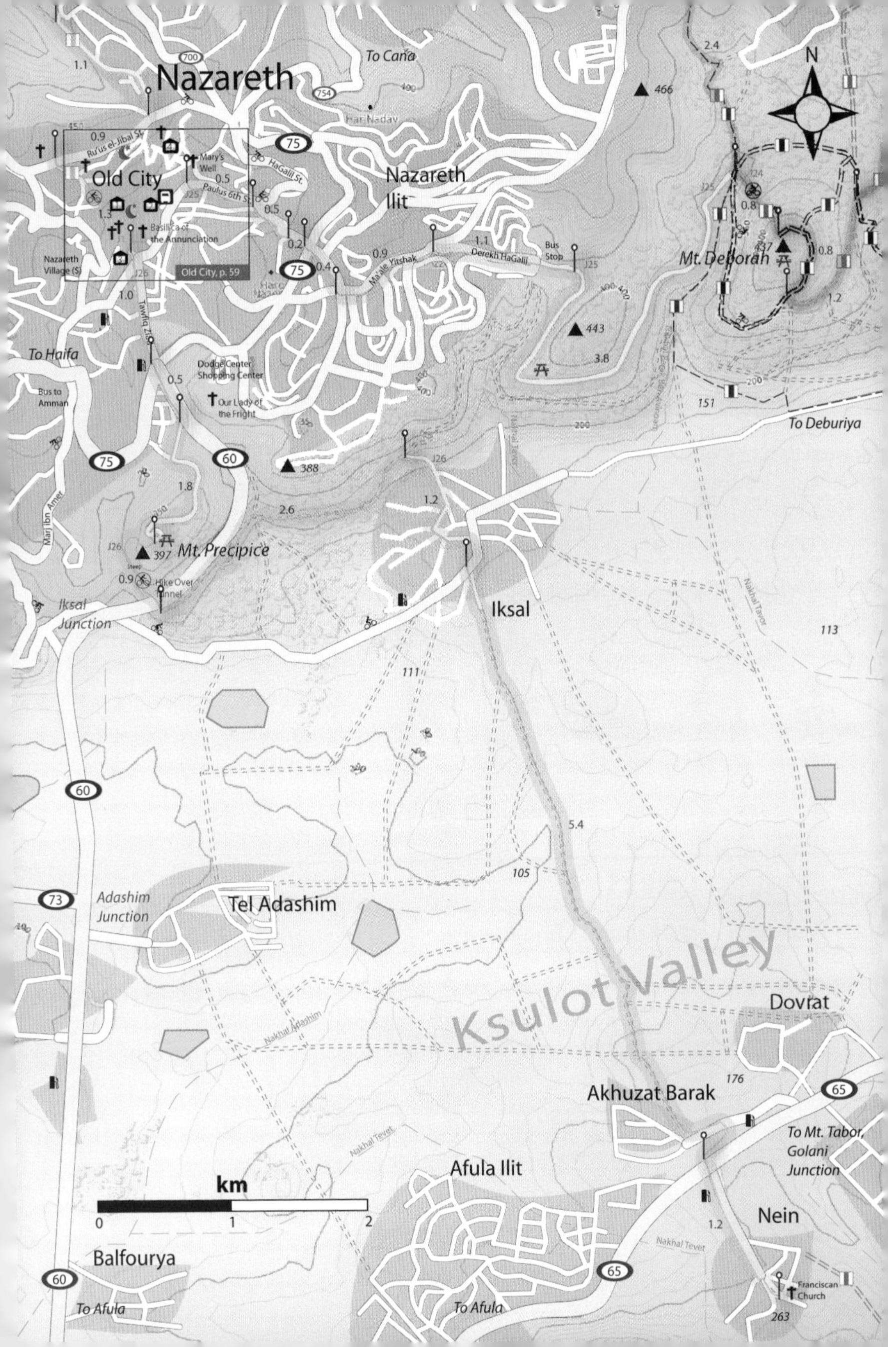

Nazareth
To Cana
Har Naday
466
N
Nazareth Ilit
Old City
Ru'us el-Jibal St.
Mary's Well
HaGalil St.
Paulus 6th St.
Basilica of the Annunciation
Nazareth Village ($)
Old City, p. 59
Ma'ale Yitshak
Derekh HaGalil
Bus Stop
Mt. Deborah
437
443
To Haifa
Bus to Amman
Dodge Center Shopping Center
Our Lady of the Fright
Tawfiq Ziad
388
To Deburiya
151
Nakhal Tavor
Marj Ibn Amer
Mt. Precipice
397
Steep
Hike Over Tunnel
Iksal Junction
Iksal
113
111
105
Adashim Junction
Tel Adashim
Ksulot Valley
Dovrat
Nakhal Adashim
Akhuzat Barak
176
To Mt. Tabor, Golani Junction
Nakhal Tevet
Afula Ilit
km
0
1
2
Nein
Balfourya
To Afula
To Afula
Franciscan Church
263

Mount Precipice

הר הקפיצה
جبل القفزة

They got up, drove [Jesus] out of the town, and took him to the brow of the hill on which the town was built, in order to throw him down the cliff. Luke 4:29

The peak of the Nazareth mountain ridges, just south of Nazareth, is known as **Mt. Precipice**, the traditional site of the cliff that an angry mob attempted to throw Jesus from after his bold proclamation in the Nazareth synagogue (Luke 4:16-30). The site offers a panoramic view of the patchwork Jezre'el Valley and Mt. Tabor, especially nice at sunrise.

Tourists gather at Mt. Precipice for views of Nazareth and the Jezre'el Valley

Today scholars do not find the mount a likely site for this story in Luke. Stoning traditions at the time dictated that a man could not be pushed from an elevation greater than twice his height. Victims were pushed off this smaller cliff head first and if that didn't do the trick, a large stone was pushed off the cliff on top of him. The location of the mount (2 km outside of Nazareth) also doesn't lend itself to the story as the hike out of town would have given too much time for tempers to cool or for Jesus to escape.

Excavations of Mt. Precipice found **Qafzeh Cave** with evidence of prehistoric settlement, including 13 Stone Age skeletons from the Neanderthal period. The caves were later occupied in the 6th century by Christian monks. Unfortunately, the excavations are not on display for the public. One local legend says that the cave opened up to hide Jesus from the angry mob. Another tradition says Jesus leapt from the mount, landing 9 km away on Mt. Tabor.

Mt. Precipice has been developed for tourism and has a parking lot, paved sidewalks and steps for sitting. In 2009, a

40,000-seat outdoor stadium was added on the north side of the mount for a Mass delivered by Pope Benedict XVI.

On the hill back toward Nazareth stands a small Franciscan chapel known as **Our Lady of the Fright**, imagined to be the spot Mary stood watching fearfully as the mob took Jesus to the cliff. The church lies in ruins, but is interesting to explore and affords a good view of the surrounding area.

Iksal אכסל إكسال

[The boundary] turned east... toward the sunrise to the territory of Kisloth Tabor. Joshua 19:12a

Just to the southeast of Nazareth lies the town of **Iksal**, with a population of about 12,000 inhabitants, mostly Muslim. The town is associated with the biblical town of Kisalot Tabor, mentioned in the book of Joshua and referred to as Xaloth by Josephus. Roman and Byzantine ruins have been excavated in Iksal and the ruins of a Crusader-era castle are still visible.

The view from Mt. Precipice into the Jezre'el Valley, including the town of Iksal and Mt. Tabor

Nein נײן نين

Soon afterward, Jesus went to a town called Nein, and his disciples and a large crowd went along with him. Luke 7:11

Nein is a town mentioned only once in the New Testament, as the site where Jesus raised the son of a widow from the dead. Today, Nein is a small Arab village located near Mt. Tabor about 8 km from Nazareth at the foot of Mt. Moreh, a 1815 m mountain also known as "little Hermon."

Nein is spelled in a variety of ways including **Na'in**, **Naim** and **Nin**.

Under the modern-day city are ancient ruins that have not been fully excavated. An earlier site, Tel Agor, is located 2 km from Nein. This site is identified as a possibility for the city of Anaharath from the Hebrew Bible, where Gideon's army of 300 defeated a larger Midianite army. Its earliest inhabitants were from the Epi-Paleolithic period (16,000 to 8,300 BCE). Nein was inhabited since the middle Bronze age, possibly as a continuation of the settlement at Tel Agor. A Roman-era cemetery is located east of town, perhaps the place the widow's son was being taken for burial.

One archeological finding discovered at Nein was a house from the early Roman era that had been burnt with people inside. Archeologists speculate that this may have been a casualty of the Great Revolt from 66-70 CE and that the family members may have been Jews being punished by the Roman authorities. Another option may be that the house caught ablaze during a major earthquake.

The New Testament reference to Nein mentions that it has a gate, leading to the assumption that the ancient city was walled. No remains of walls have been uncovered at Nein, so scholars speculate that the gate may have referred to an opening between houses that the road passed through.

The ruins of a 5th-century church can be seen north of Nein. There is also a **Franciscan church** from the 1880s near the center of town. The neighbors have held the keys to the church at Nein for seven generations. Ask them to unlock the door for you and leave a small donation.

Ask the neighbors for the key to enter the church at Nein

Afula العفولة עפולה

Gideon son of Joash died at a good old age and was buried in the tomb of his father Joash in Ophrah of the Abiezrites. Judges 8:32

Afula is a medium-sized Jewish city with a population of about 40,000, located in the Jezre'el Valley just south of Nazareth. The city is associated with biblical Ophrah, hometown of Gideon. The modern city was founded in 1925, and today is known for its superior falafel and roasted sunflower seeds. Visit **Falafel Golani** on Ha'Nasi Street across from the police station to verify claims of being the best falafel in the Middle East.

The famous falafel catch at Falafel Golani in Afula

J30

TEL REKHESH TO BELVOIR

12.7 km
3-5 hours

DIFFICULTY:
Steep ascent near end of segment, no water available on route.

BIKING DETOURS:
Take the black and red 4x4 tracks to Gazit. Catch the black 4x4 south past Taibe and turn east on the damaged road to Belvoir.

TRANSPORT FOR BELVOIR:
No direct transport. Take a bus from Tiberias to Beit She'an and get off at Route 717 (sign-posted). From there you'll need to walk or hitch 6 km uphill to the entrance. Access Tel Rekhesh via J22/23.

Walk remote wadi paths, watch graceful gazelle leap across the savanna, wander ancient ruins with a bird's-eye view of the Jordan Valley

From Tel Rekhesh, walk south on the red trail through Nakhal Tabor. After 0.6 km turn left on the blue trail and follow it through the valley for 2.4 km. At the four-way trail junction, turn left on the red trail. Continue through the valley, passing a junction with a black trail, then a junction with a green trail coming down from the left and a sign to Kokhav HaYarden. After 1 km, turn right on the blue trail toward Ein Be'era. Follow the blue trail up and out of the valley. Pass through a gate and walk straight across the field to pick up blue blazes again on the far side. After 1 km, turn left on a damaged road. Continue straight and follow signs to Kokhav HaYarden.

Accommodations:

No immediate accommodations. Wild camping or walk/hitch to town (Beit She'an, Tiberias or other). If you are planning to fill up water at Belvoir National Park, make sure to arrive before closing time (p. 188).

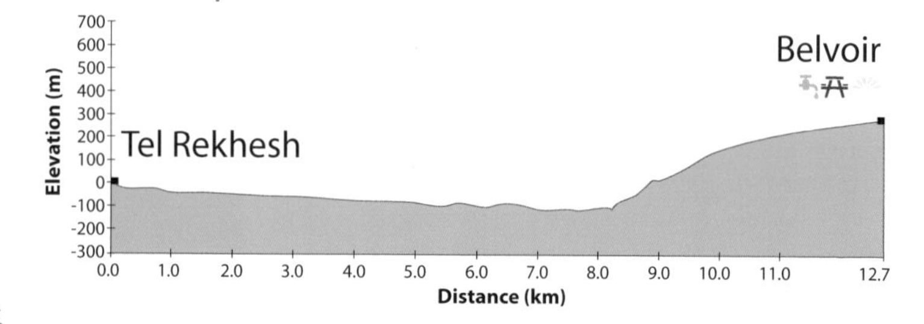

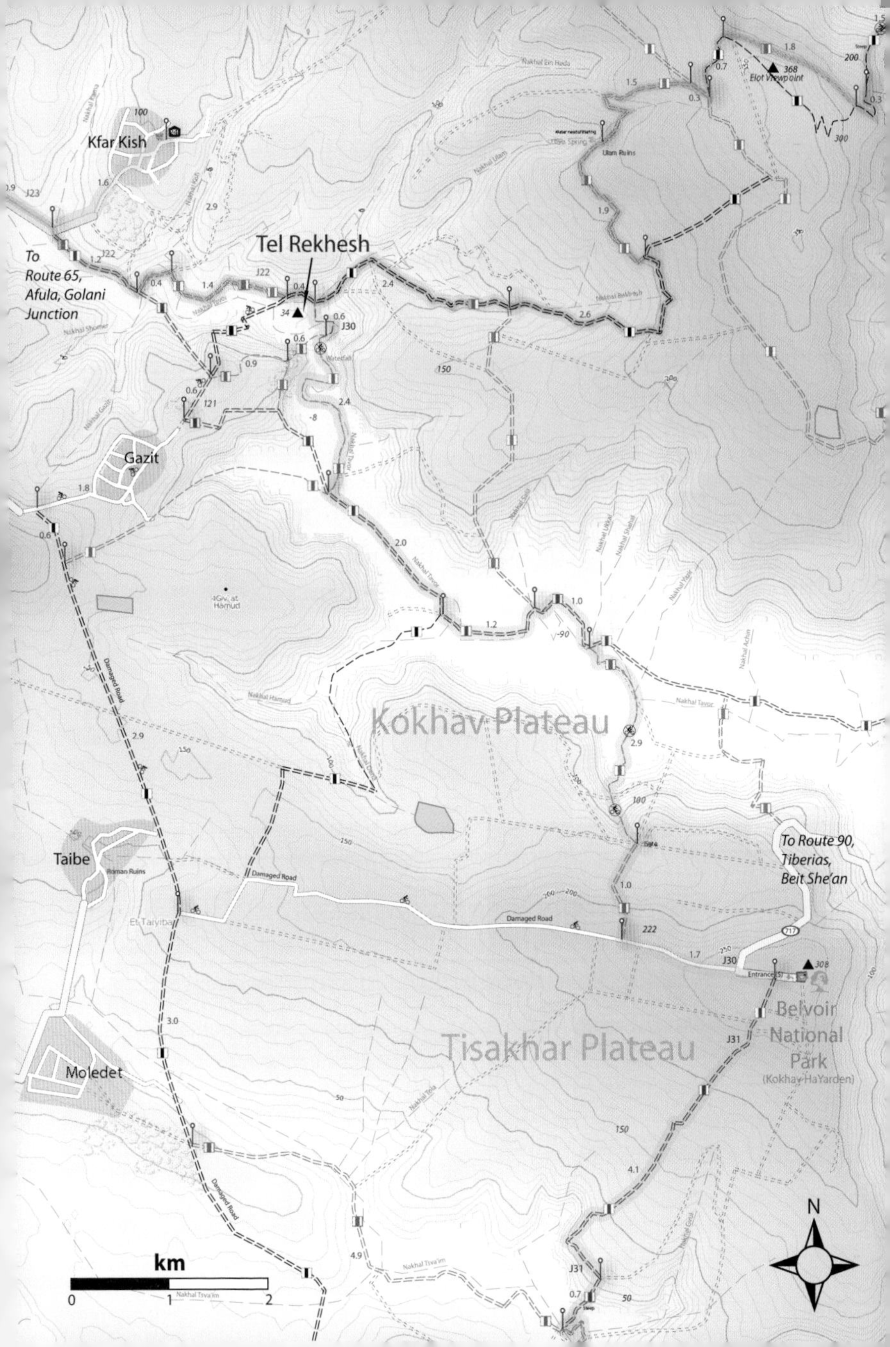

Kfar Kish
Tel Rekhesh
To Route 65, Afula, Golani Junction
Gazit
Kokhav Plateau
Taibe
Roman Ruins
Et Taiyiba
Damaged Road
Moledet
Tisakhar Plateau
To Route 90, Tiberias, Beit She'an
Belvoir National Park
(Kokhav HaYarden)
Entrance
Elot Viewpoint
Ulam Ruins
Nakhal Tavor
Nakhal Hamud
Nakhal Tsva'im
Giv'at Hamud
J22
J23
J30
J31
km
0
1
2
N

View of Nakhal Tabor and Mt. Tabor

Mountain Gazelle

As the deer pants for streams of water,
so my soul pants for you, O God. Psalm 42:1

Keep your eyes peeled for the swift mountain gazelle.

Through Nakhal Tabor, keep your eyes open for the swift and graceful Arabian mountain gazelle. **Gazelle** are medium-sized antelope that live primarily on the Arabian Peninsula. Thought to number around 3,000 in Israel, gazelle are mainly distributed in the Golan and Galilee. Until 1993, it was possible to hunt gazelle in Israel, but their declining numbers led to a protected status.

Gazelle live in small herds and graze on grass and shoots in open areas. They have adapted to go without water for long periods of time in order to survive in harsh, dry climates. Gazelle rely on their impressive speed (up to 60 km/h) to escape predators.

Za'atar (Hyssop)

زعتر זעתר

A jar of wine vinegar was there, so they soaked a sponge in it, put the sponge on a stalk of the hyssop plant, and lifted it to Jesus' lips.
John 19:29

You can't venture far into Palestinian cuisine without encountering **za'atar**, a tangy spice related to thyme, marjorie and oregano. Usually prepared as a dried green powder mixed with sesame seeds and sumac, za'atar graces everything from pizza to meat dishes to salad dressing. Wild za'atar (*origanum syriacum*) grows in the Galilee but is now a protected species due to overharvesting.

Za'atar is a likely candidate for biblical hyssop, a plant mentioned in the Bible in connection to ritual cleanliness. John's gospel records that the drink offered to Jesus on the cross was served on a stalk of hyssop. Since these stalks rarely grow longer than 60 cm (2 ft), this may mean that crosses were not as elevated off the ground as often portrayed in Christian art—the post of the cross may have only stood 2 m (7 ft).

Belvoir National Park

כוכב הירדן
كوكب الهوا

Belvoir National Park
☎04-658-1766;
adult/child 20/9NIS;
8am–5pm Apr- Sep,
8am– 4pm Oct- Mar

English:
Belvoir National Park

Hebrew:
Kokhav HaYarden

Arabic:
Kaukab el-Hawa

Well off the beaten track for most tourists, the ruins of **Belvoir Castle** are isolated on a stark basalt plateau with a plummeting view of the Jordan River Valley. The remote location enhances the feeling of connection to history for visitors to this best-preserved Crusader fortress in Israel.

Belvoir was an estate belonging to a French noblemen, who sold it to the Knights Hospitallers in 1168. The Hospitallers completed Belvoir fortress in 1173 in the concentric style of Crusader castles, surrounded by a huge dry moat. Belvoir housed about 50 knights and 450 soldiers, in addition to families and staff.

The fortress withstood an attack from Saladin's forces in 1182. However, after the battle of Hattin in 1187 as Crusaders lost ground throughout the Holy Land, Belvoir was sieged for over a year and surrendered in 1189. The inhabitants were allowed to flee to Tyre.

While little was left of the castle after being systematically destroyed, parts of the structure have been restored and give a taste of what castle life was like. As the French name ('Fair View') suggests, the castle affords a beautiful view of the surrounding area, including the Golan Heights, the Gilead mountains and Mt. Gilboa.

Interior room of Belvoir Castle

The name in Hebrew means "star of the Jordan," and in Arabic, "star of the wind."

Next to the castle there is a small sculpture park by Israeli artist Igael Tumarkin. On the other side, a vulture feeding station houses two injured griffon vultures perpetually on display on the rocks outside.

Ruins of Belvoir and view of Jordan River Valley

Belvoir National Park

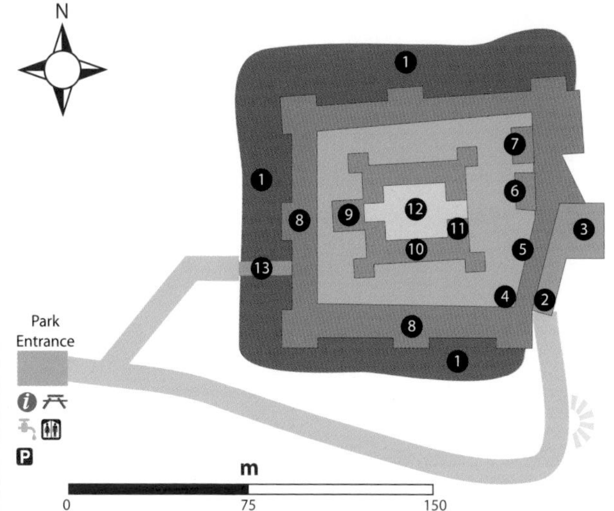

1. Moat
2. Main entrance
3. East tower
4. Inner east gate
5. Vaults
6. Cistern
7. Bathhouse
8. Sallyport (secret entrance)
9. Inner stronghold entrance
10. Dining room
11. Kitchen
12. Inner courtyard
13. West gate & drawbridge

J31

BELVOIR TO BEIT SHE'AN

16.5 km
4-6 hours

Difficulty:
Gradual elevation changes.

Biking Detours:
None. The route is possible, but has some short, steep sections.

Transport for Beit She'an:
From Afula, bus 411 and 412 run regularly to Beit She'an.

Walk on a perfect Roman *cardo*, admire ancient baths and a 4000-seat theater, imagine bustling city life 2000 years ago

Leaving Belvoir National Park, turn left on the red trail. After 4 km, cross a cattle guard and walk downhill into a wadi where you will turn left on a blue trail. At the blue/black trail junction, turn right on the black trail uphill and out of the valley.

Climb the ancient tel at Beit She'an to see remnants from ancient civilizations, such this Egyptian relief.

When the black trail meets Route 71, turn right and follow a dirt path parallel to the right side of the road. At the traffic circle, carefully cross the road and turn left on Sha'ul HaMelekh Street. Follow signs to Beit She'an National Park to left along the sidewalk along Sha'ul HaMelekh St. When you reach a traffic circle with ancient columns, the National Park entrance will be on your left.

Accommodations:

28 **Beit She'an Youth Hostel:** ☎04-606-0760; double 385NIS

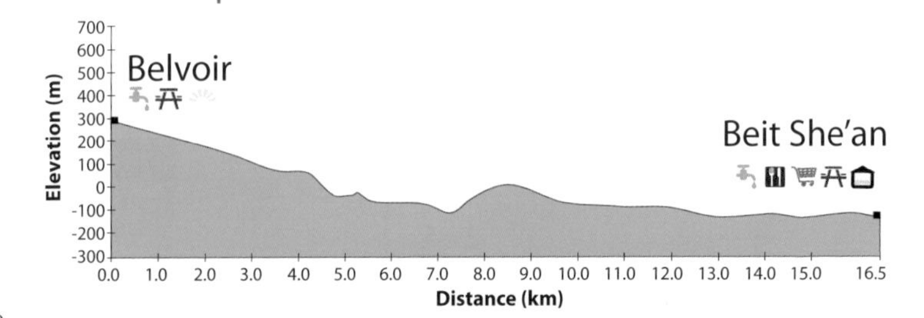

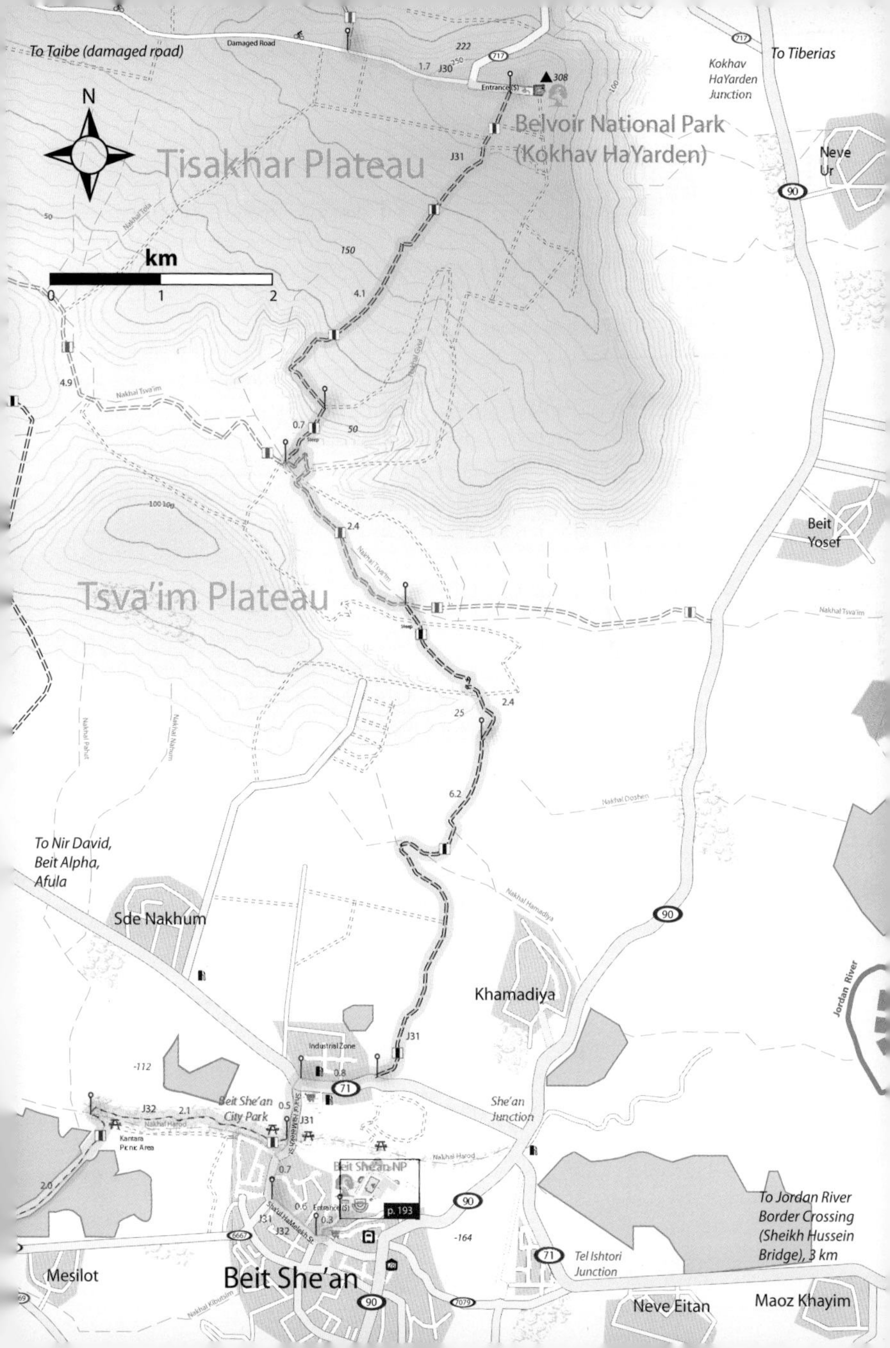

To Taibe (damaged road)
Damaged Road
To Tiberias
Kokhav HaYarden Junction
Belvoir National Park (Kokhav HaYarden)
Entrance ($)
308
Tisakhar Plateau
Neve Ur
N
km
0
1
2
Nakhal Tsva'im
Nakhal Gvul
Steep
Tsva'im Plateau
Beit Yosef
Nakhal Doshen
Nakhal Pahut
Nakhal Nahum
To Nir David, Beit Alpha, Afula
Nakhal Hamadiya
Sde Nakhum
Khamadiya
Jordan River
Industrial Zone
Beit She'an City Park
She'an Junction
Kantara Picnic Area
Nakhal Harod
Sha'ul HaMelekh St.
Beit She'an NP
p. 193
To Jordan River Border Crossing (Sheikh Hussein Bridge), 3 km
Tel Ishtori Junction
Mesilot
Beit She'an
Neve Eitan
Maoz Khayim
Nakhal Kibutsim
J30
J31
J32
90
71
717
6667
7079

Beit She'an בית שאן بيت شآن

All their valiant men journeyed through the night to Beth Shan. They took down the bodies of Saul and his sons from the wall of Beth Shan and went to Jabesh, where they burned them. 1 Samuel 31:12

Name Alternatives:
Beth Shan (Biblical)
Beisan (Arabic)
Scythopolis (Greek)
Nysa (Greek)

The archeological park at **Beit She'an** is a fascinating mish-mash of the remains of 18 cities from different time periods built on top of each other, including the best-preserved Roman theatre in the country. Located at the juncture of the Jordan River Valley and the Jezre'el Valley, it's easy to see why the city was inhabited during so many different time periods, as it was an important gateway between Jerusalem and the Galilee, and between the interior of the region and the coast.

The earliest settlement at Beit She'an was from the late Stone Age, and the city is first mentioned in Egyptian writings from the 19th century BCE when it was an administrative center for Egyptian rule over Palestine. When the Israelites arrived, Beit She'an briefly was part of the territory of Manasseh, but fell to the Philistines soon after King Saul was defeated on Mt. Gilboa (p. 200). According to 1 Samuel, Saul and his sons' bodies were displayed on the gate to Beit She'an.

Beit She'an National Park
☎04-658-7189;
adult/child 23/12NIS;
8am-5pm Sat-Thurs,
8am-4pm Fri Apr-Sept,
one hour earlier Oct-Mar

An evening **sound and light show** is available on Monday, Wednesday, Thursday or Saturday by reservation. Call ☎04-648-1122

The city took on the name Scythopolis in the 3rd century BCE, and soon thereafter became a Hellenized Greek *polis* known as Nysa. In 107 BCE John Hyrcanus brought the city under Hasmonean control and gave Gentile inhabitants the choice to be circumcised or exiled. They chose exile.

When the Romans conquered Palestine in 63 BCE, Beit She'an was made one of the Decapolis cities (p. 144) and most of its Jewish inhabitants were killed. The city was famous for its linen production, until a period of decline under Byzantine rule. In the 7th century, the city was conquered by the Arab invasion and was later destroyed by an earthquake in 749.

The view from the tel behind is well worth the climb, as are the ruins of religious structures from Egyptian, Canaanite, Israelite, Greek and Roman rule featured there.

Stroll down the Roman cardo at Beit She'an and climb the ancient tel looming behind.

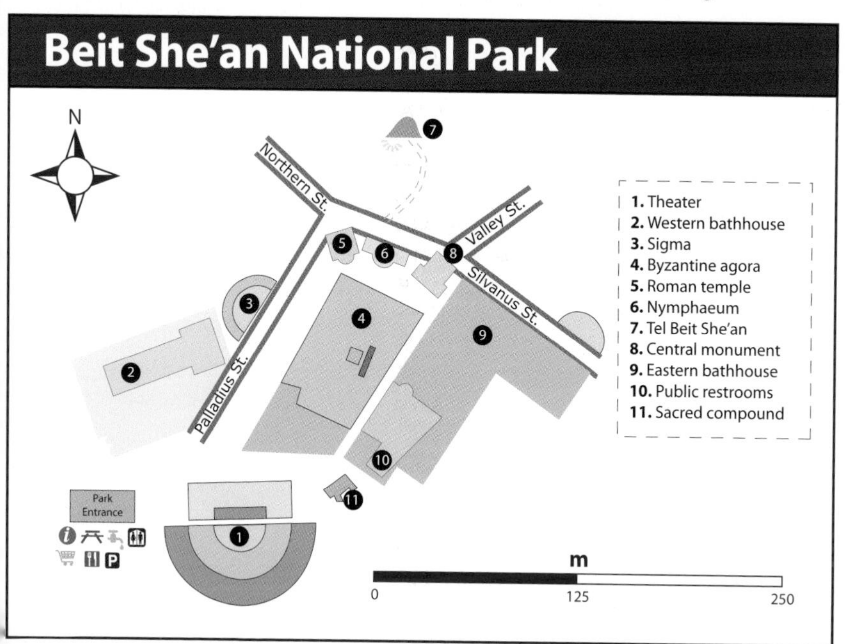

J32

BEIT SHE'AN TO GAN HASHLOSHA

8.0 km
2-3 hours

Difficulty: Flat terrain.

Admission Fees:
Optional: Beit She'an National Park, Gan HaShlosha, Gan Garoo Park.

Biking Detours:
None.

Transport for Gan HaShlosha:
From Afula or Beit She'an, catch bus 411 or 412, which run regularly.

Meander along the Harod stream, cool off in therapeutic warm pools at Gan HaShlosha, take a walk on the Australian side at Kangaroo Park

Begin at the Beit She'an National Park entrance and follow Sha'ul HaMelekh St. through the town to enter the Beit She'an city park. Turn left on the red trail along Nakhal Harod until you reach the Kantara picnic area. Follow the red marked dirt path out of the park.

Cross Route 669 to meet a black marked road. Note the tel with a lookout tower. Turn right at the parking lot for Kibbutzim Stream Nature Reserve and cross the swimming area on a green footbridge. Follow the unmarked gravel trail to the west, following the outside edge of Kibbutz Nir David. When you round the southwest corner of Nir David, turn right to enter Gan HaShlosha and Gan Garoo park.

Accommodations:

29 **Nir David Hotel:** ☎04-648-8525; www.nirdavid.net; cabin 550-800NIS; pool and fitness center

30 **Ein Harod Kibbutz Lodge:** ☎04-648-6083; www.en-harod-tour.co.il; dorm 120NIS, double 370NIS

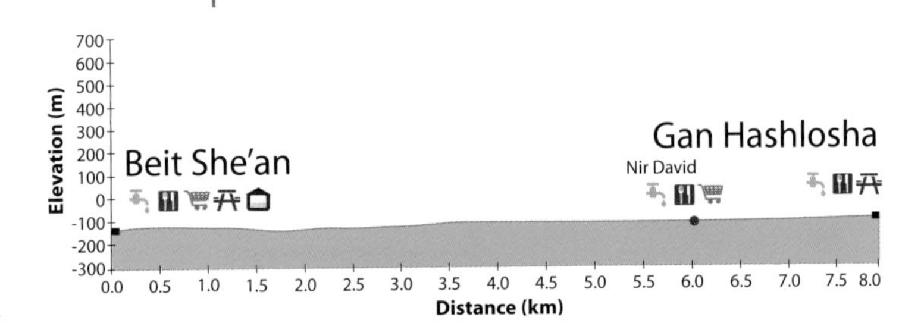

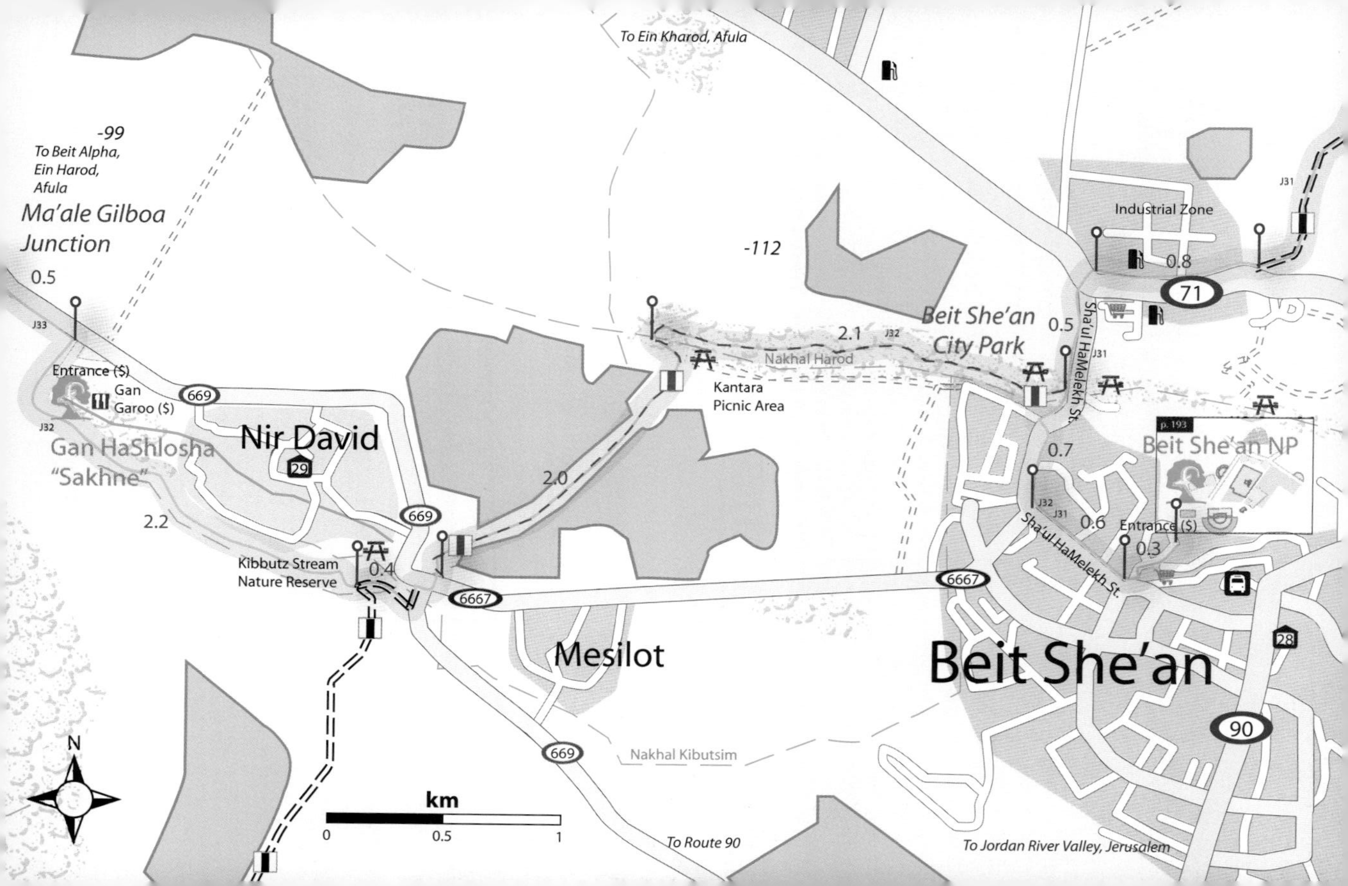

To Ein Kharod, Afula
-99
To Beit Alpha, Ein Harod, Afula
Ma'ale Gilboa Junction
0.5
J33
Entrance ($)
Gan Garoo ($)
J32
Gan HaShlosha "Sakhne"
2.2
Nir David
29
669
Kibbutz Stream Nature Reserve
0.4
2.0
6667
Mesilot
669
Nakhal Kibutsim
km
0
0.5
1
N
To Route 90
-112
2.1
J32
Nakhal Harod
Kantara Picnic Area
Beit She'an City Park
0.5
Sha'ul HaMelekh St.
J31
Industrial Zone
0.8
71
J31
p. 193
Beit She'an NP
0.7
J32
J31
0.6
Sha'ul HaMelekh St.
Entrance ($)
0.3
6667
Beit She'an
28
90
To Jordan River Valley, Jerusalem

Take a relaxing swim in the turquoise waters of Gan HaShlosha.

Gan HaShlosha גן השלושה

On a hot day, Gan HaShlosha is an inviting place to refresh in large outdoor warm pools, which are connected by waterfalls and surrounded by lush green landscaping. The expansive grounds have plenty of green space for picnics and lounging, and the pools, fed by the Amal River, are 82°F (28°C) year-round.

If you feel the need to justify such hedonism with something of educational value, the site also houses the **Museum of Mediterranean Archeology**, featuring Greek articles from the Beit She'an valley as well as a replica of Tel Amal, a tower and stockade settlement from 1938 (see Ein Gev p. 140) and a recreation of a hydro-powered flour mill.

The name means "Park of the Three" in memory of three Jewish National Council inspectors who were killed by a land mine near the village of Samaria in 1938. Locals know the park by its Arabic name, *Sakhne*, which means warm.

The park has a snack bar and restrooms with showers. Bus 412 between Beit She'an and Afula can drop you off close to the entrance.

Gan HaShlosha
Park ☎04-658-6219,
Museum ☎04-658-6352;
adult/child 33/20NIS
(half-price with national park pass);
8am-5pm Apr-Sept, Sun-Fri
8am-4pm Oct-Mar, Sun-Fri

Gan Garoo גן גורו

Feeding a kangaroo at Gan Garoo Park

Next door is one of the stranger attractions in Israel, the **Gan Garoo** (Kangaroo) park featuring a variety of wildlife and plants from Australia, including kangaroos, wallabies, koala bears, cassawary and over 20 types of eucalyptus.

Guests can wander extensive grounds including an open area to interact with different types of kangaroos, a maze and children's play areas. The unique park took six years to receive approval and faced numerous obstacles to importing rare and exotic animals, particularly the koala bear whose diet consists entirely of eucalyptus. Eucalyptus to feed the koalas is grown in nearby Kibbutz Nir David.

Gan Garoo Park
☎04-648-8060;
adult/child 32NIS;
9am-4pm Sun-Thurs,
9am-1pm Fri,
9am-5pm Sat

Beit Alpha بيت الفا בית אלפא

Just off the trail (J33) in Kibbutz Beit Alpha you can visit the ancient **Beit Alpha synagogue**. The main feature of the ruins is the well-preserved 5th-century mosaic floor featuring Jewish symbols interspersed with the signs of the zodiac. Compare the mosaics here to the fine workmanship at Sepphoris (pp. 70-72), and the Beit Alpha mosaics look crude and cartoonish, in a charming folk-art style.

Beit Alpha National Park
☎04-653-2004;
adult/child 20/9NIS;
8am–5am Apr-Sep,
8am–4pm Oct-Mar

An informative 15-minute video in the mosaic room explains the mosaic images and gives a theory for the unique style of the floor. The images portrayed on the floor include the binding of Isaac, a zodiac with misspelled Hebrew words and a depiction of the Torah ark.

Beit Alpha Synagogue

J33

GAN HASHLOSHA TO MT. GILBOA

13.6 km
4-6 hours

Difficulty:
Steep ascent up Mt. Gilboa.

Admission Fees:
None.

Biking Detours:
The green/black 4x4 ascent to Mt. Gilboa is possible but steep. Descend the same way or take Route 667 to Route 6666.

Transport for Mt. Gilboa:
No direct transport. Take bus 411 or 412 from Afula. Get off at the entrance to Beit Alpha Kibbutz on Route 669. Walk or hitch the final 7 km up the mountain.

Stalk the Gilboa iris as you romp through fields of wild flowers

From the entrance to Gan HaShlosha, follow the paved track to Route 669 and turn left. At the Ma'ale Gilboa Junction with Route 6666, turn left past the gas station and continue until you meet a green trail on the right. Follow the green 4x4, passing a quarry and turning uphill to enter Gilboa Nature Reserve. After 3.5 km, continue on a black trail where the green trail veers left. Stay on main black 4x4 as it switchbacks up the mountain.

Near the top, turn left on a red trail, leaving Gilboa Nature Reserve. Turn right up a set of stone stairs and cross a paved road into a picnic area. Enter Gilboa Nature Reserve and Mt. Barkan lookout tower area. Note the Palestinian Territory to the south, with the village of Faqu'a just across the border.

To descend the mountain, either retrace your steps to Beit Alpha or use the red trail to En Hasamal, which is intended for fit hikers only. The red trail descends steeply down the mountainside, using a series of handholds and ladders for the final section to reach the valley floor. Continue on red 4x4 track to Beit Alpha.

Accommodations:
No accommodations on Mt. Gilboa or Beit Alpha. Walk, bus, taxi or hitch to Ein Harod, Nir David, Afula or Nazareth.

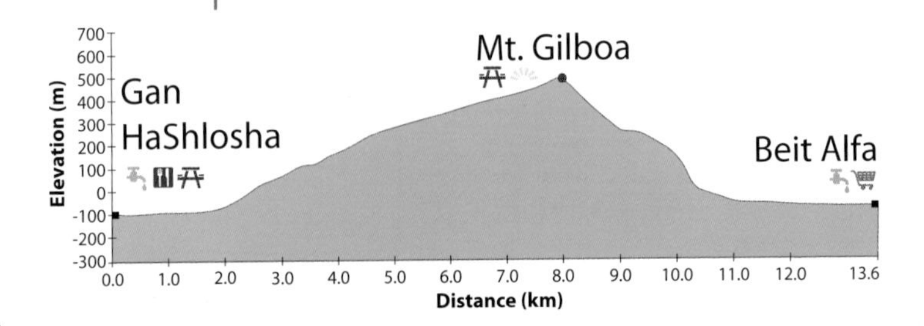

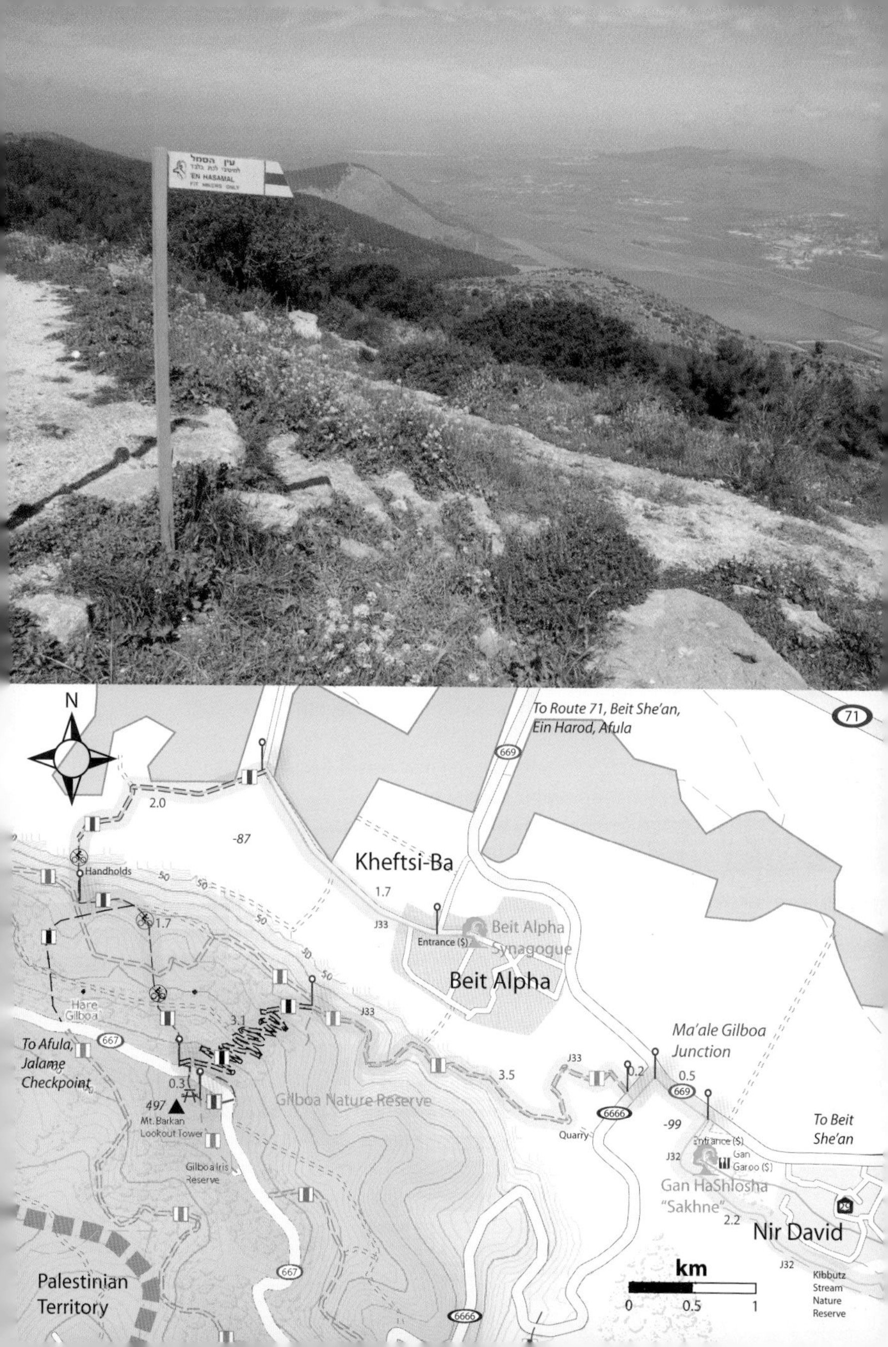

'EN HASAMAL
N
To Route 71, Beit She'an, Ein Harod, Afula
71
669
2.0
-87
Kheftsi-Ba
Handholds
50
1.7
J33
Entrance ($)
Beit Alpha Synagogue
Beit Alpha
Hare Gilboa
3.1
J33
To Afula, Jalame Checkpoint
667
Ma'ale Gilboa Junction
J33
0.2
0.5
669
3.5
0.3
497
Mt. Barkan Lookout Tower
Gilboa Nature Reserve
6666
Quarry
-99
To Beit She'an
Entrance ($)
J32
Gan Garoo ($)
Gilboa Iris Reserve
Gan HaShlosha "Sakhne"
2.2
Nir David
Palestinian Territory
667
km
0
0.5
1
J32
Kibbutz Stream Nature Reserve
6666

Mount Gilboa

הר גלבוע
جبال فقوعة

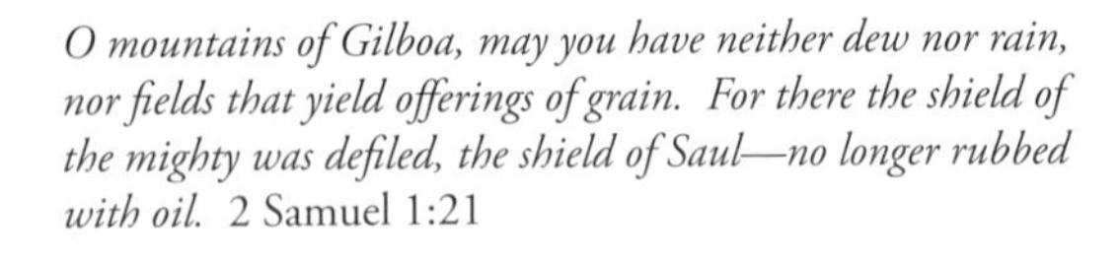

O mountains of Gilboa, may you have neither dew nor rain, nor fields that yield offerings of grain. For there the shield of the mighty was defiled, the shield of Saul—no longer rubbed with oil. 2 Samuel 1:21

Spring flowers on Mt. Gilboa, including the Gilboa iris (opposite)

Along the southern edge of the Jezre'el Valley, the mountain ridge of **Gilboa** rises about 510 m (1700 ft) above the plain. Just on the other side lies the West Bank and northern Palestinian cities such as Faqu'a and Jenin, which can be seen from atop Gilboa.

Gilboa was the site of the Israelite battle against the Philistines during which King Saul killed himself after hearing that his sons had been killed (1 Samuel 31:4). The Philistine victors then hung Saul's beheaded body from the gate of Beit She'an (see p. 192). When David heard of Saul's death, he cursed Gilboa to be barren without rain or dew (2 Samuel 1:21).

Not long ago it appeared that the curse may have taken hold, as Gilboa began to show bald spots from lack of rain, but extensive reforesting by the Jewish National Fund has restored most of the barren areas. In spring the ridge explodes with exuberant wildflowers including the rare **Gilboa iris**, which blooms in a small reserve near the summit. Nursed back from extinction by the Society for the Protection of Nature in Israel (see p. 42), the iris has become the symbol of the organization and many Israelis flock to Gilboa in March to see the flower.

At the base of Mt. Gilboa runs the spring of Harod, where Gideon thinned down his army by observing who drank water by cupping their hands and who lapped the water (Judges 7). The name Gilboa comes from the Hebrew word for "bubbling," presumably in reference to this spring.

The West Bank

הגדה המערבית
الضفة الغربية

The **West Bank** is an ear-shaped territory that stretches from just south of the Galilee down to the south Hebron hills. This area, along with the Gaza Strip, is what remains of the territory designated for Palestinians in 1948 (see historical timeline p. 221). The name comes from the location of the territory on the western bank of the Jordan River.

From the top of Mt. Gilboa, the Nativity Trail (see p. 46) in the West Bank lies only about 1 km south. This route to Bethlehem stretches through the Palestinian territory, passing through remote countryside and connecting towns and villages along the way. The trail is not marked and it is not recommended to walk without a guide, but if you were to enter the West Bank from here you would proceed to Jalame checkpoint. This main northern checkpoint to Jenin was closed in the year 2000, but recently reopened for limited hours.

The West Bank

J40

KAUKAB TO KHIRBET CANA

7.7 km
2-3 hours

DIFFICULTY:
Moderate elevation change.

BIKING DETOURS:
None.

TRANSPORT FOR KAUKAB ABU AL-HIJA:
Take bus 28א from Nazareth.

TRANSPORT FOR KHIRBET CANA:
No direct transport. Hike to Kfar Manda (+4 km) and take bus 28 to Nazareth.

Visit the grave of Saladin's Lieutenant, wander the ancient ruins of Yodfat and Khirbet Cana

From the bus stop along Route 784 outside of Kaukab Abu al-Hija, follow a blue trail past a Muslim shrine and down through olive groves. Turn left on a red 4x4 track through a small pass to arrive at Tel Yodfat. After climbing the tel to visit historic Yodfat, continue down through the wadi on the red trail. When you reach the junction with a blue trail, turn left around the side of Khirbet Cana to enter the ancient city from the north side.

Accommodations:
No accommodations at Khirbet Cana. Keep walking to Eilabun (J41, p. 212) or walk to Kfar Manda (+4 km) for a bus.

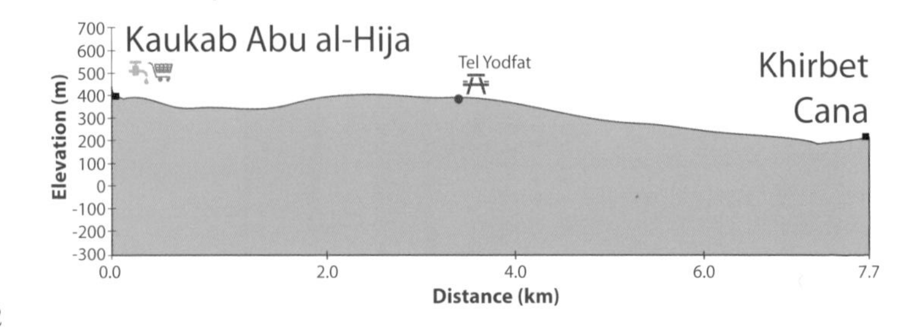

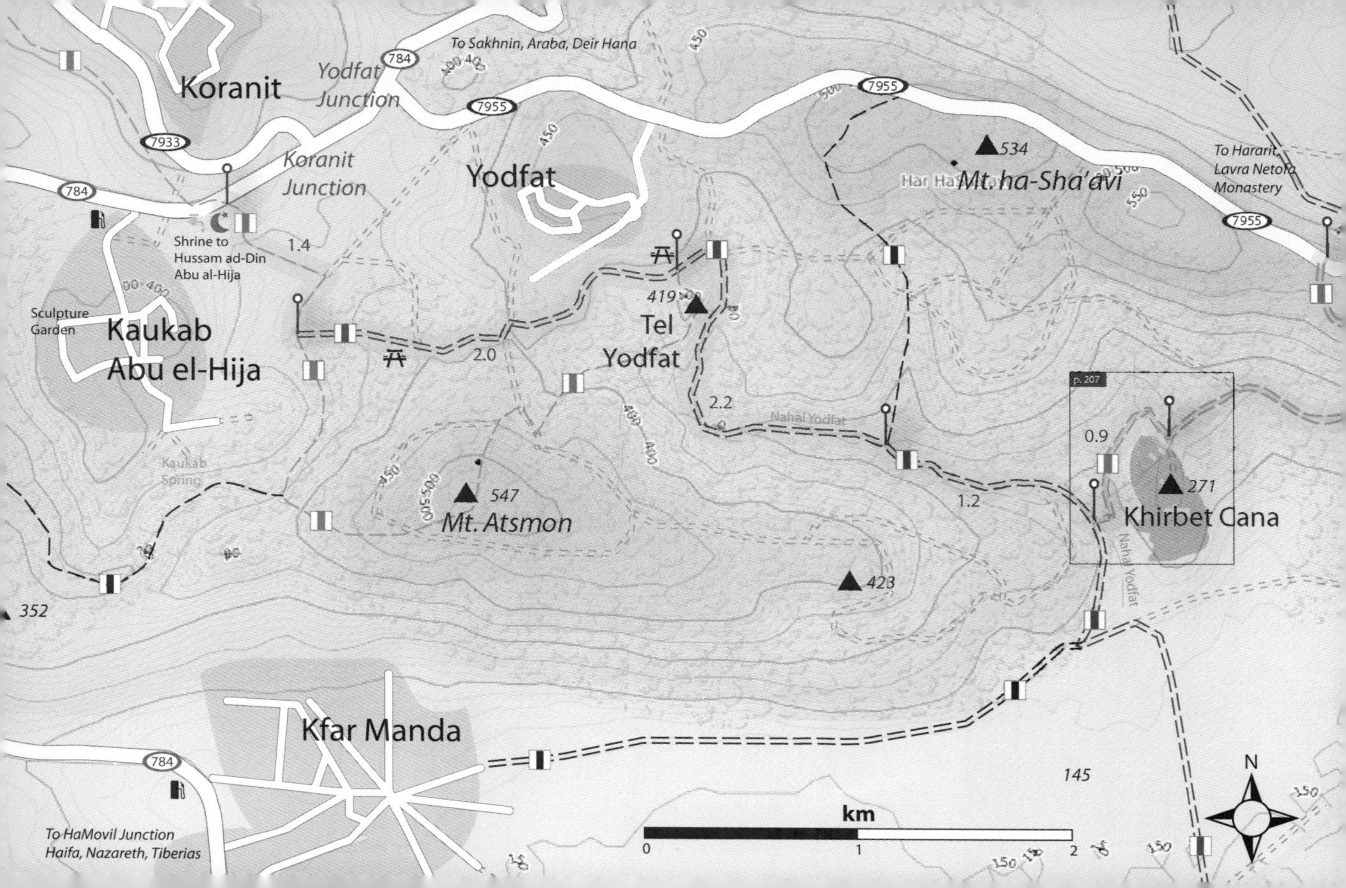

To Sakhnin, Araba, Deir Hana
784
Yodfat Junction
Koranit
7933
7955
Koranit Junction
Yodfat
784
Shrine to Hussam ad-Din Abu al-Hija
1.4
Sculpture Garden
Kaukab Abu el-Hija
2.0
419
Tel Yodfat
2.2
Kaukab Spring
547
Mt. Atsmon
352
534
Mt. ha-Sha'avi
Nahal Yodfat
To Hararit, Lavra Netofa Monastery
p. 207
0.9
271
Khirbet Cana
1.2
423
Nahal Yodfat
Kfar Manda
784
To HaMovil Junction Haifa, Nazareth, Tiberias
145
km
0
1
2
N
450
400
500
550
150

Shrine of Hussam ad-Din Abu al-Hija

Kaukab abu al-Hija

כוכב אבו אל-היג'א
كوكب أبو الهيجا

Kaukab Abu al-Hija is a predominantly Muslim town with a population of about 2,800. The word *Kaukab* means "star" in Arabic, and Abu al-Hija refers to the grave shrine just outside of town which distinguishes this town from others named Kaukab. The town features a **sculpture garden** with about 30 works of art by both Israelis and Palestinians. Take a look at the green-domed **shrine to Hussam ad-Din Abu al-Hija**, a lieutenant in Saladin's army.

Yodfat

יודפת جفات

Known as the "Masada of the Galilee," **Yodfat** was an ancient fortified city best known for its battle led by Josephus (see right) against Vespasian's army in 67 CE. It was originally settled by the Israelites in the Iron Age, but most likely destroyed by the Assyrians in 732 BCE and later repopulated.

During the Great Revolt against the Romans, Josephus fortified the city with thick walls to protect against Roman efforts to crush the revolt. In 67 CE, Josephus' record tells us that Vespasian's troops laid siege to the city with battering rams, a ramp, javelins and other projectiles. After 47 days, the Romans entered the city and slaughtered the inhabitants.

Josephus and his forty men hid in a cave for three days. When they heard the Romans coming for them, all committed suicide save the brave leader (Josephus himself). This motif of valiant suicide-rather-than-surrender is also used by Josephus in his telling of the battles of Masada and Gamla, though no archeological evidence has been found that confirms the story.

Today **Tel Yodfat** is a great place to clamber about among ruins and explore the ancient cistern and cave system as well as remnants of the fortified walls and siege ramp.

Josephus Flavius

The primary extra-biblical historical source about the time of Jesus is the writing of **Josephus Flavius**, a 1st-century Jewish historian and apologist from the Galilee known in Hebrew as Yosef Ben-Matityahu. Josephus came from a priestly family and prided himself on being a loyal and observant Jew. He was a military leader against the Romans in the First Jewish-Roman War but was defeated at Yodfat, taken to Rome and later became a Roman citizen.

Josephus' most important writings are *The Jewish War*, chronicling the Great Jewish Revolt against Rome from 66-70 CE, and *The Antiquities of the Jews,* which offers a Jewish perspective on world history. As both a Jew and a Roman citizen, Josephus offers a unique perspective that holds these two identities in balance, even when they are at war with each other, portraying each side as gracious and courageous in both victory and defeat. His strong loyalties indicate he often wrote with political motives and took creative freedom with the facts, so his writings must be read carefully. Even so, his contributions have been invaluable for both Jewish and early Christian history.

At the fortified city of Yodfat, the Romans defeated the Jews under the command of Josephus.

The remote ruins of Khirbet Cana are a likely location of Jesus' miracle of turning water into wine.

Khirbet Cana خربة قانا חורבת כנא

Another contender for the site of Jesus' first miracle of turning water to wine is **Khirbet Cana**, a site of Roman and Byzantine ruins located in the Netofa Valley about 9 km northwest of Nazareth. The site is only partially excavated which, along with its remote location, lends it an air of mystery and timelessness. There are no entrance fees or salesmen hawking their wares here, just a hill of ruins surrounded by agricultural fields and scattered houses. While not nearly as popularized as Kfar Cana (home of the Wedding Church, see p. 76), evidence suggests that this may be the more authentic of the candidates.

Cana is frequently mentioned in early pilgrimage literature, which suggests that both Khirbet Cana and Kfar Cana were known as pilgrimage sites. In the 17th century, favor shifted to regarding Kfar Cana as the authentic site on the grounds that it had a church and was located on the main Sepphoris-Tiberias highway. In recent years the tides have turned to regard Khirbet Cana as the more authentic according to archeological exploration.

On the northern and western sides of the hill are ruins of dozens of Roman and Byzantine houses. Watch out for hidden entrances to the cistern system which make for tripping hazards. The most impressive structure is located on the southwest area of the hilltop, with a columned stone-paved building that may have been a synagogue or church. Pilgrim graffiti found inside this structure suggests it may have been a place that the miracle of the wine was remembered. See if you can find the steps into a pool by the structure, which may have been a Jewish *mikveh* or ritual bath.

Other evidence for the authenticity of this site include its location without running water, suggesting that drinking water would have been stored in stone jars, appropriate to the story. Also, Josephus mentions Cana as a city fortified for the Great Revolt, and Khirbet Cana is just a short distance from Yodfat, another fortified city. The ruins of Khirbet Cana are older and more extensive than in Kfar Cana. Whether or not this is the site of the miracle, the ancient ruins are well worth exploring in a half-day trip.

Khirbet Cana Historic Site

N
To 7955
1. North structures
2. South structures
3. Synagogue/ church
4. Eastern village
To Yodfat
To Kafr Manda
m
0
250
500

J41 KHIRBET CANA TO EILABUN

15.3 km
4-6 hours

DIFFICULTY: Strenuous elevation change.

BIKING DETOURS:
None. The ascent from Khirbet Cana to Route 7955, the descent from Mt. ha-Akhim and the descent from Route 7955 to Eilabun are steep but possible.

TRANSPORT FOR EILABUN:
Take buses 28, 29 or 30 from Nazareth or 28א (return to Nazareth only).

Prayerfully meditate at the peaceful Lavra Netofa Monastery, relax in the welcoming village of Eilabun

From Khirbet Cana, continue on the blue trail up to Route 7955 and carefully walk east along the road, leaving it for a short detour up Mt. Akhim on a green trail. Continue east on the road straight through the junction with the road to Araba, passing Avtalyon until you meet a black blazed 4x4 trail. If you wish to visit Hararit and the Lavra Netofa Monastery, follow the road up to the left. To continue to Eilabun, follow the black 4x4 downhill past the Netofa spring and the ruins of Netofa in the valley, crossing Route 806 on the edge of town.

In town, follow the route (3 km) outlined on the Eilabun town map on p. 213. Make your way to the historic center of the old town near the old Catholic church and then back through the modern main street to cross Route 65 near the gas station.

Accommodations:

- 31 **Beit Pardess** (Hararit +1 km off route): ☎04-678-0782; double 600-1300NIS wifi P
- 32 A network of **family stays** is being developed in **Eilabun.** Contact Ramez Eid to coordinate: ☎054-311-8824, ramezeid@yahoo.com, dorm 100NIS P

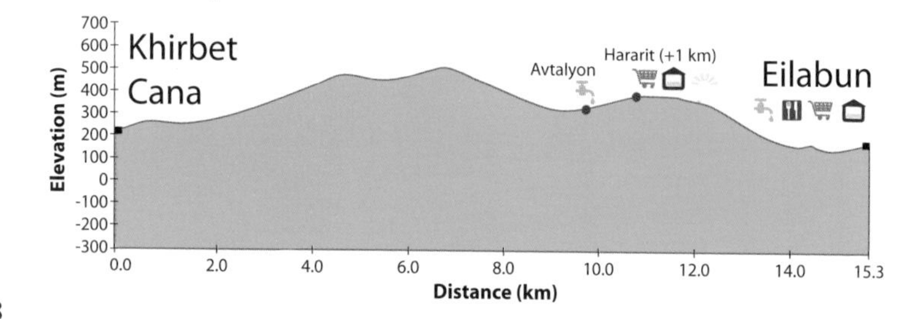

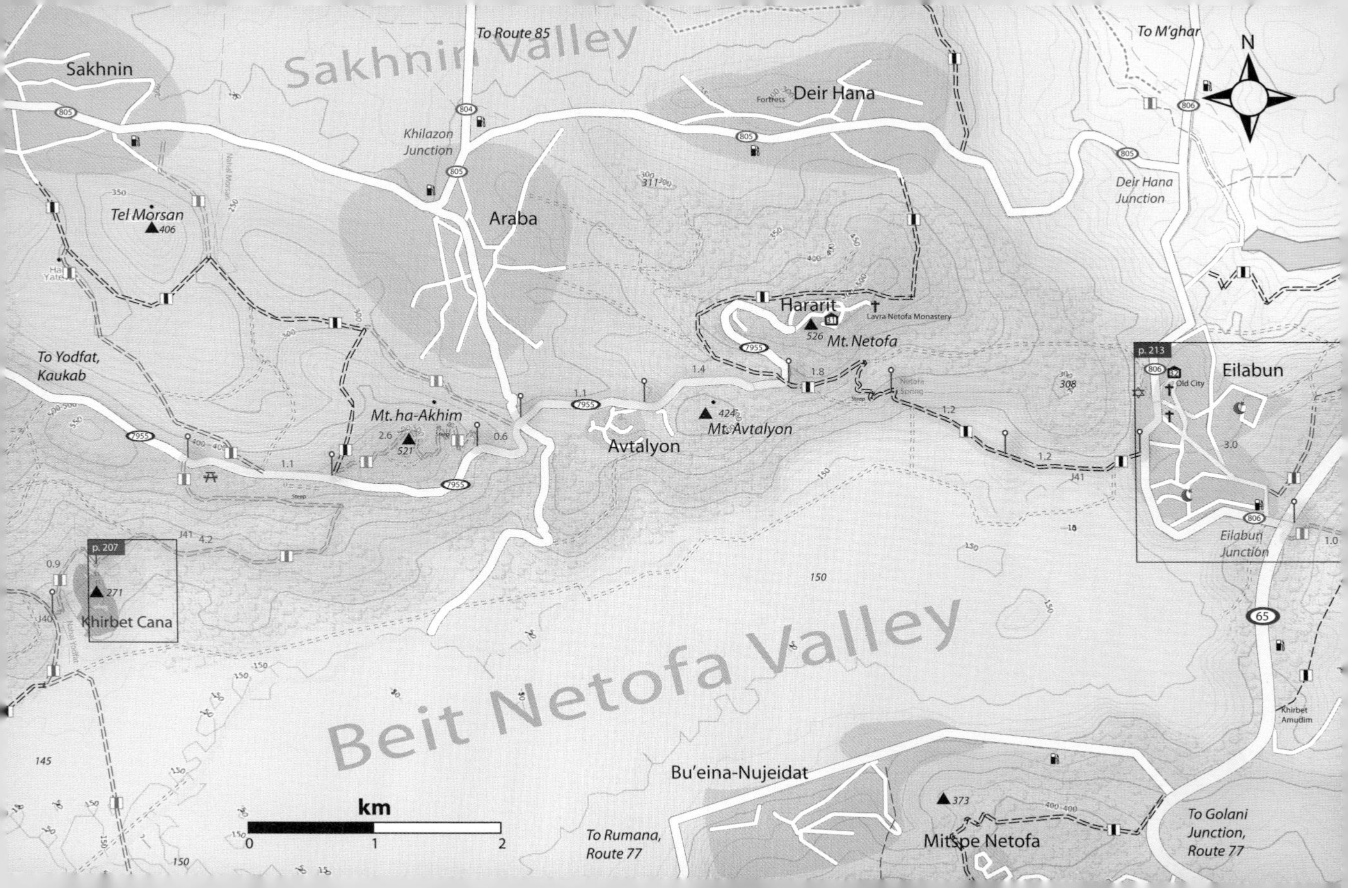

Sakhnin Valley
To Route 85
Sakhnin
Deir Hana
Fortress
To M'ghar
N
Khilazon Junction
Deir Hana Junction
Araba
Tel Morsan
406
Hararit
Lavra Netofa Monastery
526
Mt. Netofa
Eilabun
p. 213
Old City
To Yodfat, Kaukab
Mt. ha-Akhim
521
Avtalyon
Mt. Avtalyon
424
308
3.0
1.4
1.8
1.1
1.2
0.6
2.6
4.2
0.9
1.0
J41
J40
Netofa Spring
Steep
Eilabun Junction
p. 207
271
Khirbet Cana
Nahal Morsan
Nahal Yodfat
150
145
Beit Netofa Valley
Bu'eina-Nujeidat
km
0
1
2
To Rumana, Route 77
373
Mitspe Netofa
To Golani Junction, Route 77
Khirbet Amudim
805
804
806
7955
65

A table spread at Beit Pardess, Hararit

Hararit הררית

The small community of **Hararit**, perched on Yodfat ridge about 1 km off route, was founded in 1980 by a group of Transcendental Meditation practitioners. The 55 families in the community still practice TM together twice a day. This peaceful area commands expansive views of the Beit Netofa Valley and up into the Golan Heights.

Hararit has several boutique B&Bs and also runs workshops in TM and holistic treatments. **Beit Pardess** (p. 208), run by the charming Ruthy and Joe, is a unique B&B and restaurant built using the golden ratio. This means, according to Joe, that everyone who enters the house leaves smiling.

Just outside of Hararit lies the **Lavra Netofa Monastery** (☎04-678-3944), started in 1967 by a Dutch Trappist monk, Father Ya'aqov Willebrands, known locally as Abuna Yacob. Abuna Yacob's uncle, also a priest, protested against the Nazis in Holland and was imprisoned in Dachau concentration camp where he developed an affinity for the Jewish people. Crippled by his term at Dachau, he was unable to travel to the Holy Land himself, so asked his nephew to go in his place.

After twelve years of negotiating to receive permission from the Catholic Church, Abuna Yacob indeed finally came to the Galilee and spent another three years negotiating a land purchase from the Khattib family of nearby Deir Hana.

Abuna Yacob began his monastery in a Canaanite-era cistern, a cave which he expanded through three years of chiseling the rock. He learned Arabic and Hebrew and built strong relationships with local communities. Eventually he aligned himself with the local Melkite Church and focused on living simply in emulation of the life of Jesus and the early church founders. After Abuna Yacob's death in 2005, the monastery passed over to a small French order, with several monks and nuns living there today.

A visit to the original cistern chapel is a worthwhile detour. To be sure it is not in use, you can call ahead. The monks and nuns practice a regular schedule of silent meditation, so at certain times, no one will answer. If you visit Lavra Netofa, please respect the silent and peaceful vibe of the community by keeping your voices low.

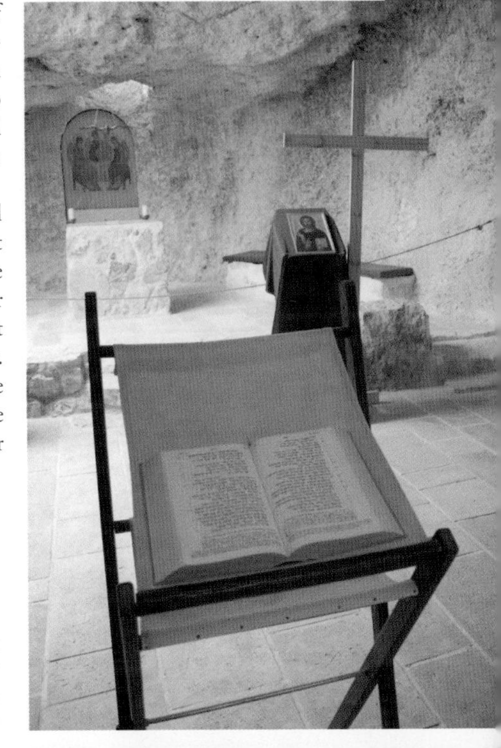

The chapel at Lavra Netofa Monastery interior (right), exterior (below)

The town of Eilabun, perched on the eastern edge of the Beit Netofa Valley

Eilabun عيلبون עילבון

Eilabun is a predominately Christian town with a population of about 5,000. In the War of 1948, the Israeli army entered Eilabun while inhabitants sought refuge in the church. Even after surrender, twelve men from Eilabun were lined up and shot in the head in front of the church. Most of the inhabitants were then expelled to Lebanon. Some reports suggest that the attack may have been in retaliation for the killing of two Israeli soldiers six weeks earlier in a nearby encampment at 'Arab al-Mawasi.

This bleak history took a surprising turn when Eilabun inhabitants were allowed to return to their village several months after being expelled. Their return was negotiated by religious leaders with pressure from the Vatican. In 2007, a documentary film about the town's history was released, entitled *The Sons of Eilaboun*.

A breakfast feast at the Eid family home in Eilabun

Today, Eilabun is a pleasant town with a small Old City built upon a rising hill, a sign of the layers of previous settlements beneath. Evidence of Greek, Roman, Byzantine, Crusader and Arab settlements have been discovered, as well as a system of underground tunnels and caves from an unknown time period.

The present-day town of Eilabun began about 400 years ago and was expanded by Christian families in the 19th century. Locals are keen to welcome visitors and are developing a homestay network and volunteer program. For information, contact Ramez Eid (see p. 208).

The church in Eilabun where town members sought refuge in 1948 (opposite top)

Eilabun

1. The old Catholic church
2. Christian cemetery
3. Tomb of the Rabbi (Mittia Ben Haresh)
4. High school
5. Catholic church
6. Orthodox church
7. Office of Culture
8. Muslim cemetery
9. Local honey store (Georgette Khouri)
10. Village spice shop
11. Local history museum (Nayef Sama'an)

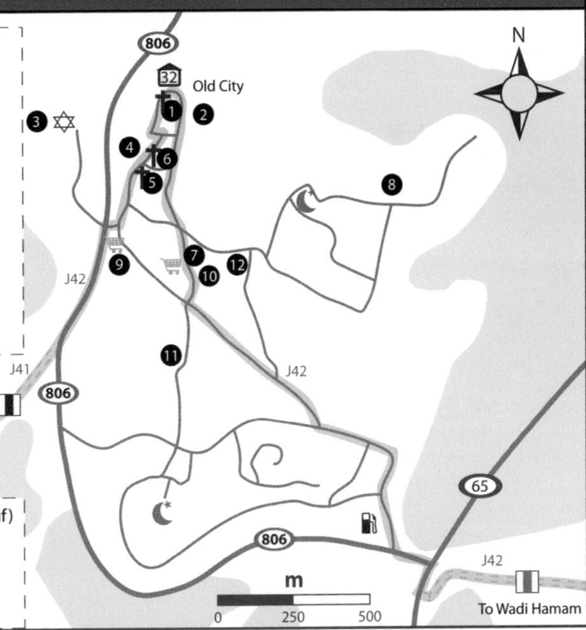

12. Iron artist (Abdullah Yusuf)
13. National Water Carrier

 Eilabun family stay (Ramez Eid)

J42 EILABUN TO WADI HAMAM

12.9 km
2-3 hours

Difficulty: ▬☐☐
Gradual downhill with steady footing.

Biking Detours:
None. You may need to walk your bike for a short section at the end of Nakhal Arbel near Wadi Hamam.

Transport for Wadi Hamam:
From Wadi Hamam, walk via J7 for 1 km to Route 807, and another 1 km to Route 90 at Migdal Junction. Take a taxi or bus 841/963 to Tiberias.

Stroll through the Old City of Eilabun, walk the gentle valley of Nakhal Arbel, drink refreshing water from Arbel spring

Begin where the bus stop is located on the west side of Eilabun near Route 806 and walk through town, using the detailed town map on p. 213.

Exit Eilabun at the junction of Route 65 and Route 806 outside of town Walk south about 100 m along Route 65 until you see a green blaze on the left. Take the green trail for 1 km, then turn left on the black trail. After 4.5 km you will meet the blue blazed and orange dotted Jesus Trail main route (J5). Follow this trail for about 3 km until you come to an abandoned building where the blue trail turns right up and out of the valley. Do not climb up out of the valley, but continue straight on an unmarked 4x4 which will turn into a green marked trail. In 1.5 km you will arrive at the spring and village of Wadi Hamam where it joins the Israel Trail and main Jesus Trail route and the junction of J6/7.

Accommodations:
No immediate accommodations. Walk out to Migdal Junction (2 km) to take a bus for overnight in Tiberias or other.

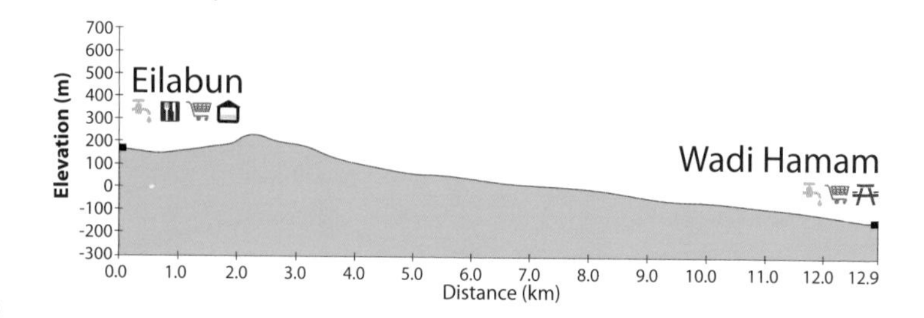

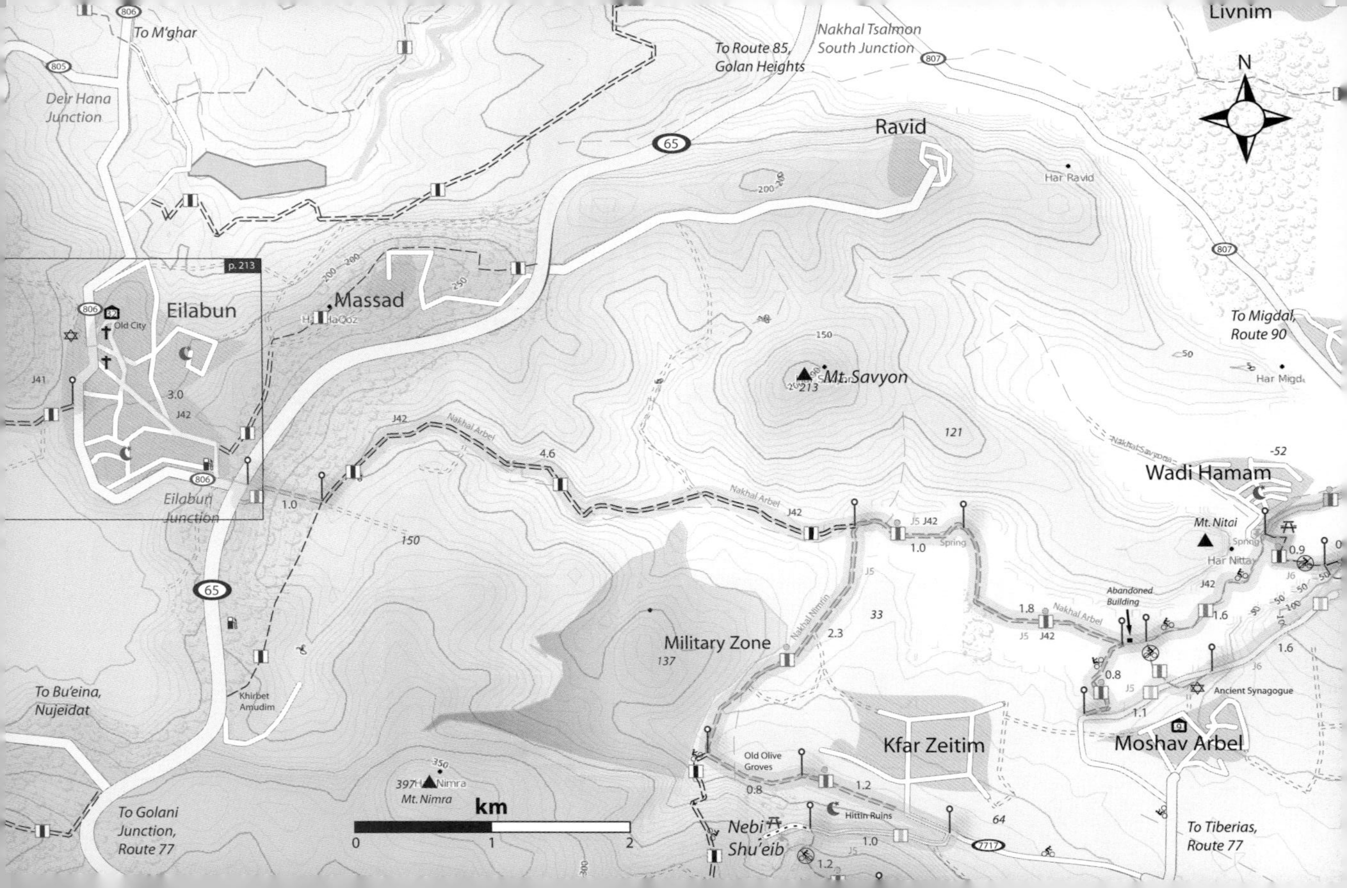

Livnim
N
To M'ghar
806
805
Deir Hana Junction
To Route 85, Golan Heights
Nakhal Tsalmon South Junction
807
Ravid
65
Har Ravid
To Migdal, Route 90
Har Migd
p. 213
Eilabun
Old City
Massad
3.0
J41
J42
4.6
Nakhal Arbel
Mt. Savyon
213
150
121
-52
Wadi Hamam
Mt. Nitai
Spring
Har Nittai
0.9
J5
1.0
1.8
1.6
1.1
0.8
Abandoned Building
Ancient Synagogue
Moshav Arbel
Eilabun Junction
806
150
Nakhal Nimrin
2.3
33
Military Zone
137
Kfar Zeitim
To Bu'eina, Nujeidat
Khirbet Amudim
To Golani Junction, Route 77
397
Nimra
Mt. Nimra
350
km
0
1
2
Old Olive Groves
1.2
Hittin Ruins
Nebi Shu'eib
64
7717
To Tiberias, Route 77

A single pillar still stands at Khirbet Amudim.

Khirbet Amudim חורבת עמודים

Just south of the Netofa Valley, all that remains of the ancient city of **Amudim** is a lone column and a few scattered ruins in a field, easily visible from the passing highway. The town dates to the 4th century, and was home to one of the biggest synagogues in the region.

Wadi/Nakhal وادي נחל

Wadi is the Arabic term, now common in English also, that refers to a dry river valley with periodic water flow in wet seasons. The Hebrew term is ***nahkal.*** In the Galilee, wadis create a connected system of drainage for rainfall. From Eilabun to Wadi Hamam, you will walk through Wadi Arbel, which channels rainwater into the Sea of Galilee. See p. 109 for Wadi Hamam.

Flash floods can be a real danger in wadis during the rainy season. When in doubt, call the flash flood hotline: ☎02-622-2211.

Side Route:
To visit Khirbet Amudim (+1.5 km each way), turn right on the black trail 1 km after Route 65.

Bedouin بدو בדואים

The ravens brought [Elijah] bread and meat in the morning and bread and meat in the evening. 1 Kings 17:6a

Historically, **Bedouin** were nomadic desert-dwelling tribal groups that lived throughout the Middle East. The descendants of these tribes are still called Bedouin, even though most of them are no longer nomadic, having settled into towns or began sedentary farming. Bedouin are ethnically Arab and the majority are Muslim.

In 1 Kings there is a story about the prophet Elijah being fed by ravens in the desert. It has been suggested that the Hebrew word used for ravens (*orebim*) may have actually referred to "Arabians" or "Bedouin," which would make sense with the tradition of hospitality among Bedouin.

A bemused goat grazes with Arbel Cliff in the background (opposite above).

A young shepherd tends his flock near Wadi Hamam (opposite below).

Historical Timeline of the Holy Land

An overview of historical developments with an emphasis on the Galilee region.

Stone Age (600,000-4,000 BCE)

Human skeletons dating from the Stone Age have been found in the Galilee, particularly on the shores of water sources. Flint tools from this period have also been discovered, as well as the evidence of large animals on the savannas that would have been hunted. Evidence of the use of fire dates to about 200,000 BCE. In 14,000 BCE, a major social shift took place from hunting and gathering to food production. Toward the end of this period, once nomadic peoples became more sedentary as their economy shifted from hunting to farming.

Stone Age skeletons have been discovered in a cave on Mt. Precipice, just outside of Nazareth (p. 180) and in Wadi Amud, west of Tabgha (p. 113). An important Stone Age camp called Ohalo has been discovered on the southwest shore of the Sea of Galilee.

Copper and Bronze Ages (4000-1200 BCE)

During this period, the region of Palestine was made up mostly of small independent city-states, rather than large empires such as those found in Egypt and Mesopotamia. Canaanites built their city-states inland, while Philistines settled along the coast. Trade began during this era, as farming techniques allowed for surpluses that could be bartered. Abraham and his ragtag nomadic tribe arrived on the scene around 1800 BCE, migrated to Egypt and were led back out of Egypt by Moses around 1250 BCE. In the Galilee, early remnants from Tel Megiddo and Beit She'an show evidence of Canaanite settlement. The wall at Tel Rekhesh is from the Bronze Age.

Iron Age (1200-586 BCE)

The Israelites consolidated their tribal system into a monarchy under Saul, David and Solomon successively. The Galilee is mentioned as a reward given by Solomon to Hirem for his loyalty. After Solomon died, the northern part of the kingdom seceded, forming the Kingdom of Israel, separate from the Kingdom of Judah in the south. In the 8th century BCE, the Assyrians conquered the Kingdom of Israel. The Assyrian Empire weakened and was conquered by the Babylonians, and the people of Judah were exiled from Jerusalem in 586 BCE. The gate at Bethsaida and model shrine at Tel Rekhesh are from the Iron Age.

Persian Period (538-332 BCE)

The Jews were allowed to return in 538 BCE, as an isolated province of a vast empire. By the 5th century BCE, a Jewish governor was appointed and the Jews achieved pseudo-independence.

Hellenistic Period (332-63 BCE)

Alexander the Great conquered the region in 331 BCE, dividing it into rule by the Seleucids and Ptolemics, though the Seleucids eventually conquered the Ptolemics. The Seleucids dominated the Jews by appointing one of their own as high priest, instigating the Maccabean revolt in 167 BCE. The descendants of the Maccabees later reemerged as the Hasmoneans, a Jewish dynasty which briefly had self-rule over the region before being squashed by the Romans.

Roman Period (63 BCE-324 CE)

During the Roman period, Palestine served as a buffer zone for Rome and was treated as a client state, with Herod the Great as king. After his death, control of the Galilee was given to his son, Herod Antipas. The ministry of Jesus in the Galilee took place during this period, from about 27-30 CE. Shortly after the time of Jesus, the Great Jewish Revolt (66-70 CE) resulted in the destruction of the Jewish temple in Jerusalem by Rome, forcing Jews to shift the focus of their religious practice. Again in the 2nd century, the Romans put down another Jewish uprising known as the Bar Kokhba Revolt. A Roman city was built on the ruins of Jerusalem. Exiled from the holy city, Jews migrated north to the Galilee where cities such as Tiberias and Sepphoris became centers of Jewish life and culture.

Christianity was born during this time of political upheaval for the Jews, and adherents were largely persecuted and forced to conduct their religious life in secret. This all changed with the Constantinian shift in 313 AD, when the emperor Constantine promoted tolerance of Christianity after having had a dream of conquering in battle under the sign of the cross. Constantine and his mother, Helena, traveled the Holy Land determining the location of key events from the life of Christ, and building churches and shrines to commemorate them.

Byzantine Period (324-640 CE)

The Roman period blends into the Byzantine period during the rule of Constantine, with power gradually shifting away from Rome to Constantinople in Asia Minor. With Christianity legalized and churches built in key locations in the Holy Land, a wave of Byzantine pilgrims came to the region, many leaving detailed records of what they encountered. The churches at Bereniki, Tabor, Nazareth

(Basilica of the Annunciation grotto), Sepphoris, Magdala, Tabgha, Kursi, and many other pilgrimage sites were built during this period. Mosaic arts, such as those displayed in Sepphoris, thrived and reached their high point in quality in Byzantine times.

Early Arab Period (640-1099 CE)

Conquerors from Arabia took over the region in the 7th century. Jerusalem, already holy to Judaism and Christianity, became a holy city for Muslims as well. For the most part minority religions were allowed to continue their own pilgrimages and pass freely. When Jerusalem was captured by Seljuk Turks in 1071, they refused to allow Christian pilgrimage to the Holy Land, sparking Pope Urban II in 1095 to call for a crusade to liberate the holy places.

Crusader Period (1099-1291)

In 1099, Crusader forces took Jerusalem and massacred the Muslim inhabitants. A feudal system was put into effect, and castles, abbeys and other European-style buildings were installed throughout the region. Belvoir castle, the ruins at the Horns of Hattin, the Synagogue Church in Nazareth and St. Anne's Church at Sepphoris are examples of Crusader architecture.

Mamluk Period (1250-1517)

The Crusaders were defeated by Saladin, who was subsequently defeated by the Mamluks of Egypt, who largely ignored the region. Pilgrims of all religions were, for the most part, allowed to come to Jerusalem. Few records of Christian pilgrimage exist from this time period.

Ottoman Period (1517-1918)

The Turkish Ottomans conquered the region in 1517, but after a few strong sultans, carried on with no central leadership. A tribal system of local leadership emerged that was inadequate to maintain administration and development of the region. Much of the Nazareth Old City is from this time period, including the White Mosque and the Fauzi Azar mansion. Some of the early kibbutzim in the Galilee, such as Kibbutz Kinneret, were founded toward the end of this time period.

British Mandate Period (1918-1948)

The Ottoman Empire fell shortly after World War I, in which the Ottomans sided with the Germans. Britain was given governing power over Palestine. Jewish migration to the region increased in response to intensifying persecution in Europe and Russia that culminated in the tragic events of the Holocaust. Britain eventually turned over the region to the United Nations to be partitioned into two states, Jewish and Arab, with the region of the Galilee being given to the Jewish state.

State of Israel (1948-Present)

War broke out after the British withdrew, leading to an armistice in which Jordan took control of the West Bank and Egypt took control of Gaza, while an expanded Jewish territory was under control of the state of Israel. While many Arabs living in what became the state of Israel fled, some remained and became Israeli citizens, particularly in the Galilee region. In the War of 1967, Israel took control of the territories of the West Bank, Gaza, Sinai and the Golan. The Sinai Peninsula was returned to Egypt through peace negotiations in 1978; the Golan Heights were effectively (but not formally) annexed by Israel in 1981; and the West Bank and Gaza remain Palestinian territories under Israeli military occupation, with some areas under administration of the Palestinian Authority.

From 1987-1993 and again in the early 2000s, Palestinians reacted in opposition to the occupation, sometimes violently, in waves of resistance known as the First and Second *Intifadas* (Arabic for "shaking off"). The Israeli military responded with increased restrictions on movement, speckling the West Bank with hundreds of checkpoints and road barriers. In 2004, Israel began building a wall around the West Bank, loosely following the 1949 Armistice line (known as the Green Line), though dipping inside this line to route around Jewish settlements and include them on the Israeli side of the wall, resulting in the *de facto* annexation of about 9.5% of the land area of the West Bank.

In spite of the political tensions between Israelis and Palestinians, particularly centering around Jerusalem, Gaza and the West Bank, the Galilee has remained a stable region where Jewish Israelis and Arab/Palestinian citizens of Israel have lived in relative peace, though racial tensions and discrimination remain.

First-Century Context of Jesus

Jesus and his disciples went on to the villages around Caesarea Philippi. On the way he asked them, "Who do people say I am?" Mark 8:27

We all read biblical and historical texts through a lens deeply shaped by our own culture and time period. In the same way, the Bible was influenced by the 1st-century culture of its authors, riddled with clues about the context of its time and audience. Deciphering these clues leads to deeper knowledge of the context of the Bible, and ultimately, richer understanding of its meaning for us today.

In a movement starting in the mid-18th century known as the "Quest for the Historical Jesus," scholars began to consider extra-biblical sources and apply scientific techniques to the study of Jesus to better understand the historical context in which he lived and ministered. These techniques included archeological and geographical study, textual criticism, linguistic and sociological analysis and comparison to extra-biblical texts. This movement has re-emerged in recent years as scholars study everything from the political, economic and religious environment of the 1st century to what Jesus may have eaten or what clothes he may have worn.

These insights can help us be more attuned to the nuanced significance that Jesus' words and actions may have had in their original cultural context. By attempting to hear with 1st-century ears, we can draw fresh understanding into the biblical story that is both more accurate to the mind and more illuminating to the soul.

Politics in the Time of Jesus

"Shall I crucify your king?" Pilate asked.
"We have no king but Caesar," the chief priests answered. John 19:15b

Jesus was born into Jewish society shortly after the region of Palestine came under Roman occupation. Herod the Great, a client king for the Romans, ruled the region until his death in 4 BCE. The account in Matthew places the birth of Jesus as during the rule of King Herod, as Herod orders the killing of all boy children under two years old in the vicinity of Bethlehem, a story which calls to mind Moses, who also escaped a systematic slaughter of young boys.

Most scholars place the birth of Jesus between 6 and 4 BCE. During the life of Jesus, the ruler of the Galilee was Herod the Great's son, Herod Antipas. Caesar Augustus was emperor of the Roman Empire when Jesus was born, but Tiberius

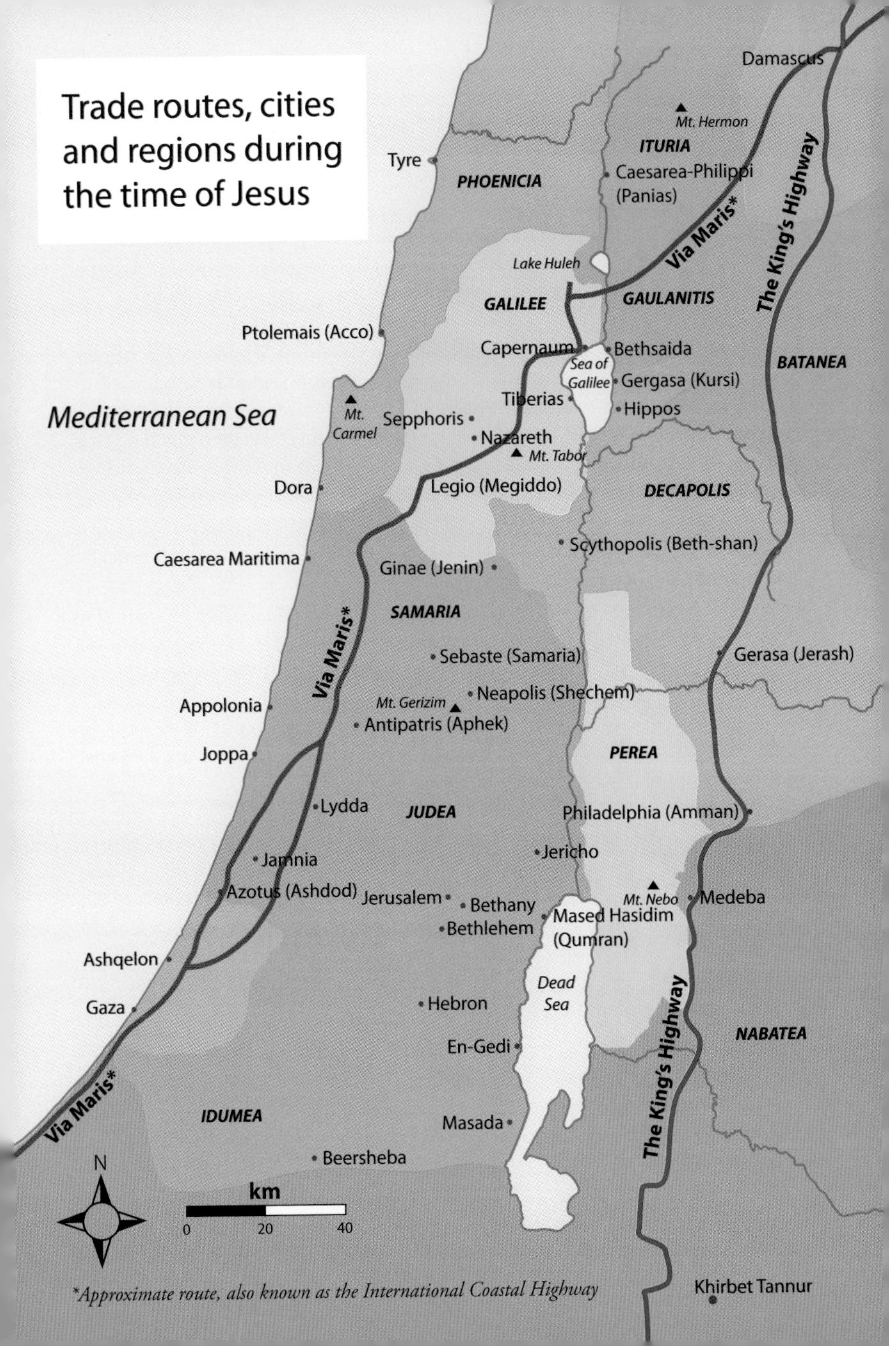

Trade routes, cities and regions during the time of Jesus
Damascus
Mt. Hermon
ITURIA
Tyre
PHOENICIA
Caesarea-Philippi
(Panias)
Via Maris*
The King's Highway
Lake Huleh
GALILEE
GAULANITIS
Ptolemais (Acco)
Capernaum
Bethsaida
Sea of
Galilee
Gergasa (Kursi)
BATANEA
Tiberias
Hippos
Mediterranean Sea
Mt.
Carmel
Sepphoris
Nazareth
Mt. Tabor
Dora
Legio (Megiddo)
DECAPOLIS
Scythopolis (Beth-shan)
Caesarea Maritima
Ginae (Jenin)
SAMARIA
Via Maris*
Sebaste (Samaria)
Gerasa (Jerash)
Neapolis (Shechem)
Mt. Gerizim
Appolonia
Antipatris (Aphek)
Joppa
PEREA
Lydda
JUDEA
Philadelphia (Amman)
Jericho
Jamnia
Mt. Nebo
Azotus (Ashdod)
Jerusalem
Bethany
Medeba
Mased Hasidim
(Qumran)
Bethlehem
Ashqelon
Dead
Sea
Gaza
Hebron
NABATEA
En-Gedi
The King's Highway
Via Maris*
IDUMEA
Masada
Beersheba
N
km
0
20
40
*Approximate route, also known as the International Coastal Highway
Khirbet Tannur

became emperor in 14 CE and would have governed during Jesus' adult life. The governor in Judea was Pontius Pilate (confirmed extra-biblically by tablets found at Caesarea).

Rome concerned itself very little with border areas like Palestine, and Roman governors were in place almost entirely to collect taxes and keep the peace. Revolts were quickly and brutally snuffed out by Rome's strong and ruthless military.

At the beginning of Herod Antipas' rule, a revolt in Sepphoris led by Judas ben Hezekiah resulted in a crushing defeat by the Romans. Sepphoris was burned to the ground, and the rebels were sold into slavery or crucified. Other messianic figures arose, promising freedom and self-determination for the Jews. Jesus quite possibly grew up hearing stories of the heroism and bravery of these revolutionaries against the pagan and exploitative Roman oppressors. During the time of Jesus, several of these messianic figures rose to prominence, and people at the time of Jesus may have considered Jesus to be in this category of political revolutionary.

Understanding the political system at the time of Jesus can give new nuance to how his words in the gospels may have sounded to those living in the 1st century. For example, the gospels record Jesus as speaking often about the "kingdom of God," or "kingdom of heaven," contrasting it sharply to the pagan empire of Rome. The Greek words used in the New Testament for "kingdom" and "empire" are the same, so this term could also be translated, "the empire of God."

Some of the terms and concepts used to describe Jesus were also terms used to describe Caesar, as an integral part of the political/religious ideology of the emperor cult. These terms and concepts include: divine savior; God manifest; son of God; one who brings peace, prosperity and salvation; righteous; just; faithful and ruler of a kingdom (empire) without end. The Greek word *evangelion*, which is commonly translated as "gospel" or "good news," was also used as a term to describe the rule of Caesar over Rome.

Economy in the Time of Jesus

> *But woe to you who are rich, for you have already received your comfort.*
> Luke 6:24

First-century Palestine was a time of economic extremes. Wealthy elite Romans and Jewish leaders such as the Pharisees and Sadducees ate and drank in the lap of luxury, while the majority of people were at the edge of starvation. Heavy taxes against the poor drove many to be in debt beyond what they could ever repay. The elites of society made up only about 2-3% of the population, but economically dominated the non-elites, exacting from the poor taxes from 20-50% of their crops and earnings.

While scholars have different theories about the economic status of Jesus, most assume he was born into a poor but not destitute family. We know little about his income, except that he worked as a *tekton* (carpenter or builder). Scripture also suggests that Jesus may have been 'sponsored' by some wealthy women, in order to devote full time to his ministry (Luke 8:3). Jesus was most likely literate, or at least could read if not write, and probably multi-lingual (Aramaic, Greek and Hebrew). It appears that he was religiously educated and most likely had committed the Hebrew Jewish scriptures to memory.

Jesus often criticizes the Jewish elites for mimicking the unjust system of the pagan Roman Empire, rather than caring for the needs of the people and rejecting the pagan empire. Particularly in the writings of Luke, Jesus speaks frequently about economic justice and criticizes those who participate in unjust economic activity. He preached a message of mutual sharing and care for the destitute, even in economically challenging times when many peasants would have had the mentality of hoarding resources rather than sharing.

Religion in the Time of Jesus

> *Then some Pharisees and teachers of the law came to Jesus from Jerusalem and asked, "Why do your disciples break the tradition of the elders? They don't wash their hands before they eat!"* Matthew 15:1-2

First-century Palestine was a place of religious diversity, both among the Jewish minority and the pagan majority. Starting with Caesar Augustus, the religion of the Roman Empire was the emperor cult, which regarded the emperor as a divine being. Citizens and subjects of Rome were required to offer prayers to and for the emperor, and to participate in festivals and public displays of patriotism and worship. Emperor worship fused politics and religion, and strict hierarchy was reinforced by pyramids of patronage. The message of emperor divinity permeated public space, and communicated to people that to oppose the political system was to oppose God, and that the order, hierarchy and violence of the empire were divine tools.

Overall, Rome was relatively unconcerned with the religious practices of its subjects, except where they interfered with maintaining peace and order. The Jews were permitted to practice their faith and even had certain exemptions and privileges that allowed them to live out their religious life for the most part, including an exemption from emperor worship, permission to collect and regulate temple taxes, permission to have their own court system and some exemptions from state duties required on the Sabbath.

There was no one dominant definition of Judaism in the 1st century. Many splinter groups existed and fought within and amongst themselves. Some of the main Jewish factions were Pharisees, Sadducees, Essenes, revolutionaries and ordinary practitioners. Pharisees belonged to a learned school of thought that sought to follow the law exactly. They were opposed to and by the Sadducees, about whom little is known except that they did not believe in the resurrection of the dead, and were perhaps considered more of a political party as opposed to a school of learning like the Pharisees. These two groups were wealthy elites who collaborated with Rome in order to maintain their power balance.

The Essenes were a withdrawn Jewish sect with particular mystical practices. They rejected marriage, remaining celibate, and rejected participation in commerce, sharing all their possessions in common. They viewed the Roman Empire as evil and demonic. Many scholars believe it was the Essenes who lived at Qumran, where the Dead Sea Scrolls were found. Revolutionary groups, such as the zealots, opposed Roman occupation and believed they had to violently resist domination. Often the leaders of these groups saw themselves as messiah figures and believed themselves to be divinely appointed to free their people. Ordinary non-elite Jews primarily lived out their agrarian lifestyles, trying to practice their religion and thrive in spite of excessive taxation, poverty, disease and a generally poor standard of living.

Further Study and Exploration

Two thousands years after the life of Jesus, many pieces of his life are difficult or impossible to recreate with extra-biblical sources and scientific methods. Respected scholars have come out with radically different pictures of Jesus and the 1st-century world. Even if not proven, these theories can help spark our imagination and curiosity, inspiring all to examine more deeply the context and culture of Jesus in interpreting the Bible.

Some of the foremost Historical Jesus scholars include Albert Schweitzer (1875-1965), Marcus Borg, John Dominic Crossan, N.T. Wright and Ekkehard Stegemann.

For further study and exploration, the following are recommended resources:

Historical Jesus

- *Archaeology and the Galilean Jesus: A Re-examination of the Evidence,* by Jonathan L. Reed, 2002.
- *Excavating Jesus: Beneath the Stones, Behind the Texts*, by John Dominic Crossan and Jonathan Reed, 2001.
- *Galilee: History, Politics, People,* by Richard Horsley, 1995.
- *The Nazareth Jesus Knew,* by Joel Kauffmann, 2005.
- *The Quest for the Historical Jesus,* by Albert Schweitzer, 2010 (originally published in German in 1906).

History

- *The Holy Land: An Archeological Guide from Earliest Times to 1700,* by Jerome Murphy-O'Connor, 2008.
- *The Jesus Movement: A Social History of its First Century,* by Ekkehard Stegemann and Wolfgang Stegemann, 1995.
- *Travel in the Ancient World,* by Lionel Casson, 1994.

Suggested Reading

Guidebooks

- *Fodor's Israel,* edited by Linda Cabasin and Rachel Klein, 2009.
- *Hike the Land of Israel: A Complete Guide to the Israel National Trail,** by Jacob Saar, 2008.
- *Hiking in Israel: 36 of Israel's Best Hiking Routes,* by Ya'akov Shkolnik and Yadin Roman, 2008.
- *Israel: National Parks & Nature Reserves,* by Azaria Alon, 2008.
- *Israel's Northern Landscapes: Guide to the Golan Heights, Eastern Galilee and Lake Kinneret,** by Aviva Bar-Am, 2008.
- *Lonely Planet: Israel & the Palestinian Territories,* by Michael Kohn et al., 2010.
- *Walks in Palestine: Including the Nativity Trail,* by Di Taylor and Tony Howard, 2001.

Regional Flora and Fauna

- *A Field Guide to Jordan,* by Jarir Maani, 2008.
- *Pocket Guides to the Flora & Fauna of Israel,** Noam Kirshenbaum. talituly@zahav.net.il
- Society for the Protection of Nature in Israel Maps #1,2,3 (Hebrew only)*

Pilgrimage & Travel Philosophy

- *Explorations in a Christian Theology of Pilgrimage,* by Craig Bartholomew and Fred Huges, 2004.
- *Jerusalem Pilgrims Before the Crusades,* by John Wilkinson, 2002.
- *The Art of Pilgrimage,* by Phil Cousineau, 2000.
- *The Way of the Lord: Christian Pilgrimage Today,* by N.T. Wright, 1999.
- *Travel as a Political Act,* by Rick Steves, 2009.

Hebrew and Arabic Language

- *Colloquial Hebrew,* by Zippi Lyttleton and Tamar Wang.
- *Yalla Nihki Arabi (Let's Speak Arabic): A Course in Colloquial Jerusalem Arabic for Beginners,* by Omar Othman. Available for sale in East Jerusalem.

Recent History

- *Arab and Jew: Wounded Spirits in a Promised Land,* by David Shipler, 2001.
- *Blood Brothers,* by Elias Chacour, 2003.
- *The Lemon Tree: An Arab, a Jew, and the Heart of the Middle East,* by Sandy Tolan, 2007.

**Mainly available in bookstores in Israel*

Web Resources

It is said that any guidebook is out of date by the time it goes to print. We have done our best to ensure that the information contained in this book is accurate. However, things change, so the best source of up-to-date information about the trail is the official website, **www.jesustrail.com.**

There you can find:

- Any **updates** to this book, including changes in route, accommodations, contact information, availability, etc.
- **GPS files** of every hike in this book, free to download to your personal device for foolproof navigation.
- An interactive **hiker's forum** made up of Jesus Trail hikers and hiking hopefuls, where you can ask and answer questions about the trail.
- **Reviews of accommodations** written by other hikers.
- **Volunteer information** for Jesus Trail and other opportunities in the area.
- Additional **trail resources** as they become available.

J#	Route Beginning and End	Distance (km)	Distance (miles)	Time (hours)	Difficulty
J0	Nazareth	1-2	0.6-1.2	1-2	
J1	Nazareth to Zippori	7.8	4.8	2-3	
J2	Zippori to Cana	5.6	3.4	1.5-2	
J3	Cana to Kibbutz Lavi	14.4	8.9	3.5-5	
J4	Kibbutz Lavi to Nebi Shu'eib	6.1	3.8	1.5-2.5	
J5	Nebi Shu'eib to Moshav Arbel	9.6	6.0	2.5-4	
J6	Moshav Arbel to Wadi Hamam	3.6	2.2	2-3	
J7	Wadi Hamam to Tabgha	10.1	6.4	2-3	
J8	Tabgha to Capernaum	2.3	1.4	:30-:45	
J9	Tabgha to Mt. of Beatitudes	1.4	0.9	:20-:30	
J10	Capernaum to Bethsaida	12.4	7.7	3-5	
J11	Bethsaida to Kursi	15.8	9.8	4-6	
J12	Kursi to Ein Gev	5.8	3.6	1.5-2.5	
J13	Ein Gev to Susita (return)	8.0	5.0	3-5	
J14	Ein Gev to Yardenit	14.5	9.0	3-5	
J20	Mt. Arbel to Tiberias	6.1	3.8	1.5-2.5	
J21	Tiberias to Yardenit	13.1	8.1	3-5	
J22	Yardenit to Kfar Kish	19.4	12.0	6-8	
J23	Kfar Kish to Mt. Tabor	11.0	6.8	3-5	
J24	Mt. Tabor to Mt. Deborah	13.1	8.1	3-5	
J25	Mt. Deborah to Nazareth	7.4	4.6	2-3	
J26	Nazareth to Nein	15.1	9.4	4-6	
J30	Tel Rekhesh to Belvoir	12.7	7.9	3-5	
J31	Belvoir to Beit She'an	16.5	10.3	4-6	
J32	Beit She'an to Gan HaShlosha	8.0	5.0	2-3	
J33	Gan HaShlosha to Mt. Gilboa	13.6	8.5	4-6	
J40	Kaukab to Khirbet Cana	7.7	4.8	2-3	
J41	Khirbet Cana to Eilabun	15.3	9.5	4-6	
J42	Eilabun to Wadi Hamam	12.9	8.0	2-3	

Accommodations Near Destination	Pages	Connects to	Points of Interest
1-4	58-67	J1, J25	Nazareth
5	68-73	J0, J2, J25	Zippori NP
6	74-79	J1, J3,	Churches at Cana
7-8	80-89	J2, J4,	Roman road
-	90-95	J3, J5	Horns of Hattin
9	96-103	J4, J6, J42	Arbel Valley
9-10	104-109	J5, J7, J42	Arbel NP
10-16	110-117	J6, J8, J42	Churches at Tabgha
10-16	118-125	J7, J9, J10	Capernaum
10-16	126-127	J7, J8	Mt. of Beatitudes
10-16	128-133	J8, J11	Bethsaida, Jordan River
-	134-137	J10, J12	Kursi NP
17	138-141	J11, J13	Ein Gev
17	142-145	J12, J14	Susita/Hippos
18-19	146-149	J12, J14, J21, J22	Jordan River
20-23	150-155	J6, J21	Tiberias
18-19	156-161	J20, J22, J13	Jordan River
24-26	162-167	J21, J23, J13, J30	Ein Ulam, Tel Rekhesh
25-27	168-171	J22, J24, J30	Mt. Tabor
-	172-175	J23, J25	Mt. Deborah
1-4	176-177	J24, J0, J1	Nazareth
-	178-183	J22, J23, J31	Mt. Precipice, Nein
-	184-189	J2, J24, J25	Belvoir Castle NP
28	190-193	J30, J32	Beit She'an NP
29-30	194-197	J31, J33	Gan HaShlosha Park
29-30	198-201	J32	Beit Alpha, Mt. Gilboa
-	202-207	J41	Yodfat and Cana ruins
31-32	208-213	J40, J42	Eilabun
9-10	214-217	J6, J7, J41	Arbel Valley

Accommodations

Accommodation Name	Location	J#	Type	Prices*
1. Fauzi Azar Inn	Nazareth	J0/1/25	Guesthouse	70/300-400
2. Al-Mutran	Nazareth	J0/1/25	Guesthouse	—/470
3. Sisters of Nazareth	Nazareth	J0/1/25	Convent	60/150-250
4. St. Margaret Hostel	Nazareth	J0/1/25	Convent	140/400
5. Zippori Country Cottages	Zippori	J1	B&B	—/450
6. Cana Wedding Guesthouse	Cana	J2	Family Stay	100/300
7. Yarok Az Organic Farm	Ilaniya	J3	Family Stay	100/300
8. Kibbutz Lavi Hotel	Kibbutz Lavi	J3	Hotel	—/400
9. Arbel Guesthouses (Shavit)	Moshav Arbel	J5	B&B	100/350
10. Beit Bracha	Migdal	J7	Guesthouse	180/360
11. Ginosar Inn	Ginosar	J7	Guesthouse	—/400+
12. Karei Deshe Youth Hostel	Tabgha	J7	Youth Hostel	120/320
13. Pilgerhaus Tabgha	Tabgha	J7	Hotel	—/650+
14. Vered HaGalil	Korazim	J10	Cabins	—/480+
15. Frenkel's B&B	Korazim	J10	B&B	—/500
16. Sea of Galilee Guest House	Almagor	J10	B&B	100/450
17. Ein Gev Holiday Resort	Ein Gev	J12/13	Cabins	—/535
18. Ohalo Manor	Kibbutz Kinneret	J14/21	Hotel	—/380
19. Miki's Place	Kinneret Moshava	J14/21	Family Stay	100/—
20. Tiberias Hostel	Tiberias	J20/21	Youth Hostel	75-85/350
21. Aviv Hostel	Tiberias	J20/21	Youth Hostel	70/250-300
22. Scots Hotel	Tiberias	J20/21	Hotel	—/1100+
23. Tiberias YMCA	Tiberias	J20/21	Hotel	—/450
24. Land of Galilee	Kfar Kish	J22	Family Stay	100/—
25. Mount Tabor Inn	Kfar Tavor	J23/24	Hotel	—/450
26. Hooha Cyclist's House	Kfar Tavor	J22/23	Guesthouse	150/480
27. Rashad Family Stay	Deburiya	J23/24	Family Stay	100/400
28. Beit She'an Youth Hostel	Beit She'an	J31	Youth Hostel	—/385
29. Nir David B&B	Nir David	J32	Cabins	—/550+
30. Ein Harod Kibbutz Lodge	Ein Harod	J33	Guesthouse	120/370
31. Beit Pardess	Hararit	J41	B&B	—/600+
32. Eilabun Family Stay	Eilabun	J41	Family Stay	100/—

Amenities Symbols:

- Guest kitchen
- Breakfast included
- Meals available
- Laundry
- Internet access
- wifi Free wifi
- Free pickup from nearest town or bus stop
- Credit cards accepted

Accommodations

Phone	Website/email	Amenities
054-432-2328	www.fauziazarinn.com	wifi
04-645-7947	www.al-mutran.com	wifi
04-655-4304	-	
04-657-3507	-	P
04-646-2647	www.zipori.com	wifi P
050-400-7636	-	P
054-255-8791	www.yarokaz.com	P
04-679-9061	www.lavi.co.il	P
04-679-4919	www.4shavit.com	wifi P
04-679-2338	www.cmj-israel.org	P
04-670-0311	www.ginosar.co.il	wifi P
02-594-5631	www.hihostels.com	wifi P
04-670-0100	www.heilig-land-verein.de	wifi
04-693-5785	www.veredhagalil.com	wifi P
04-680-1686	www.thefrenkels.com	wifi P
04-693-0063	www.seaofgalileeguesthouse.com	wifi P
04-665-9800	www.eingev.com	wifi P
04-667-5526	www.ohalo.com	wifi P
052-247-9057	-	P
04-679-2611	www.tiberiashostel.com	wifi P
04-671-2272	www.avivhotel.com	wifi P
04-671-0710	www.scotshotels.co.il	P
04-672-0685	www.ymca-galilee.co.il	wifi P
052-860-6311	www.landofgalilee.com	P
04-662-0124	www.mount-tabor-inn.co.il	wifi P
077-708-0524	www.hooha.co.il	wifi P
050-730-9578	-	P
04-606-0760	beitshean@iyha.org.il	wifi P
04-648-8525	www.nirdavid.net	
04-648-6083	www.en-harod-tour.co.il	wifi P
04-678-0782	ruthpardess@gmail.com	wifi P
054-311-8824	ramezeid@yahoo.com	P

P Free parking
Swimming pool
Jacuzzi

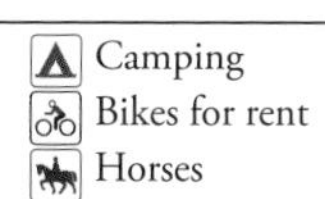
Camping
Bikes for rent
Horses

*Prices are **dorm per person/double per room in NIS**, and are subject to change, availability and season. Some amenities may not be included in room rates.

Bus Routes

From	To	Bus #	Time Range	Every
Ben Gurion Airport	Nazareth	Train to Haifa, exiting at the Haifa Center HaShmona or Lev Hamifrats (schedules at www.rail.co.il/EN), bus 331[2,3] to Nazareth		
Nazareth	Zippori, HaMovil J., Kafr Manda, **Kaukab Abu el-Hija**, Akko (343)	343[1], 28א[2,6]	06:40-17:00	1-2 hours
	Mash'had, Cana, Tur'an, **Golani J.**	24[3], 28[2,6], 28א[2,6], 29[2], 30[2], 31[3]	06:30-20:15	15-30 min
	Mash'had, Cana, Tur'an, Golani J., Lavi, **Tiberias**	431[2]	06:10-20:15	1-2 hours, none 11:00 -15:00
	Golani J., **Eilabun**	28[2], 29[2], 30[2]	06:00-20:00	1-2 hours
	Iksal J., **Afula**, Tel Aviv	823[1]	05:30-17:20	1-2 hours
	Poriya, **Yardenit**, Deganya	31[3]	06:55-18:20	1-2 hours
	Haifa	331[2,3]	05:00-21:10	30-60 min
	Jerusalem	955[1]	05:48, 08:48	2 daily
	Amman, Jordan (reserve day before at ☎04-601-0458)	NTT special bus	08:30	Sat, Sun, Tues, Thur
Tiberias	Migdal J. (Wadi Hamam), Migdal, Ginosar, Karei Deshe J., Capernaum J., Mt. Beatitudes J., **Korazim J.**	63[1], 941[1], 963[1] (56[1] to Migdal)	06:50-02:25	1-2 hours
	Kinneret, **Yardenit**	15[1], 18[1], 19[1], 24[1]	09:15-19:10	1-2 hours
	Ha-On, Ein Gev, **Kursi**	15[1], 18[1], 19[1], 22[1]	12:00-19:10	1-2 hours
	Ramot J., **Yehudiya J.**	15[1]	13:15, 16:00, 18:35	3 daily
	Kokhav HaYarden J., **Beit She'an**	28[5], 961[1]	06:30-21:30	45 min
	Tel Aviv	835[1], 836[1], 841[1]	05:00-21:00	30-45 min
	Haifa	430[1]	05:30-21:00	30-45 min
	Jerusalem	961[1], 962[1], 963[1]	06:30-20:45	1-2 hours
Afula	Deburiya, **Shibli**	350[4]	10:00-19:00	1-2 hours
	Nein, Tabor J., Gazit, J., **Golani J.**	442[1], 830[1], 835[1], 841[1]	05:45-0:00	30 min
	Beit Alpha, Gan HaShlosha, **Beit She'an**	411[4] (direct), 412[4]	05:30-23:15	30-60 min

Bus Companies:

[1] **Egged**, schedules: www.egged.com, no Shabbat service
[2] **Nazareth Transport & Tourism**, limited Shabbat service
[3] **GB Tours**, limited Shabbat service
[4] **Kavim**, no Shabbat service
[5] **Veolia**
[6] Denotes circular route, only logical for return to Nazareth

- J. = Junction
- Destination in **bold** is farthest on bus line in this book
- Weekend schedules vary (Fri. sundown -Sat. sundown)
- Does not include all minor routes

Up-to-date, comprehensive and expanded timetable list at **www.jesustrail.com/transportation**

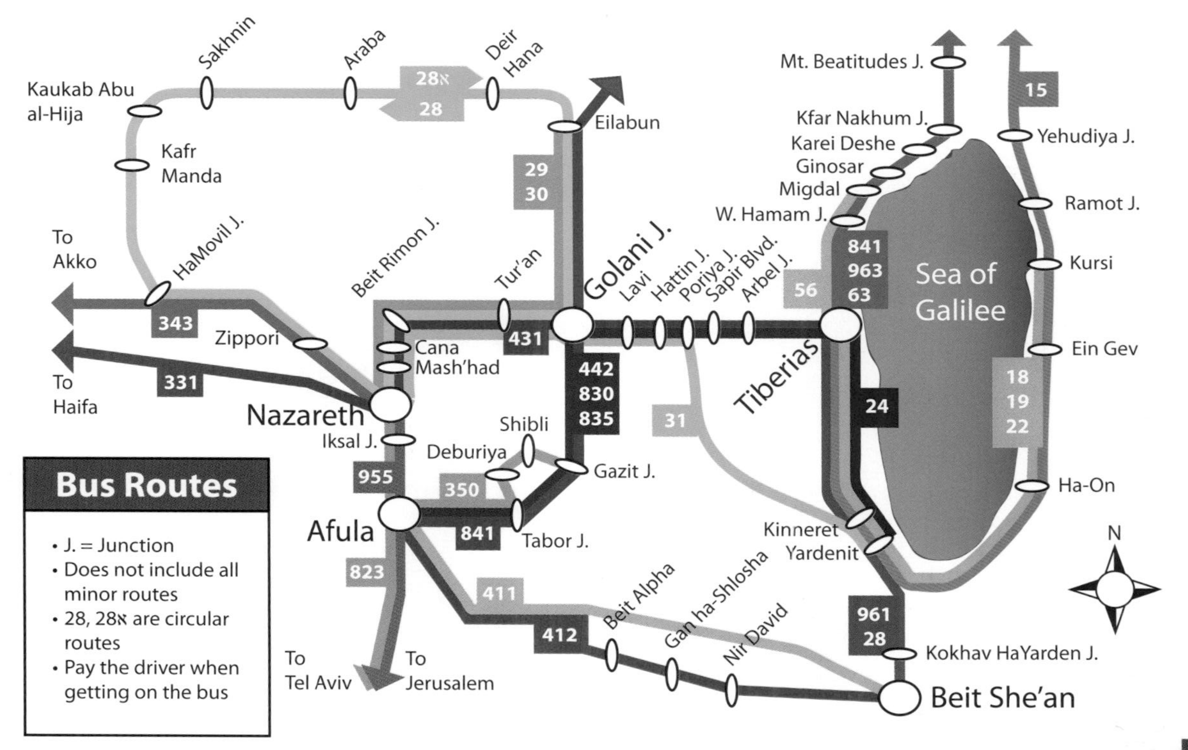
Bus Routes
Kaukab Abu al-Hija
Sakhnin
Araba
Deir Hana
28א
28
Eilabun
Kafr Manda
29
30
Mt. Beatitudes J.
15
Kfar Nakhum J.
Karei Deshe
Ginosar
Migdal
W. Hamam J.
Yehudiya J.
Ramot J.
Kursi
Sea of Galilee
Ein Gev
18
19
22
Ha-On
841
963
63
56
To Akko
HaMovil J.
Beit Rimon J.
Tur'an
Golani J.
Lavi
Hattin J.
Poriya J.
Sapir Blvd.
Arbel J.
343
Zippori
431
Cana
Mash'had
To Haifa
331
Nazareth
442
830
835
31
Tiberias
24
Iksal J.
Shibli
Deburiya
Gazit J.
955
350
Afula
841
Tabor J.
Kinneret
Yardenit
N
823
411
Beit Alpha
Gan ha-Shlosha
Nir David
412
961
28
Kokhav HaYarden J.
To Tel Aviv
To Jerusalem
Beit She'an
Bus Routes
• J. = Junction
• Does not include all minor routes
• 28, 28א are circular routes
• Pay the driver when getting on the bus

Hebrew Alphabet

א	a
ב	b
ג	g
ד	d
ה	h
ו	v/u
ז	z
ח	h
ט	t
י	y
כ	kh/k
ל	l
מ	m
נ	n
ס	s
ע	a
פ	p/f
צ	ts
ק	k
ר	r
ש	sh/s
ת	t

Phrasebook Notes

Arabic and Hebrew are both Semitic languages with many similarities to each other in structure, vocabulary and sounds. We highly recommend memorizing a few key phrases, such as greetings, as a way to show respect for local cultures. No matter how badly you butcher the pronunciation, your effort will be appreciated. See suggested reading (p. 228) for recommended language learning books.

Both languages have long and short vowel sounds. In transliteration, we use a double vowel to indicate long vowel and single vowel for a short sound (*ee* to mean a long vowel, as in "street;" *i* to mean a short vowel, as in "trip"). Both Hebrew and Arabic are read from right to left and in both, short vowels are not normally written. We use M and F to indicate masculine and feminine forms for the speaker, and "to M" or "to F" to indicate forms used when addressing a male or female. The syllables of polysyllabic words are separated by a hyphen with the accented syllables appear in **bold**.

Hebrew Pronunciation

The Hebrew language was not spoken for hundreds of years, but used as a liturgical language in Judaism. Modern Hebrew was revived in the late 19th and early 20th centuries as part of the development of the ideology of Zionism. Eliezer Ben-Yehuda is considered the father of modern Hebrew for his work in reviving the language. He raised his son using only Hebrew, making the son the first "native" speaker of Modern Hebrew. Hebrew language schools spread throughout Jewish settlements and by the British Mandate period was the primary language spoken among Jews in the region. Today about 5 million people speak Hebrew.

Assume consonants are pronounced in a similar way to English **except:**

- **r = ר** Pronounced in the back of the throat, like a Parisian "r."
- **kh = ח or כ** Hard sound in the back of the throat, as in the Scottish word "loch" or Yiddish word "chutzpah," similar to the sound of clearing your throat.
- **g = ג** Hard sound as in "goat," not a soft sound as in "gym."

Arabic Pronunciation

Over 200 million people speak Arabic as a first language, making it the world's fifth-largest language. Arabic can be difficult for English speakers to pronounce, as the Arabic alphabet contains letters and sounds not found in the English language. This presents a problem when transliterating words from Arabic into Roman letters. For the sake of simplicity, we do not differentiate between the Arabic letters س [seen] and ص [saad], د [daal] and ض [daad], ق [qof] and ك [kaf], ت [taa] and ط [Taa], ث [tha] and ظ [Tha], ح [Ha] and ه [ha] since the difference in sound to English speakers is slight. Emphatic consonants are indicated with capital letters in the alphabet at right.

Assume consonants are pronounced in a similar way to English **except**:

- **kh** = خ Hard sound in the back of the throat, as in the Scottish word "loch" or Yiddish word "chutzpah," similar to the sound of clearing your throat.
- **'** = ع A guttural voiced contraction of the throat. When in doubt pronounce as an "ah" and you should be understood.
- **g** = غ Not a hard sound as in "goat" but similar to a Parisian "r" from the back of the throat (like the Hebrew "r").
- **r** = ر Flipped sound in the front of the mouth, as in Romance languages.

Pronunciation in Arabic varies greatly by region, so the accepted pronunciation in Nazareth may differ from that in Bethlehem, with some minor differences even between neighboring villages.

Spoken dialects vary considerably from standard written Arabic. In fact, many of the everyday words used in Arabic are never written down, only spoken! While spoken dialects vary by region, written Arabic is standardized so that while a Moroccan Arabic speaker and an Iraqi Arabic speaker may not understand each other when speaking, they could most certainly communicate by writing. Formal written Arabic is not normally spoken on the street, but is used for television news and other formal communication.

Arabic Alphabet

ا	a
ب	b
ت	t
ث	th
ج	j
ح	H
خ	kh
د	d
ذ	dh
ر	r
ز	z
س	s
ش	sh
ص	S
ض	D
ط	T
ظ	Th
ع	'a
غ	g
ف	f
ق	q
ك	k
ل	l
م	m
ن	n
ه	h
و	w
ي	y

Phrasebook

English	Hebrew	Arabic
Greetings and Small Talk		
Hello	Sha-**lom**	**Mar**-ha-ba/**Ah**-lan
Goodbye	Le-hi-tra-**ot**	Bai/Ma-'a-sa-**la**-may
Good morning	**Bo**-ker tov	Sa-**bah** il-**kheer**
Yes/no/maybe	Ken/lo/u-**lai**	**Ai**-wa/la/**mum**-ken
How are you?	Ma shlom-**kha**? (to M), Ma shlom-**ekh**? (to F)	Keef **hal**-lak? (to M), Keef **hal**-lik? (to F)
I am fine.	A-**nee** be-**se**-der	Min-**eeh** (M), Mi-**nee**-ha (F)
Where are you from?	Me **ei**-fo a-**ta**? (M), Me **ei**-fo at? (F)	Min wain **in**-ta? (to M), Min wain **in**-tee? (to F)
I'm from…	A-**nee** me…	**An**-a min…
Thank you	To-**da**	Shu-**kran**
You're welcome	Be-va-ka-**sha**	**'Af**-wan
Excuse me	Sli-**kha**	**As**-sef (M), **as**-sef-ay (F)
Please	Be-va-ka-**sha**	Min **fad**-lak (to M), Min **fad**-lik (to F)
Welcome!	Bru-**khim** ha-ba-**im**!	**Ah**-lan wa **sah**-lan
Nice to meet you.	Na-**im** le-ha-**kir**	Char-**af**-na
Useful Phrases		
Do you speak English?	A-**ta** me-da-**ber** ang-**lit**?	Bi-**teh**-ki in-**glee**-zee?
I don't speak Hebrew/Arabic.	A-**nee** lo me-da-**ber** iv-**rit**/a-ra-**vit**	**An**-a ma **beh**-ki ib-**ra**-ni/ **'ar**-a-bee
Where is the...?	**Ei**-fo ha…?	Wain il...?
bathroom	She-ru-**teem**	Ham-**mam**
hospital	Beit kho-**leem**	Mu-**stash**-fa
pharmacy	Beit mer-**ka**-khat	Far-ma-**shi**-ye
Where can I find water?	**Ei**-fo ha-ma-**im**?	Wain fee **ma**-ye?
Directions		
Where is…?	**Ei**-fo..?	Wain…?
Is there ...?	Yesh ...?	Fee ...?
Right	Ya-**meen**	Ya-**meen**
Left	**Smo**-la	Shmal
Straight	Ya-**shar**	**Du**-ga-ry
North	Tsa-**fo**-na	Sha-**mal**
South	Da-**ro**-ma	Ja-**noob**

English	Hebrew	Arabic
West	Ma-a-**rav**	**Gha**-reb
East	Miz-**rakh**	Shark
Here	Po	Hon
There	Sham	Hun-**ak**
Up	Le-**ma**-la	Fok
Down	Le-**ma**-ta	**Ta**-het
Come!	Bo	Ta-**'al** (M), Ta-**'a**-le (F)
Can you show me on the map where I am?	A-**ta** ya-**khol** le-har-**ot** li al ha-ma-**pa ei**-fo a-**nee**?	Bte-a'-**dar** twar-**jee**-ne **'a**-la el kha-**ree**-ta wain **an**-a?
How many kilometers to…?	**Ka**-ma kee-lo-**me**-trim ad…?	A-**kam** ki-**lo**-me-ter **bid**-na **'ash**-an no-**wa**-sal la..?
Walking		
Way	Shveel	Ta-**reek**
Trail	**De**-rekh	Ta-**reek**
Map	Ma-**pa**	Kha-**ree**-ta
Spring	Ma-a-**yan**/ein	Ein
Well	Be-er	Beer
Village/Town	Kfar/Ir	**Kir**-ye/**Ba**-lad
Small valley (seasonal river)	Na-**khal**	**Wa**-di
Valley	**Em**-ek	Marj
Tower	Mig-**dal**	Borj
Mountain	Har	**Je**-bal
Garden	Gan	Bu-**stan**
Cave	Me-a-**ra**	Mu-**ga**-ra
Cliff(s)	Tsok(**im**)	**Jar**-ef
Steep/Flat	Ta-**lol**/Ma-**toon**	Mun-had-**ar** sha-**deed**/ **Du**-ga-ree
Easy/Difficult	Kal/Ka-**she**	**Sa**-hel/ **Sa**-'eb
Stream	Ze-**rem/Va**-dee	Ta-**yar**
Lookout	Tats-**peet**	**Nok**-tat mo-**ra**-ka-ba
Forest	Ya-**ar**	**Ga**-bi
Summit	Pis-**ga**	**Kem**-ma
Route	Mas-**lool**	Ma-**sar, ma**-slak
Bridge	**Ge**-sher	**Ji**-ser
Park ranger	Pa-**kakh**	Mo-**ra**-keb

English	Hebrew	Arabic
Gear and Clothing		
Tent	**O**-hel	**Khae**-meh
Sleeping bag	Sack she-**na**/Sa-**kash**	Kees lal nom
Raincoat	Me-**eil ge**-shem	Ka-**but**
Backpack	Tik	**Shan**-ta
Batteries	Ba-ta-ri-**ot**	Ba-ta-ri-**at**
Cooking pot	Sir bi-**shul**	**Ton**-ja-ra lil ta-**bikh**
Boots	Ma-ga-**fa**-im	**Jaz**-me
Camp stove	Ga-zi-**ya**	**Mou**-ki-de gaz
Water bottle	Bak-**book ma**-im	Ka-**nee**-net mai
Fuel canister	Mey-**khal de**-lek	Bar-**meel**
Pocket knife	O-**lar**	**Shaf**-ra
Sleeping mat	Miz-**ron** ti-yu-**lim**	**Far**-shit noom
Sunscreen	Krem ha-ga-**na**	Creem **wa**-kee min el **sha**-mis
Flashlight	Pa-**nas**	**Mis**-bah **ya**-da-wee
Walking poles	Mak-**lot** ha-li-**kha**	**A**-sal lil **ma**-shi
Transportation		
How do I get to...?	Eikh a-**nee** ma-**gi**-a le…?	Keef **baw**-sal la...?
Bus station	Ta-kha-**nat** ha-o-to-**bus**	Ma-**ha**-tet bas
Train station	Ta-kha-**nat** ha-ra-**ke**-vet	Ma-**ha**-tet ki-**tar**
Airport	Sde ha-te-u-**fa**	Ma-**tar**
When does the next/first/ last bus leave?	Ma-**tai** ha-o-to-**bus** ha-**ba**/ha-ri-**shon**/ha-a-kha-**ron** yo-**tse**?	**Win**-ta **bee**-jee el bas el **ja**-yai/el **aw**-al/el **akh**-er
I want a ticket for one-way (round-trip).	A-**nee** ro-**tse** kar-**tis** le ki-**vun** e-**khad** (ha-**lokh** va-**shov**)	**Bid**-dee **kar**-et la e-tee-**jah wa**-had (ih-ti-ja-**hain**)
I want to go to…	A-**nee** ro-**tse** le-ha-**gi**-a le…	**Bid**-dee **aw**-sal la…
Accommodations		
I'm looking for a…	A-**nee** me-kha-**pes**	**An**-a ba-**da**-wer
Hotel	Ma-**lon**	**Foon**-dook, ho-**tel**
Private room	**Khe**-der pra-**tee**	**Gur**-fa **khas**-sa
Dorm	Me-o-**not**	**Se**-ken
Do you have any rooms available?	Yesh la-**khem** kha-da-**rim** pnu-**im**?	Fee **ʿind**-kum **gur**-fa **fad**-yeh?
Do you have a cheaper room?	Yesh la-**khem khe**-der yo-**ter** zol?	Fee **ʿind**-kum **gur**-fa **ar**-khas?

Phrasebook

English	Hebrew	Arabic
Camping		
Where is a good place to camp?	**Ei**-fo yesh ma-**kom** tov le-**camp**-ing?	Wayn fee ma-**kan** mo-**na**-seb lal takh-**yeem**?
Can I pitch my tent here?	Ef-**shar** le-ha-**kim** et ha-**o**-hel she-**lee** kan?	**Mum**-kin **an**-sob **khae**-meh hon?
Is it permitted?	Ze mu-**tar**?	**Mum**-ken?
Campsite	**Camp**-ing	Takh-**yeem**
Shower	Mik-**la**-khat	Doosh
Weather		
What is the weather like?	Ma i-hi-**ye me**-zeg ha-a-**vir**?	Keef rah ya-**koon** el taks?
It's rainy/sunny/ cloudy/windy/clear	Akh-**shav** ga-**shum/she**-mesh/ me-u-**nan/ru**-akh/ba-**hir**	**Es**-a **ma**-tar/ma-**sham**-es/ ma-**ga**-yem/**ha**-wa /**sa**-fi
Flash flood	Shi-ta-**fon**	Fa-ya-**dan**
Temperature	Tem-pe-ra-**tu**-ra	Da-ra-**jet** el ha-**ra**-ra
Rain	**Ge**-shem	**Shi**-ta/**Ma**-tar
Storm	Su-**fa**/Se-a-**ra**	**As**-ef-a
Snow	**She**-leg	**Tha**-lej
Hospitality		
You are so kind.	Nekh-**mad** me-**od** mi-tsi-**dkha**	**In**-ta ki-**teer** la-**teef** (M) **In**-tee ki-**teer** la-tee-fa (F)
This is excellent!	Ze me-tsu-**yan**	**Ha**-da mom-**taz**!
I would love some.	A-**nee** es-**makh** lek-**tsat**	Min **fad**-lak.
No, thanks.	Lo, to-**da**.	La, shu-**kran**.
I'm full.	A-**nee** ma-**lay**	Sh-**be**-'et.
Sorry, I'm in a hurry.	Sli-**kha**, a-**nee** me-ma-her.	**As**-ef, **an**-a me-**sta**'-jel (M), **As**-sef-ay, **an**-a me-**sta**'-je-la (F)
I'm a vegetarian.	A-**nee** tsim-kho-**n/it** (M/F)	**An**-a na-**ba**-te
Food		
Market	Shook	Sook
Restaurant	Mis-a-**da**	Mat-**'am**
Water	Ma-**im**	**Ma**-ye
Food	**O**-khel	**Ak**-ul
Bread	**Le**-khem	**Khub**-iz
Fruit	Pei-**rot**	Fa-**wa**-ke
Vegetable	Ye-ra-**kot**	**Khu**-dra

English	Hebrew	Arabic
Coffee	Ka-**fe**	**Kah**-way
Tea	Te	Shai
Shop	Kha-**nut**	Dook-**kan**
Shopping		
How much does it cost?	**Ka**-ma ze o-**le**?	Ad-**esh** bi-**ka**-lif?
Grocery store	Kha-**nut** ye-ra-**kot**	**Su**-per-mar-ket
Gear store	Kha-**nut** tsi-**yud**	Dook-**kan**-et ma-'a-**dat** takh-**yeem**
I want to buy…	A-**nee** ro-**tse** lik-**not**...	**An**-a **bid**-dee **ash**-tu-ree...
Problems		
Is it dangerous?	Ha-**im** ze me-su-**kan**?	Hal el **ish**-ee kha-**teer**?
I'm lost.	A-**nee** a-**vud.**	Ana **da**-ye'.
I'm hungry/thirsty	A-**nee** ra-**ev**/tsa-**me**.	**An**-a jo-**'an**/'at-**shan**.
Help me!	A-**zor** li!	Sa-**'ed**-ne!
Call the police!	Kra la-mish-ta-**ra**!	**Its**-el bel **shur**-ta!
Call a doctor!	Kra le-ro-**fe**!	**Its**-el bel doc-**toor**!
Go away!	Lekh mi-**kan**!	**Roo**-eh min hon!
Signs		
Entrance	Kni-**sa** כניסה	**Met**-khel مدخل
Exit	Ye-tsi-**a** יציאה	Kho-**rooj** خروج
No entry	Ein kni-**sa** אין כניסה	Mam-**nu**-'a el do-**khool** ممنوع الدخول
Closed	Sa-**gur** סגור	Em-**sek**-ker مغلق
Open	Pa-**tu**-akh פתוח	Maf-**too**-eh مفتوح
Prohibited	A-**sur** אסור	Mam-**nu**-'a ممنوع
Toilets	She-ru-**teem** שירותים	Ham-**mam** الحمامات
Danger!	Sa-ka-**na**! סכנה!	**Khat**-ar! خطر!
Land mines!	Mok-**sheem**! מוקשים!	Al-**gam**! الألغام!

English	Hebrew	Arabic	
Numbers			
0	**E**-fes	**Sif**-er	٠
1	E-**khad**	**Wa**-had	١
2	Shta-**im**	Ti-**nain**	٢
3	Sha-**losh**	Ti-**la**-te	٣
4	**Ar**-ba	**Ar**-ba-'a	٤
5	Kha-**mesh**	**Kha**-msa	٥
6	Shesh	**Si**-te	٦
7	**She**-va	**Sa**-b'a	٧
8	Shmo-**ne**	Ta-**ma**-nya	٨
9	**Te**-sha	**Tis**-'a	٩
10	**E**-ser	**Ash**-a-ra	١٠
11	A-**khat** es-**re**	Ih-**da'sh**	١١
12	Shtaim es-**re**	It-**na'sh**	١٢
13	Shlosh es-**re**	Ta-la-**ta'sh**	١٣
14	**Ar**-ba es-**re**	Ar-ba-**ta'sh**	١٤
15	Kha-**mesh** es-**re**	Kha-mis-**ta'sh**	١٥
16	Shesh es-**re**	Sit-**ta'sh**	١٦
17	Shva es-**re**	Sa-ba-**ta'sh**	١٧
18	Shmo-**na** es-**re**	Ta-man-**ta'sh**	١٨
19	Tesha es-**re**	Ti-sa-**ta'sh**	١٩
20	Es-**rim**	Ash-**reen**	٢٠
30	Shlo-**sheem**	Ta-la-**teen**	٣٠
40	Ar-ba-**eem**	Arb-**'een**	٤٠
50	Kha-mi-**sheem**	Kham-**seen**	٥٠
60	Shi-**sheem**	Sit-**teen**	٦٠
70	Shiv-**eem**	Sab-**'een**	٧٠
80	Shmo-**neem**	Ta-ma-**neen**	٨٠
90	Tish-**eem**	Tis-**'een**	٩٠
100	**Me**-a	**Mi**-yei	١٠٠
1000	**E**-lef	**Al**-ef	١٠٠٠

Bible References by Location

Place name	Biblical name	Bible References	Claim to fame
Arbel	Beth Arbel	Hosea 10:14	Israelite battle
Beit She'an	Beth Shan	Joshua 17:11-16, Judges 1:27, 1 Samuel 31:10-12, 2 Samuel 21:12, 1 Kings 4:12, 1 Chronicles 7:29	Israelite battle
Bethsaida	Bethsaida	Matthew 11:21, Mark 6:45, 8:22, Luke 9:10, 10:13, John 1:44, 12:21	Healings, hometown of Philip, Andrew and Peter
Cana	Cana	John 2:1, 2:11, 4:46, 21:2	Jesus' first miracle
Capernaum	Capernaum	Matthew 4:13, 8:5, 11:23, 17:24, Mark 1:21, 2:1, 9:33, Luke 4:23, 4:31, 7:1, 10:15, John 2:12, 4:46, 6:17, 6:24, 6:59	Base of Jesus' ministry
Korazin	Korazin	Matthew 11:21, Luke 10:13	Rebuked for lack of faith
Kursi	Gerasene region	Mark 5:1	Exorcism of demons into pigs
Jordan River	Jordan River	Joshua 1:2, Matthew 3:6, Mark 1:5	Geographic landmark, baptism of John and Jesus
Mash'had	Gath Hepher	2 Kings 14:25	Birthplace of Jonah
Migdal	Magdala (Magdalene)	Matthew 27:56-28:1, Mark 15:40-16:9, Luke 8:2, 24:10, John 19:25	Hometown of Mary Magdalene
Mount of Beatitudes	Not specified	Matthew 5-7	Sermon on the Mount
Mt. Gilboa	Gilboa	1 Samuel 28:4, 31:1, 31:8, 2 Samuel 1:6, 1:21, 21:12, 1 Chronicles 10:1-8	Site of battle where Saul and Jonathan die
Mt. Precipice	"The brow of the hill"	Luke 4:29	Where a crowd tried to throw Jesus off a cliff
Mt. Tabor	Tabor	Joshua 19:22, Judges 4:6, 4:12, 4:14, 8:18, 1 Samuel 10:3, 1 Chronicles 6:77, Psalm 89:12, Jeremiah 46:18, Hosea 5:1	Geographic feature
Nein	Nain	Luke 7:11	Healing of widow's son
Nazareth	Nazareth	Matthew 2:23, 4:13, 21:11, 26:71, Mark 1:9, 1:24, 10:47, Luke 1:26, 2:4, 2:39, 2:51, 4:16, 4:34, 18:37, 24:20, John 1:45, 1:46, 18:5, 18:7, 19:19, Acts 2:22, 3:6, 4:10, 6:14, 10:38, 22:9, 26.9	Hometown of Jesus
Tiberias	Tiberias	John 6:1, 6:23, 21:1	Geographic reference, administrative city

Holiday	2010	2011	2012
Orthodox Christmas	January 7	January 7	January 7
Purim*	February 28	March 20	March 8
Mawlid al-Nabi* (Muhamed's birthday)	February 26	February 15	February 4
Passover*	March 30-April 6	April 19-26	April 7-14
Roman Easter	April 4	April 24	April 8
Orthodox Easter	April 4	April 24	April 15
Yom Hashoah* (Holocaust Remembrance Day)	April 11	May 1	April 19
Israeli Memorial Day*	April 18	May 8	April 25
Israeli Independence Day*	April 19	May 9	April 26
Ramadan begins*	August 11	August 1	July 20
Eid al-Fitr* (Ramadan ends)	September 9	August 30	August 18
Rosh Hashanah* (Jewish New Year)	September 9-10	September 29-30	September 17-18
Yom Kippur*	September 18	October 8	September 26
Eid al-Adha* (Feast of the Sacrifice)	November 16	November 6	October 26
Chanukkah*	December 2-9	December 21-28	December 9-16
Islamic New Year*	December 7	November 26	November 15
Roman Christmas	December 25	December 25	December 25

*Jewish and Islamic holidays begin at sundown the day before the holiday.

Index

A

B

C

T

U

V

W

Y

Z

Map and Diagram Index

Overall Map

Itinerary Routes

Historic Maps & Diagrams

Detailed Maps

Cities, Towns, Villages and Parks

Acknowledgements

This trail and guidebook would not have been possible without the help of many remarkable people who have generously offered their support, expertise and time. The project advanced far more quickly and smoothly than we could have ever imagined, and key people all over the world have helped the trail move from dream to reality.

First, we would like to thank Maoz Inon, owner of the Fauzi Azar Inn and our business partner, co-visionary and friend. Thanks to the Azar family, especially Suraida Shomar Nasser, for catching the vision and providing such a perfect place to launch Jesus Trail hikers. Thanks to long-term Jesus Trail volunteer Linda Hallel, whose selfless service and enthusiasm has been a great benefit to the trail. Thanks to the Society for the Protection of Nature in Israel, especially Gili Greenbaum, Moti Ben Shitreet and Ohad Kohavi for marking the Jesus Trail and offering their expertise in trail development.

Thanks to our tireless research assistant, Kevin Butrick, whose precise editing, fact-checking, diagram-making and other contributions were truly invaluable to the final product. Many of our friends and family volunteered their time to edit and provide feedback to our manuscript at various stages. Thanks to Betsy and Steve Dintaman, Rosemary and Steve Landis, Reta Halteman Finger, Nancy Heisey, Hannah Stutzman, Rachel Miller, Steve Kriss, Conrad Erb, Nate Herr, Joel Stern and others for reviewing all or portions of the manuscript. Thanks to Gerald McDermott, Craig and Mariella Lorge, Nathan Seth and all others who field tested sections of the book and provided feedback. Thanks to Ohad Sharav and Danny Schapiro of Steinhart Katzir Publishers Ltd., Michael King of Cascadia Publishing House and Dawn Ranck for providing advice and support as we delved into the world of publishing.

Thanks to Professor Linford Stutzman, author of *SailingActs: Following an Ancient Voyage,* and Janet Stutzman for support, inspiration and advice. Linford and Janet were our leaders in an Eastern Mennonite University study semester that brought both of us to the Middle East for the first time. Dr. Stutzman's seminary course about the 1st-century context of Jesus provided a vital backdrop to all of our research, as did Dr. Paul Wright's biblical geography course at Jerusalem University College.

Acknowledgements

Thanks to Nate Herr and Matt Cooper, who wrote the first turn-by-turn databook for the trail. Thanks to Anita Rhodes Clymer for contributing recipes and the sidebar about 1st-century food. Thanks to the schoolchildren of Nazareth, Mashhad and Cana for picking up trash along the trail with energy and enthusiasm.

Local residents generously provided us with invaluable local knowledge and insight. Thanks to Ramez Eid, Ronny Eid, Jonathan and Rina Ritter, Farah Bellan, Sarah and Israel Shavit, Alon Kafry, Marwa Abu Rany, Gabi Ashkar and many others. Your hospitality and encouragement blessed us richly. The phrasebook could not have been completed without the assistance of astute native speakers Magen Inon (Hebrew), Reham Bishara (Arabic) and Rabea Helou (Arabic).

Many thanks to our families for their support, insight and advice. David's parents, Steve and Rosemary Landis, cheerfully allowed us to over-run their dining room with our research materials. Anna's parents, Steve and Betsy Dintaman, provided support and feedback, and will be among the first to hit the trail with the published guide.

Our apologies to anyone we may have overlooked in this non-exhaustive list of supporters and friends of the project. Any mistakes in the text are solely the fault of the authors. If you find errors in the book, please contact us at info@jesustrail.com.

To all supporters and contributors, Thank you! תודה רבה شكرا كثيرا

About the Authors

David Landis and Anna Dintaman at Mt. Precipice in Nazareth

Anna Dintaman has lived, worked and traveled in South America, the Middle East, Eastern Europe and beyond. She studied religion and anthropology, as well as NGO management, and has worked in non-profit development and responsible tourism initiatives. Anna's trekking experience includes Torres del Paine in Patagonia and the Camino de Santiago in Spain, though her favorite outdoor adventure spot is still her home area in the Shenandoah Valley of Virginia.

David Landis is an experienced outdoor adventure specialist whose hiking repertoire includes trails as varied as Everest base camp and other trails in the Himalayas, Camino de Santiago in Spain, the Saint Paul Trail in Turkey, the Inca Trail in Peru, Torres del Paine in Patagonia and the Israel Trail. In 2004, he embarked on a round-the-world trip that took him to over 40 countries on four continents. He has also led a group of young adults on a bicycle trip across the continental USA. When he is not traveling or bicycling, he works with web development and communications projects. David cofounded the Jesus Trail in 2007 along with his Israeli friend and business partner, Maoz Inon.

David and Anna have been working together with the Jesus Trail since 2007. Their research for the book involved hiking thousands of kilometers in the Galilee, visiting countless historical and religious sites, holing up in libraries surrounded by a fort of research materials and walking the 800-km length of the Camino Frances in Spain in order to learn more about pilgrimage. In May 2010, they plan to be married and continue to work with the Jesus Trail and other pilgrimage trails in the region.

We welcome your feedback, comments and corrections.

Contact the authors at:
anna@jesustrail.com
david@jesustrail.com

Legend

Trail Markings

	Hiking route described in this guide
	Marked hiking trails of various colors
	single track (green)
	double track (black)
	Israel National Trail
	Golan Trail
	Sea of Galilee Trail
0.5	Distance between pins

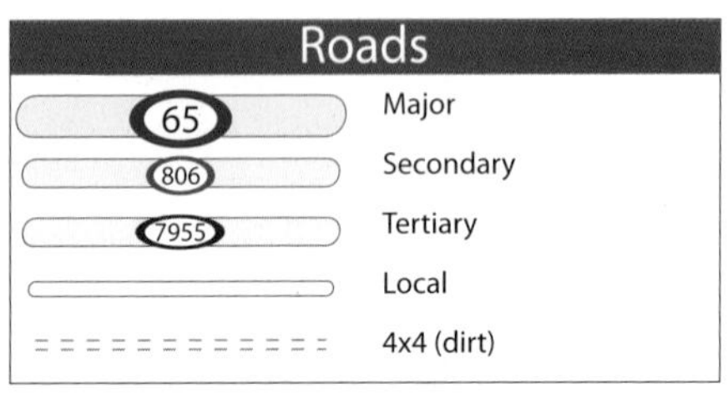

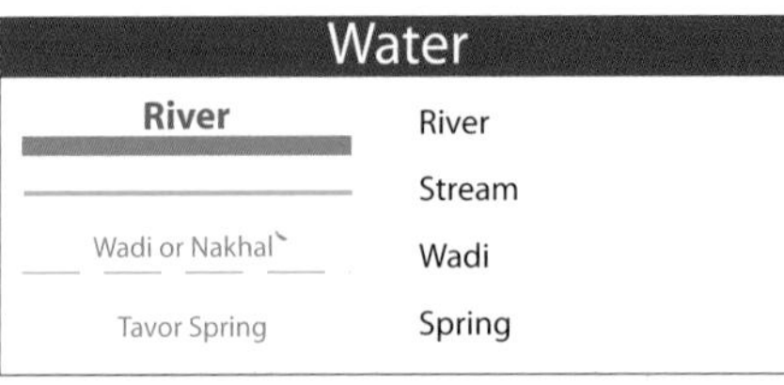

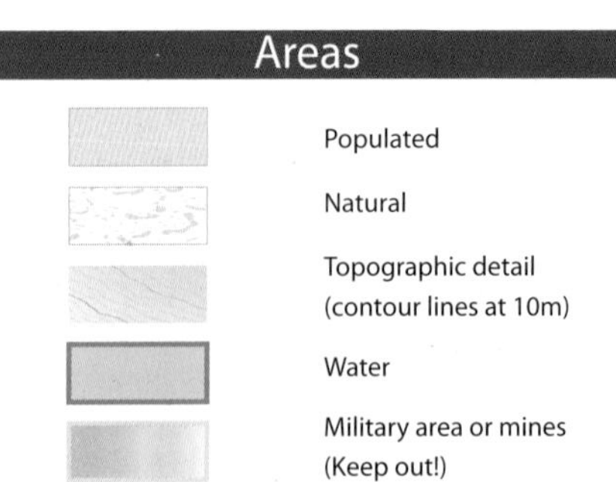

Symbols

	Tourist information
	Picnic area
	Water
	Toilets
	Supermarket
	Restaurant/Cafe
	Viewpoint
	Parking
	Campsite
	Accommodation
	Bus station/stop
	Church or Christian site
	Synagogue or Jewish site
	Mosque or Muslim site
	Gas station
181	Mountain (meters)
	Biking impossible or strongly discouraged
	Bike detour
($)	Entry Fee
	Park